The Honoured Society

The Honoured Society

The Sicilian Mafia Observed

NORMAN LEWIS

ELAND
London

First published by William Collins in 1964
First published by Eland in 1984

This edition published by Eland Publishing Limited
61 Exmouth Market, London ECIR 4QL in 2003

Cover designed by Robert Dalrymple
Cover image: Salvatore Giuliano © Bettmann/CORBIS
Map © Reginald Piggott

Text set in Great Britain by Antony Gray
Printed in Spain by GraphyCems, Navarra

Contents

Illustrations

Illustrations 1, 2, 3, 7, 11, 15, 16, 17 and 18 photographs by Scafidi;
Illustrations 4, 5, 6, 9, 10, 12 and 13 photographs by James McNeish;
Illustration 8 photograph by Camera-Press Ltd;
Illustration 14 photograph by Le Ore, Milan;
Illustration 19 photograph by the author

To S. J. Perelman

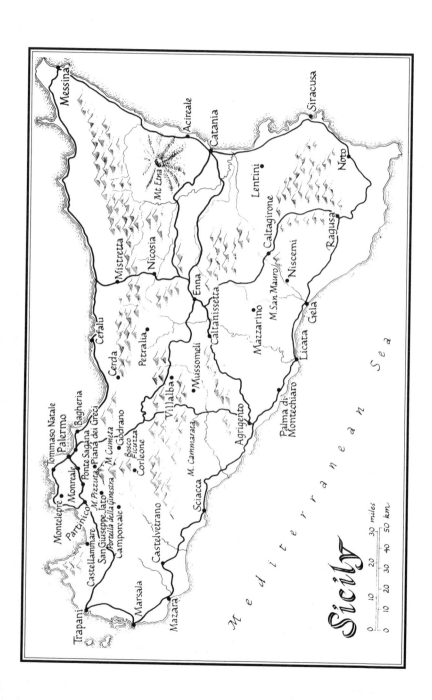

I

ON JULY 10TH, 1943, the allied armies landed on the south coast of Sicily and, thrusting northwards, began their conquest of the island. The task of occupation was divided between the American and combined British and Canadian forces, the former including in their command a small contingent of Free French. The Anglo-Canadian army advancing up the east coast found an enemy poorly equipped to offer resistance. A great deal of ingenuity had gone into the construction of painted wooden cannon, artfully contrived to discharge firecrackers and thus draw fire, which deceived nobody. Key positions were defended by captured Russian guns which could not be fired because no one had been able to translate the operational manuals. Some battery commanders had no idea that they were about to be attacked as the telephone lines connecting them to their headquarters had not yet been laid. In one case, infantry rushed into battle had received an emergency issue of mouth organs but no ammunition. Yet all things considered, despite the fact that they were out-gunned, outnumbered by five to one, and faced by battle-toughened veterans of the Africa campaign, the Italians fought back well and sometimes desperately. It cost the British and Canadian army five slogging weeks, some stiff engagements, and several thousand casualties to reach their objective : the town of Messina on the northeast tip of the island.

The Americans, to whom had been allotted the seemingly stiffer proposition of subduing the mountainous centre and western half of the island, carried out their share of the operation with great speed. After a short initial period when the American Seventh Army seemed almost to be awaiting the signal to move, it suddenly began a brisk advance up two main roads towards Palermo, reaching the north coast of Sicily in only seven days and with hardly a shot fired. General Patton was to describe this campaign as 'the fastest blitzkrieg in history'. It was certainly the least costly : casualties, once the Seventh Army had broken out of its beachheads, being negligible.

The key-point in the Italo-German defence system was the area of Mount Cammarata near the towns of Villalba and Mussomeli, and here, in positions dominating both main roads along which the Americans were certain to advance, a mixed brigade of motorised artillery, anti-aircraft guns and 88mm anti-tank guns, plus a squadron of German tanks, including several Tigers, waited to give battle. The Cammarata redoubt had been most carefully chosen. This craggy solitude, with its concealed ravines and its caves reached by secret paths, had been the home of armed resistance since Roman antiquity and had sheltered slave rebellions that had taken decades to quell. Only a few miles away, and in similar terrain, the bandit Giuliano was shortly to hold two fully equipped divisions in check with a force of only a hundred men. In command of the defenders was a Colonel Salemi, a veteran described as possessing an inflexible sense of duty. The Colonel was pessimistic about the final outcome of the battle in view of the lack of air-cover, but he had no doubt of his ability to halt the American advance for a valuable period of days, or even weeks. Cammarata might, in fact, have supplied a foretaste of the unhappy experience of Cassino.

*   *   *

On the morning of July 14th, four days after the landing, an American fighter plane flew low over the town of Villalba, circled and returned to drop a packet which fell near the church. A yellow flag with the letter L in black had been stretched over the side of the plane's cockpit, and when the packet was picked up its contents were found to include a small replica of this flag. Packet and contents were handed over to Carabinieri Lance-Corporal Angelo Riccioli, now a sergeant-major in the service at Palermo, who has no objection to discussing the occurrence with an interested visitor. Next day the plane returned and a second packet was dropped, this time a short distance from the house of Villalba's leading citizen – Calogero Vizzini – for whom it was intended. The packet was recovered by a servant of the Vizzini family, Carmelo Bartolomeo, who must have been looking over his employer's shoulder when it was opened, as he later told a newspaperman that he had seen a yellow silk handkerchief bearing the initial L. Bartolomeo's employer, Calogero Vizzini – generally known as Don Calò – was the head of the Mafia of all Sicily, and as such considered by most Sicilians to be the most powerful man in the island.

Next morning, July 15th, a messenger left Villalba on horseback for the neighbouring town of Mussomeli. He was carrying a letter on behalf of Don Calò to Giuseppe Genco Russo, regarded at that time as second to Don Calò in the Mafia hierarchy. This letter, which the messenger had

Don Calogero Vizzini (1877–1947), Mayor of Villalba and Mafia chief, in characteristic attire

been told to swallow if intercepted, was couched in Mafia jargon, and its substance was that a certain Mafia chieftain known as Turi would be leaving on July 20th to accompany the American motorised division as far as Cerda (within five miles of the north coast), while he, Don Calò, would be going on the same day with the main body of the army. Genco Russo was asked to do all he could in Don Calò's absence for the security and the comfort of the Americans.

On July 20th, in fact, while the advance guard of the Seventh Army was still thirty miles away, a solitary jeep made a dash to reach Villalba and carry off the indispensable Don Calò. The jeep, however, took a wrong turning, came under fire from an Italian patrol, and one of its crew was killed. Later that day three American tanks repeated the attempt and were successful. One of these was flying the by now familiar yellow flag with the black L, and when in the main square an officer climbed out of its turret, he spoke in the authentic Sicilian dialect of the region.

Citizens of Villalba who were present at the encounter between this officer and the formidable Don Calò say that the American seemed surprised by the presence in the flesh of the legendary Mafia chief. Characteristically, Don Calò appeared on the scene in his shirtsleeves and braces, waddling unemotionally towards the group of nervous and excited American soldiers standing under the guns of their tanks. At this time he was sixty-six years of age, a man of bulky features and inert expression, but with eyes that moved like lizards. Don Calò's slovenly dress and laconic speech were typical Mafia affectations. It was not done for a Mafia chieftain to show off in the matter of his clothing or any other way, and sometimes, as in Don Calò's case, this lack of concern for appearances was carried to extremes. From the Prince of Lampedusa's description, Don Calò might well have been the twin brother of Don Calogero Sedara, the unshaven and unscrupulous mafioso mayor of *The Leopard*.

Reaching the shadow of the guns, Don Calò pulled out of his pocket the yellow handkerchief that had been dropped by the plane, and showed it to the officers. He and a nephew, Domiano Lumia, who had returned from the United States a short time before the outbreak of war, were invited to get into one of the tanks, which then moved off, followed by the others. During the whole confrontation Don Calò – true to his reputation for preferring action to speech – is reported not to have opened his mouth.

Next morning, July 21st, on the heights of Cammarata, visible from the town, two-thirds of Colonel Salemi's men were found to have deserted. Some of them have since said that during the night they were approached by Mafia agents, who convinced them of the hopelessness of their position and supplied them with civilian clothes and whatever else was needed to get home to their families. The same day, the Italian Commander himself was arrested by a trick while passing through Mussomeli, and confined by the Mafia in the Town Hall. At four o'clock on the afternoon of the 21st, Moroccan troops under General Juin, who

Giuseppe Genco Russo, Don Calò Vizzini's successor, beside his late chief's coffin

had been waiting since dawn at the village of Riffi for an order to advance, received the expected signal from a Sicilian agent coming from Mussomeli and began to move forward. The battle of Cammarata was over without a shell having been fired.

Don Calò was away from his capital for six days. During this time the Seventh Army divided itself in two columns, one of which, striking directly north along the Agrigento-Palermo road, reached Cerda, where it was joined by the other column which had carried out a wide encircling movement through Gela, Piazza Armerina, Nicosia, Mistretta and Santo Stefano – all of them notorious as Mafia towns. As indicated in the letter to Genco Russo, Don Calò considered his mission to end at Cerda. Here other Mafia potentates were ready to shoulder his responsibility.

In reality, although at this time Don Calò was the accepted head of the Mafia, there were certain weak links in his chain of command. Mussolini's vigorous attack on the 'Honoured Society', as it was called by its members, had shaken its structure and left it weaker, probably, than it had ever been. Many of the best Mafia brains had been hastily converted to Fascism. Others, in 1943, were still in *confino* and only just about to be released. In the heart of western Sicily, the stronghold of great feudal estates, Don Calò – who had been too wily even for Mussolini – remained absolute master; but in the coastal plain between Cerda and Palermo the Mafia satraps had become used to their independence and had to be handled with diplomacy. It would be Don Calò's first task to repair this weakness in the organisation.

By the time Calogero Vizzini returned to Villalba the war in western Sicily was at an end. He had dedicated the whole of his life to what the Mafia calls 'winning respect', and his prestige was now enormous. He had been nicknamed by the Allies 'General Mafia'. Whether or not he was responsible for American strategy in western Sicily, his followers certainly gave him the credit for it, and no one could deny that the Mafia had most efficiently cleared all obstacles in the path of the American advance, while in the east the British and Canadians were still fighting their way round the slopes of Etna and it was to be three more weeks before they reached their goal at Messina.

But the war in western Sicily had been terminated bloodlessly, rapidly, and to the satisfaction of all but a few diehard senior Axis officers like the unfortunate Salemi. The Sicilians, always anti-Fascist, to all intents and purposes were now anti-Italian too. In so far as the loyalties of kinship were felt they were towards America, where by 1943 two million Sicilians, or first-or second-generation Americans of Sicilian origin, were living in a prosperity that was almost incredible by island standards. Many islanders were totally dependent on money sent back by relations in the States. Moreover, American Intelligence had seen to it that the Sicilian component of the invading force was as high as fifteen per cent. Hatred of the war had become so intense that, shortly after the invasion began, there were cases of Sicilian civilians attacking and destroying Italian military camps left unguarded by the rushing of troops to the beach-heads. To the Sicilians, resistance of any kind only signified a painful delay in an occupation wholeheartedly desired by all.

*   *   *

There was a precedent for the display of yellow flags and handkerchiefs which heralded this happy conclusion of hostilities on the western Sicilian front. The exchange of silk handkerchiefs was commonly practised among the Mafia and had become the equivalent of a password when an identity had to be established. In 1922 a certain Lottò, an associate-member of the Mafia of Villalba, committed a murder so outrageously ill-planned and with such an arrogant disregard for any attempt at concealment, that his arrest and conviction were inevitable. This kind of overconfidence was in breach of Mafia rules, which called for consultation and approval at high level before a liquidation could be carried out. But, to have left a 'man of honour' to his fate would have damaged the authority and prestige of the Mafia and have caused Don Calò himself serious 'loss of respect'. He therefore arranged to have Lottò declared insane and transferred to a criminal lunatic asylum at Barcellona, where Mafia infiltration had been particularly successful. Soon after Lottò's arrival, he officially died. The 'corpse' was removed for burial in a specially prepared and ventilated coffin, after which Lottò was supplied with false identity documents and smuggled away to the United States. On arrival in New York, he was met by a group of friends who had been warned to expect him, and to these he identified himself by the production of a yellow silk handkerchief given to him by Don Calò, which in this instance carried the initial C.

The bold black L on the flags flown at Villalba on these fateful days in July stood for Luciano. Lucky Luciano, originally Salvatore Lucania, had been born in Lercara Friddi, the next town of any size along the main road from Villalba to Palermo, and as head of the Mafia in the United States – which he had almost certainly become – Luciano would undoubtedly have been in regular contact with his opposite number in Sicily. In 1943, Luciano, who had been found guilty on sixty-two counts of compulsory prostitution, was serving a thirty–fifty years' prison sentence. He had recently been transferred at the US Navy's request from the State Penitentiary at Dannemara, a maximum security prison known to the criminal fraternity as 'Siberia', to the Great Meadows Penitentiary, where he was more conveniently accessible to parties of naval officers in plain clothes who went there to confer with him.

In February of that year – five months before the invasion of Sicily took place – he appealed through his lawyer, George Wolf, for a reduction of his sentence in consideration of 'services rendered to the nation'. Following this, he appeared in 1945 before the State Parole Board, where some squeamishness seems to have been displayed by naval intelligence officers called upon to testify on his behalf. Whatever had been promised Luciano in return for his co-operation – and Luciano protested that it was his freedom – the naval authorities refused to be drawn in, and the fact that Luciano was eventually freed and deported to Italy was due to the action as a private individual of Commander Haffenden, a naval officer prominent in these negotiations, and his confidential letters to members of the Parole Board.

The late Senator Estes Kefauver, Chairman of the Senate Crime Investigating Committee 1950–1951, has referred in his book *Crime in America* to the background of these circumstances.

During World War II there was a lot of hocus-pocus about allegedly valuable services that Luciano, then a convict, was supposed to have furnished the military authorities in connection with plans for the invasion of his native Sicily. We dug into this and obtained a number of conflicting stories. This is one of the points about which the committee would have questioned Governor Dewey, who commuted Luciano's sentence, if the Governor had not declined our invitation to come to New York City to testify before the committee.

One story which we heard from Moses Polakoff, attorney for Meyer Lansky, was that Naval Intelligence had sought out Luciano's aid and had asked Polakoff to be the intermediary. Polakoff, who had represented Luciano when he was sent up, said he in turn enlisted the help of Lansky, an old associate of Lucky's, and that some fifteen or twenty visits were arranged at which Luciano gave certain information.

... On the other hand, Federal Narcotics Agent George White, who served our committee as an investigator for several months, testified to having been approached on Luciano's behalf by a narcotics smuggler named August Del Grazio. Del Grazio claimed he "was acting on behalf of two attorneys ... and ... Frank Costello who was spearheading the movement to get Luciano out of the penitentiary," White said.

'He [Del Grazio] said Luciano had many potent connections in the Italian underworld and Luciano was one of the principal members of the Mafia,' White testified. The proffered deal, he went on, was that Luciano would use his Mafia position to arrange contacts for undercover American agents "and that therefore Sicily would be a much softer target than it might otherwise be." '

There have been many apocryphal versions of what followed these transactions, some of them wildly improbable. It has, for example, been reported that Luciano was secretly released from prison in 1943 to accompany the invasion force, that he was freely to be seen in the town of Gela where the Seventh Army's first headquarters were established, and even that he was a member of the crew of the tank that picked up Don Calò at

Villalba. There is no evidence of Don Calò and Luciano getting together, however, until 1946, when they occupied adjoining suites in a Palermo hotel during the formation of the Sicilian Separatist Party.

*   *   *

The day after Don Calò's return to his capital, an intimate little ceremony took place in the barracks of the carabinieri at which he was appointed Mayor by the American Officer of Civil Affairs. A sketch made from a photograph taken at the time captures the spirit of the historic moment. It shows Don Calò, who has agreed to put on an untidy jacket for the occasion, listening while the Civil Affairs Officer, who has been told that the new Mayor is illiterate, reads out the document conferring the honour upon him. The artist shows Don Calò's attention as incompletely held by the ceremony, an eye swivelled sideways as if distracted by something that is happening behind his back. In fact, in the square below a cheering crowd had gathered, and among the cheers Don Calò was slightly embarrassed to hear cries of 'Long live the Allies. Long live the Mafia.'

That evening the new Mayor gave a party for the Allied officers – 'the sheep' as Don Calò called them – and a number of his selected friends. The friends were the members of the Mafia of Villalba and such Mafia notabilities from the surrounding districts as could attend at short notice. Some of them wore their hair closely cropped, and their faces still bore the pallor of Mussolini's prisons. Don Calò introduced them to the officers as victims of Fascism, as indeed they were. His enthusiastic recommendations easily persuaded the military authorities to issue fire-arms permits all round – 'to guard against the possibility of any attempted Fascist coup'. Thus Don Calò had restored to him the armed bodyguard that had been taken away by Mussolini in 1924. The first of many victims of this resurgence of democracy was Pietro Purpi, the very carabinieri noncommissioned officer whose rueful task it had been to countersign the firearms permits.

Don Calò's next step was a more important one – so important indeed that Sicily has not yet recovered from its far-reaching effects. He

Funeral notice of Don Calò affixed to the church door and proclaiming his virtues:

'*Calogero Vizzini. With the skill of a genius he raised the fortunes of a distinguished household. Wise, dynamic, tireless, he was the benefactor of the workers on the land and in the sulphur mines. Constantly doing good, he won himself a wide reputation in Italy and abroad. Great in the face of persecution, greater still in adversity, he remained unfailingly cheerful. And today, with the peace of Christ and in the majesty of death, he receives from friends and foes alike that most beautiful of all tributes: He was a gentleman.*'

compiled a list of suitable candidates for the office of mayor throughout the whole of western Sicily, and this too was found acceptable. Many of these partisans of democracy, as Don Calò pointed out, had spent long years in confinement. No one seems to have had time to investigate his claim that his nominees had suffered for their political ideals, rather than for crimes ranging from armed train-robbery to multiple homicide. In a matter of days, half the towns in Sicily had mayors who were either members of the Mafia or were at least closely associated with it. One or two had been bandits into the bargain. A noteworthy appointment was that of Serafino Di Peri to be Mayor of Bolognetta near Palermo. Di Peri's first task as head of the municipality was to form a band of 109 desperadoes, who thereafter terrorised the outskirts of Palermo for the next five years. Thus for the first time, due to the military authorities' complete incomprehension of the situation in which they found themselves, the Mafia ruled directly, instead of, as in the past, exerting its influence indirectly through the control of corrupt public officials. Within days the maleficent genius of Don Calò had been able to repair much of the damage done to the 'Honoured Society' in the twenty years of Fascism. Now, in the absence of a constituted government, the Mafia chieftains had become the real rulers of Sicily.

A ceremony with a strangely archaic flavour brought this period to a close. A whispered suggestion to the Allies set the ball rolling with a gift to the municipality of Villalba of two Fiat trucks and a tractor taken from an abandoned Italian depot. The trucks were usefully employed in the black market, and the tractor was sold for scrap iron. Following this lead, presents for Don Calò began to pour in from all over Sicily. Every notability contributed to this avalanche of flour, cheeses, pasta, and stolen military equipment. Under the innocent gaze of the Allied Military Government a spontaneous revival took place of an ancient custom dating back to the days of Roger the Norman. Don Calò had become, for the second time in his life, a feudal ruler, and these gifts were the tributes of vassals who accepted him as their overlord.

*   *   *

Strangely, not all those who came to press Don Calò's hand or to present their ceremonial offering were sycophants. Aside from the natural awe they felt for him, many people genuinely admired the head of the Mafia, and even those he had victimised sometimes seemed unable to repress their grudging esteem. Don Calò was a natural artist in the control of men, through their affections as well as through their fears. His immense dignity, the Johnsonian pithiness of his rare but massive utterances, the majestic finality of his opinions, appealed to the human search for leadership. Even men of education and intellectuals admitted their susceptibility to a strange power of attraction not uncommonly possessed by a capo-Mafia, and certainly highly evident in Don Calò. The Mayor of Villalba would have shaken his head at the puerility of anyone who could really have believed he was a criminal. He almost certainly saw himself as the head of a self-created aristocracy of the intellect, to which had been committed, as if by some divine right, the arcana of government. He believed in himself as only a mafioso could and with the stolid unwavering faith of religious fanaticism – and almost as though by telepathic contact, he forced those around him to become believers too. Don Calò knew that only he, the inspired realist in command of the Mafia, could rule Sicily as it should be ruled, and had anyone dared to oppose this assumption – which he would never have bothered to claim in so many words – he would have pointed to the total ruin Mussolini had left behind after a mere twenty years of Fascist rather than Mafia rule. Such mafiosi of the old school were only criminals in the eyes of the law and of abstract justice – and in a more confused and unfocused way in those of the peasantry they exploited. To the rest of the community they were 'men of respect', and of sincere if inscrutable purpose.

A conversation fifteen years later between a newspaperman and Don Calò's chauffeur, after the old capo-Mafia's death, illuminated a curious facet of his remarkable character.

'Did Don Calò pay you well?'

'He never gave me a lira.'

'You mean you never had any wages? In that case, how did you live?'

'I suppose you might say I robbed him. I used to tell him we needed a new set of tyres for the car. Or maybe it was petrol or oil. Once I told him we had to have a new engine. I just put the money in my pocket. He never said a word.'

'But didn't he realise what was happening all the time?'

'Of course he did. Nothing ever got past him. Don Calò knew everything that was going on. He just wanted it that way. He never gave me any wages, so I cheated him and he pretended not to notice it. That was the way he wanted it.'

2

THE WORD MAFIA probably derives from the identical word in Arabic and means 'place of refuge'. As such, it no doubt recalls the predicament of the relatively civilised Saracens after the conquest of Sicily by the Normans in the eleventh century. The Arabs had introduced smallholdings and scientific irrigation. Their rule by comparison with anything the island had known before (or since) was mild and beneficent. Had they remained, there is no reason why the prosperity and civilisation of Sicily should not have equalled that of Spain, but the Normans dislodged them and plunged the country back into the polar night of feudalism. Most of the Arab smallholders became serfs on the reconstituted estates. Some escaped to 'the Mafia'.

These are the dry bones of probability as unearthed by the historians. But scratch below the surface and the evidence of an even earlier origin comes to light. One discovers archaic – even Bronze Age – ingredients in the seemingly down-to-earth, devil-take-the-hindmost materialism of the men of the 'Honoured Society'. In times of crisis, men like Don Calogero Vizzini tend sometimes to behave not so much like big-scale black-market operators of the twentieth century as like the *personae* of a Greek tragedy, whose motives are often so remote from our own as to be incomprehensible. This – from our viewpoint – irrational element in Mafia behaviour comes out strongly in the great feud between the Barbaccia and Lorello families of Godrano, near Palermo.

The two families quarrelled back in 1918 over the possession of a wood. This in itself is perhaps significant, because the wood, standing unaccountably intact in a country denuded of trees since Roman times, may have survived through its supposed possession of sacred or magic attributes. The dispute over this ragged patch of stunted oaks and thorny underbrush cost these two families dozens of lives, until, it is supposed,

Don Calò Vizzini – that great advocate of Mafia unity – intervened in 1942 to help repair the quarrel. Following age-old custom, the thing now would have been to arrange a marriage between two suitable members of the opposing families. This could not be done through lack of mutually acceptable candidates, and in 1944 the war flared up again with the commission by the Lorellos of what to the men of honour is considered the most odious of all crimes: Francisco Barbaccia, head of his family, was kidnapped and never seen again. It is at this point that the archaic component of the Mafia mentality – its utter separation from the outlook of the ordinary criminal of modern times – is apparent. The killing of Barbaccia was bad enough, but the final offence – held to be ten times more execrable than the killing itself – was the concealment of the body so that vengeance could not be ritually sworn 'in the presence of the corpse'. By 1960, nearly one-tenth of the population of Godrano had become casualties as the feud developed and spread, the latest victim – in the absence of eligible adults – being a boy of twelve.

The Mafia stands outside Christian morality, but the uncorrupted form of the Mafia found in feudal Sicily has an iron morality of its own. No mafioso sees himself as a criminal, and the Mafia has always been the enemy of petty crime – and therefore, to a limited extent, the ally of the police, both in Sicily and the United States. The organisation demands blind obedience from its members, but will defend them in return through thick and thin – and in an alien land even extends its powerful protection to all immigrants of Sicilian birth. It can be regarded as a form of primitive human society that has somehow survived in the modern Western world; its cruel laws are those of tribesmen exposed to continual danger who can only hope to survive by submitting to the discipline of terrible chieftains. The capo-Mafia considers himself a lawgiver, concerned with the welfare of his people, and prides himself on watching over the advancement of deserving juniors in the organisation with the assiduousness of the master of novices of a religious order. In his own eyes, he never steals from the community, but he can see no objection to exploiting his power over men to enrich himself. To delinquents he awards only one punishment, usually after a warning:

death. He is self-righteous and full of justifications. Listen to Nick Gentile, an American capo-Mafia, discussing the ethics of eliminating an uncontrollable young criminal: 'There was nothing we could do with him, so he had to be rubbed out. We embalmed the body and sent it back to his people in Sicily. His folks were poor – they didn't have anything – so we put a diamond ring on his finger, the way they'd see it as soon as they opened the casket. I guess we did the right thing. We figured otherwise he'd have finished up in the chair or the gas-chamber. That way they wouldn't even have had his body back.'

A primeval law transcends the bonds of blood-relationship, and Mafia honour demands precedence over ordinary human loyalties. Between 1872 and 1878 there took place in the neighbourhood of the towns of Bagheria and Monreale the most calamitous vendetta known to history. The two clans involved, the Fratuzzi and the Stoppaglieri, were both active in the same area, frequently treading on each other's toes but on the whole successful in keeping on terms of limited hostility. In 1872 Giuseppe Lipari, a member of the Fratuzzi clan, committed what the Mafia calls *infamità* by denouncing a Stoppaglieri to the police. The Stoppaglieri sent an emissary to their opponents describing what had happened, and calling upon the Fratuzzi to observe Mafia law and execute Lipari. This the Fratuzzi failed to do, and the feud was on. Within a short time all the close relations of the original disputants had been killed, and as more remote degrees of kinship were forced into the vendetta, the whole population began a terror-stricken rummaging back into its ancestry in search of dangerous ties of blood. By 1878 a man might be approached by some enshrouded, tragic crone he had never seen before – the female head of one of the clans – who would inform him that he was now the surviving head of the Fratuzzi, or the Stoppaglieri, and that he must consider himself in a state of ritual vendetta with some cousin he had never seen or heard of and who might even have had the foresight to take refuge in Tunisia or the USA. A case occurred of a young boy being assisted to fulfil his ritual duty by an outsider, who charitably loaded his blunderbuss for him and carried it to the place where it had been decided to stage an ambush. By the time the feud ended, fear of involvement had brought about the depopulation of the countryside. The survivors of the two clans were reconciled in characteristic fashion. A survivor of the Fratuzzi, Salvatore D'Amico, who had lost all his family, went to the police and told all he knew of the malfeasances of the Stoppaglieri. It was an act tantamount to suicide, of a man tired of life, as D'Amico made quite clear in his statement. This time the Fratuzzi did the right thing. They killed their clan member, and to make sure of his recognition, his body was displayed prominently, with an amulet of the kind worn by the Fratuzzi, made from a vestment stolen from an image of the Madonna, placed over each eye.

There are mild and rustic men, goatherds and ploughmen, drawn without hope of escape into these ancient, tragic games whose rules were established perhaps before their ancestors reached the shores of the Mediterranean. In 1944 I was engaged in army duties in Naples which committed me to a number of lugubrious visits to the prison of Poggio Reale. There I was introduced by the head warder to a Sicilian, D'Agostino, who had committed five vendetta murders. The maximum sentence for an 'honour' killing in Italy is ten years, so that D'Agostino was serving a total of fifty years. He was put on display for the benefit of privileged visitors with what can only be described as a sort of modest pride. D'Agostino was treated with immense respect. He was the only prisoner, not excluding a general occupying a cell in Poggio Reale at that time, who was addressed in the third person singular, being given a courteous *lei* instead of the familiar and slightly contemptuous *tu*. D'Agostino was small, puzzled, and yet resigned. He was slightly under five feet in height, with tiny hands and feet and hardly more than the frame of a child. His crime had been committed with an axe – the tomahawk-like weapon that Prefect Mori, Mussolini's destroyer of the Mafia, had permitted shepherds to keep – and he had wiped out a whole family. This was the end of a period of close confinement, and on the assumption that after three years the prisoner had come to a working arrangement with despair, the forty-seven years that remained would pass under a slightly relaxed prison régime. D'Agostino always expected to be asked whether he would commit his crime again could the clock be put back, and his reply was always the same: 'Surely you don't imagine I had any choice, one way or the other? Honour's honour and a vendetta's a vendetta. You might say that destiny put its big fat thumb in my neck and squashed me like a beetle.' The warders nodded their sympathy and their agreement. That was the way it was.

What would Don Vito Cascio Ferro, who established his image as a forward-looking man by making a pioneer trip in a balloon and was head of all the Mafia until his final arrest by Prefect Mori, have said to anyone who pointed out to him that the organisation he commanded was psychologically still entangled in the prehistory of humanity? The sophisticated Don Vito can hardly have realised, either, that Mafia symbolism – the system of graded warnings from the cutting down of a vine and the maiming of an ass or mule, to the depositing at a man's door of his beheaded dog or a sheep with its throat cut – is shared with certain African tribes of the Republic of Mali. How strange, too, that the custom of vendetta of Corsica, Sardinia and Sicily – whose peoples have presumably been separated for thousands of years – should be so similar in all its curious detail: the ritual denunciation of the slayer by the professional mourners at the funeral (ignorance of his identity will be feigned, if necessary, up till this point); the entrusting of the vendetta to the male nearest-of-kin by the senior female member of the household; the kissing, even the pretended sucking of the wounds, by close relations such as mother, wife or brother, followed by the spoken formula: 'In this way may I drink the blood of the man who killed you'; the final consummation of the act of vengeance, which ideally should take place, after a period of ritual preparation, in full sunshine – an archaic blueprint for the *mise-en-scène* of *High Noon*.

*   *   *

The vendetta was the weapon ready to hand of the poor and otherwise defenceless in a society where law did not exist and justice meant the baron's court and the baron's torture chamber. Sicily – the America of the ancient world – has been a colony exploited by the use of slave labour, either openly or in a disguised form, for two thousand years. The

Roman armies marched to the conquest of Gaul and Britain on bread made from corn grown by Sicilian slaves. When, with the fall of Rome, the Papacy took over the great Sicilian estates, it was the chain gangs of Sicilian peasant labourers that provided three-fourths of its wealth. Sicily was exploited by Norman, German, Frenchman, Aragonese, Spaniard, and finally the Bourbons, but nearly always from a distance. After the Germans there was no central government, no monarch, no court, no resident hierarchy. So long as the corn was shipped out of Sicilian ports each year, nothing else mattered. Defining the seemingly endless ice-age of feudalism in Sicily, Filangieri, the social historian, said that an overbearing despotism had grown up to separate the Crown from the people. As a result, Sicily was a political hermaphrodite, neither monarchy nor republic, 'which suffered from all the dependency of the former, while lacking the advantages of a constitution, and all the turbulence of the latter, although deprived of its liberties'.

And then, just at the time when the first stirrings of the modern world were visible elsewhere in Europe, another tragic yoke was laid upon the Sicilian neck by the establishment of the Inquisition. And in Sicily, through the remoteness of the Crown, its effects were even more deadening than in Spain itself. More and more to the modern observer the Holy Office appears as a device concerned primarily with economic situations, and only secondarily with matters of faith. Drawing its revenues from heresy, it saw to it that heresy was abundant. In Spain heresy provided an excuse for the ruin and annihilation of a class of rich Christianised merchants of Jewish or Moorish origin. In Sicily its objectives were all-embracing, although vaguer. Heresy started as religious dissent, but as religious dissenters – understandably enough – were remarkably few, the Inquisition widened its scope to include a miscellany of bigamists, 'philosophers', usurers, sodomites, priests who married their concubines, and finally opponents of any kind, who automatically became classed as heretics. Membership of the Inquisition, like that of an exclusive club, was open only to the aristocracy, and in Sicily the barons enrolled themselves with enthusiasm as familiars. All convictions were accompanied by forfeiture of property, and the Inquisition gave no receipts. In procedural matters the scales were heavily weighted against those whose reputation for original thought or whose conspicuous possessions happened to attract the Holy Office's attention. Arrests were made on suspicion, often as the result of anonymous denunciation. The accused was presumed guilty and the functions of prosecutor and judge were combined. Women, children and slaves could be called as witnesses for the prosecution, but not for the defence. Nor could the victim be allowed a lawyer to plead his case, as this would have been tantamount to opposing the Inquisition, and, as such, an act of heresy.

The familiars of the Inquisition dominated Sicily for three centuries. Until the time of their disbanding in 1787 there were never less than two thousand of these psalm-singing marauders, each in command of his own band of retainers – all of whom enjoyed the same extra-legal privileges. They stripped rich men of their property, and sentenced them to *murus largus* – the most comfortable kind of incarceration the day had to offer. The poor were punished for their lack of seizable goods by torture and *murus strictis*, which meant that they were flung, fettered, into a deep dungeon and endured 'the bread and water of affliction' until they died. Horrified by these excesses, which he was quite powerless to check, the Spanish Viceroy, the Duke of Medinaceli, wrote: 'It would take a year to describe the things they do. Unheard of things – the most hideous and frightful enormities.' The poor man's only shield was the Mafia and the vendetta. Justice was not to be come by, but the association of men of honour, silent, persistent and inflexible, could at least exact a bloody retribution for the loss of a wife or daughter, or the burning down of a house. Colafanni, an authority on the period, sums up: 'The Mafia in Sicily under the Bourbons provided the only means for the poor and humble to make themselves respected ... To the Mafia, then, went all the rebels, all those that had suffered injuries, all the victims.'

It was in the school of the vendetta, too, that the traditional character of the mafioso was formed. The common man, a victim of absolute power, had to learn to stomach insult or injury with apparent indifference so that vengeance could be delayed until the opportunity for its consumption presented itself. The mafioso therefore developed a kind of self-control closely resembling that quality known as *giri* by the Japanese, and so much admired by them. A true man of honour never weakened his position or armed his enemy in advance by outbursts of passion or of fear. When he sustained some grave injury he made a pact with himself to be revenged, and thereafter would wait patiently and unemotionally, half a lifetime if necessary, until his moment came – often seemingly on excellent terms with the man he proposed to destroy.

But when a man lost his head, threw Mafia-inculcated secrecy and caution to the wind and struck back openly, his only chance of salvation was to take to the *maquis*. For this reason there was never a time when Sicily was without its bandits. At the end of the Second World War thirty separate armed bands terrorised western Sicily, while even in the late winter of 1962–3 motorised bandits were still staging highway robberies on the main provincial highway between Castellamare and Ballestrate. A hundred and fifty years ago the Bourbon authorities decided to deal with this situation by creating the first pseudo-police force. The only qualification for enrolment in the 'Armed Companies', as they were called, was ruthlessness. Many of these upholders of the law were ferocious criminals reprieved from the gallows and allowed to rehabilitate themselves in this way. What the familiars of the Inquisition had overlooked, the Armed Companies took. After the depredations carried out in the name of religion, Sicilians were now doomed to suffer voicelessly under the agents of the State. Since then they have quite simply turned their backs on authority of any kind. For this reason the police charged with the investigation of the highway robberies of February 1963 met with nothing but the most intractable hostility from local villagers, while even the victims of the robberies appear not to have been specially helpful. For this reason, when a man is found lying seriously wounded, possibly dying, and the police appeal to him to identify his aggressor, the reply is usually couched in a formula: 'If I die, may God forgive me, as I forgive the one who did this. If I manage to pull through, I know how to settle my own accounts.'

This is the famous Sicilian *omertà* – 'manliness', which rules the public conscience and is sustained so often even in the face of death. It is a word which calls for further examination, and is best understood by the study of an extreme case of *omertà* in action.

Some four or five years ago one of two brothers living together in a Sicilian farmhouse disappeared. The men were known to have been on the worst possible terms for years, and the younger and stronger one frequently knocked his older brother about and even threatened to kill him. Finally the older brother vanished and the police got to hear about it, searched the farmhouse, and found inefficiently cleaned-up blood-stains on the floor. It is a popular misconception that a case for murder cannot be made out if no body can be found. In this case it was decided by the examining magistrate that a *corpus delicti* existed, constituted by the threats of murder known to have been made, the man's disappearance, the bloodstains, and the suspect's immediate assumption of his brother's property. The younger brother was accordingly tried for murder, found guilty, and sentenced to imprisonment for life.

A year or two later a carabiniere, who knew the older brother, suddenly found himself face to face with the 'murdered' man. He was working quietly as a labourer on a farm in the mountains, only two miles away. It emerged that as part of his plan to be revenged on his brother, the man had changed his name, although most of his fellow labourers and some of the neighbours knew who he was all the same. This was *omertà* with a vengeance. It simply did not occur to these people to go to the police, despite the terrific injustice that had been done. It was 'manly' to solve one's own problems in one's own way and leave others to do the same, and one 'lost respect' by poking one's nose into other people's affairs.

The Sicilian conscience is further bedevilled by an unfortunate linguistic confusion, arising out of the similarity between the words *omertà* and *umiltà* – humility, the Christian virtue so much extolled in the Church. Many illiterate Siciliane have combined the two words to produce a hybrid of mixed pagan and Christian significance. The virtuous man is in Mafia fashion 'manly' and silent, and as a Christian, humble.

Far from protecting the underdog, the Mafia today has taken the place of the oppressors of old, but it still benefits from a moral climate formed in past centuries. The Sicilian is a trifle cynical and quite self-sufficient. He fights his own battles, keeps his mouth shut, and has little interest in the doings of humanity outside the circle of his family, extended perhaps to include his second cousins. 'Manliness', once a barricade raised against injustice, now serves to keep justice out.

*   *   *

In the past it was the Mafia – the product of weak government that had developed its own vested interest in governmental weakness – that whipped up the frantic *jacqueries* of 1820, 1840 and 1866. The savageries of these outbursts of peasant hatred are quite inexplicable to anyone unaware of the long years of contempt that had preceded them. As in Spain, the targets of popular fury were always the same: the landlord, the Church, the police. There is no better description of the kind of thing that could happen than that given by Giovanni Verga in his story 'Liberty', which is largely factual and based on the rising at Brontë, put down by Nino Bixio, lieutenant of Garibaldi – the man who was to have given the land to the peasants.

> Like the sea in storm, the crowd foamed and swayed in front of the club of the gentry, and outside the Town Hall, and on the steps of the church – a sea of white stocking-caps, axes and sickles glittering. Then they burst into the little street.
>
> 'Your turn first, baron! You who have had folks cudgelled by your estate guards!' At the head of all the people a witch, with her old hair sticking up, armed with nothing but her nails. 'Your turn, priest of the devil, for you've sucked the soul out of us!' . . . 'Your turn, police-sergeant, you who never took the law on anybody except poor folks who'd got nothing!' 'Your turn, estate guards, who sold your own flesh and your neighbour's flesh for ten pence a day!'
>
> Now they were drunk with the killing. Sickles, hands, rags, stones, everything red with blood. The gentry! Kill them all! Kill them all! Down with the gentry!

'Don't kill me,' pleads the priest, 'I'm in mortal sin!' Neighbour Lucia being the mortal sin; neighbour Lucia, whose father sold her to the priest when she was fourteen years old, at the time of the famine winter. But the priest is hacked to pieces on the cobblestones of the street. Then it is the turn of the apothecary, the lawyer, and the lawyer's eleven-year-old son. The estate guards fire on the crowd from the castle, but the castle is stormed and the defenders massacred, the baron's young sons trampled to death, the baroness and her baby thrown from her balcony to the street.

And then suddenly the slaughter is over. They are free of the gentry and rage is dead. Now they have their liberty, but nobody knows what to do with it. And in any case there is no time to learn, for the Army, with its firing squads, is on the way. Quietly and sadly, arms folded, they sit waiting behind closed doors.

In those days the Mafia was still with the people; then, gradually, as it gathered its power it began to draw apart. The Mafia was paid for its part in Garibaldi's triumph, it organised the plebiscite (at Lampedusa's Donnafugata – Voters, 515; Voting, 512; Yes, 512; No, zero); its chieftains, like his illiterate Sedaras, married their daughters to penniless princes. From that time on the Mafia began to elbow the feudal aristocracy aside. By 1945 the process was complete. Don Calogero Vizzini was the feudal overlord of all Sicily as well as head of the Mafia. And thereby he had become the worst single thorn in the peasants' side since the bad old days of the Bourbons.

Don Fabrizio, the ruminative and unworldly princeling of Lampedusa's novel, philosophical in his acceptance of Garibaldi and the Mafia, felt queasy at the first sight of the infant democracy newly delivered at Donnafugata. 'Something had died, God only knew in what back-alley, in what corner of the popular conscience.' People always had done, and always would do, what they were told, and he found it in some way demeaning that anyone should find it necessary to construct this elaborate edifice of pretence dedicated to the lie that free will and freedom of choice actually existed.

However sickening to Don Fabrizio's stomach the newly imported democracy might have been, for the Mafia it was an invention as promising as the new steam-engine. In the old days the Viceroy had given the orders – at most, and as a matter of courtesy, taking the advice of his council of nobles. Now it was to be the turn of anyone who could fight his way to the controls of this wonderful new machine. In 1881 communal elections were held at Villalba – the town that was to become Don Calogero Vizzini's capital – and the Marchese of Villalba, supported by the Mafia, took his precautions ten days in advance. The two hundred and fourteen citizens possessing the qualifications entitling them to vote were locked up in a granary, from which they were released, eight at a time, and escorted by the Marchese's armed guards to the polls. The Marchese was elected.

Later the Mafia invented and perfected new methods of democratic suasion. By the time the government of Giolitti reached power, the Mafia had become the only electoral force that counted in Sicily and the Government was realistic in its acceptance of the fact. Alongi, who published a study of the Mafia in 1902, describes the arrangements for voting he had witnessed a year or two previously: 'Some short distance from the polling station the road was barred by a group of sinister figures. Here each voter as he approached was seized, thoroughly bastinadoed, and forced to drink a huge glass of wine. There followed a thorough search of his person, after which the government candidate's voting slip was put into his hand and he was led or dragged to the ballot box, where the president took the slip from him and put it in.'

Later still, this physical suppression of the element of choice gradually came to be considered unnecessary; it was found that the same result could be obtained by making the voter understand what he stood to lose by voting for the wrong side. As it was never explained to the voter what programme the candidates stood for, and he was assumed to be quite ignorant of the function of Parliament, the contending parties might be represented by symbols such as the mule and the ox, and the agricultural voters warned that it was either a case of voting for the mule or looking elsewhere for work in future. The system recalls the last election held under French tutelage in parts of then colonial West Africa, where bloody disputes took place between villages over the relative merits in terms of strength, courage and sagacity of the lion and the elephant, which were the symbols adopted by two of the parties soliciting their votes.

This somewhat special interpretation of the democratic process persisted in Sicily even after the end of the Second World War. In 1945 when the Mafia and most of Sicily's aristocracy were hoping that Sicily would secede from Italy to become an American state, or at worst a British colony, a Separatist congress was convened at which Don Calogero Vizzini appeared unexpectedly and without formal invitation. When asked who he represented, he replied with proud simplicity: 'I have only to whistle, and every man in the province of Caltanisetta will vote Separatist.'

When a year or two after that the Mafia threw the idea of Separatism overboard, and became, by order of Don Calò, Christian Democrat, there was one serious breach in the Honoured Society's political unity in the person of the awe-inspiring Don Vanni Sacco, head of the Mafia of Camporeale. To the remonstrations of Don Calò, when he refused to accept a badge sent him in the form of a cross on a shield – the Party emblem – Vanni Sacco replied: 'I've been a liberal all my life, and my father before me. After all, politics, as I see it, is a stick, and I've got used to the feel of this one.' It took lunch with the Archbishop of Monreale, Monsignor Filippi, and the Archbishop's consent to Vanni Sacco's request that his daughter, Giovanna, should be granted the honour of christening the cathedral's new bell, before Don Vanni would agree to change his politics.

*   *   *

At the turn of the century, with the political machine finally and firmly under control, and the manicured hands of that distinguished ruffian Don Vito Cascio Ferro on its levers, the Mafia could go ahead and trim up the details of the 'state within a state' that existed until the coming of Mussolini, and was to re-emerge in 1945 under the generalship of Don Calogero Vizzini of Villalba.

It was Don Vito who developed with a certain artistry the system of the '*pizzi*', as he called it – an onomatopoeic and picturesque word from the Sicilian dialect which translates rather flatly into English as 'racket'. *Pizzi* means the beak of a small bird, such as a canary or a lark, and when Don Vito with his inborn habit of understatement spoke of levying a Mafia toll, he called it in Sicilian *fari vagnari a pizzi* – 'wetting the beak'. By the time Prefect Mori had succeeded in putting Don Vito away on his faked-up charge, beak-wetting was included in almost every conceivable activity in Sicily.

A great gathering of vulturine chieftains had collected to wet their beaks at the expense of the farmers, whose produce they bought dirt cheap on the spot and carried to the market in the Mafia's own beautifully decorated carts – or later, trucks. In the market only those whose place had been 'guaranteed' by the Mafia were allowed to buy or sell at prices the Mafia fixed. The Mafia wetted its beak in the meat, fish, beer and fruit businesses. It moved into the sulphur mines, controlled the output of rock salt, took over building contracts, 'organised labour', cornered the plots in Sicily's cemeteries, put tobacco-smuggling on a new and more profitable basis through its domination of the Sicilian fishing fleets, and went in for tomb-robbing in the ruins of the Greek settlement of Selinunte – the results of its archaeological excavations being offered at bargain prices to foreign tourists. Looking round for further sources of revenue, the Mafia decided to recommend the owners of country houses and estates, however small, to employ guardians for their property, and after a few stubborn landowners had declined to supply sinecures for ex-convicts and had seen their property burned down, the practice became universal. There were advantages, too, to be gained by stringing along. The Mafia gave monopolies to shopkeepers in different trades and then invited them to put up their prices – at the same time, of course, increasing their Mafia contribution. Some of the Mafia beak-wettings were picturesque in a sort of depraved oriental way. Beggars, for example, would be granted exclusive rights to a certain pitch, thus guaranteeing a display of distorted limbs freedom from competition by simulated idiocy.

The most evident of the Mafia's criminal functions – and one that had been noted by the Bourbon attorney-general back in the 'twenties of the last century – now became the normally accepted thing. The Mafia virtually replaced the police force, offering a form of arrangement with crime as a substitute for its suppression. When a theft, for instance, took place, whether of a mule, a jewelled pendant, or a motorcar, a Mafia intermediary was soon on the scene, offering reasonable terms for the recovery of the stolen object. In this way the matter was usually settled rapidly, and to the satisfaction of all concerned. The victim got his property back without delay. The thief received a relatively small sum, but at least escaped the risk of police interference, since no one would have dared to call in the police once the Mafia had interested itself. The Mafia intermediary, of course, wetted his beak at the expense of both parties. The situation was and is an everyday one in Sicily. The police charge nothing to restore stolen property but are only successful in one case out of ten. The Mafia is expensive, and may impose a commission charge of thirty-three and a third per cent. However, the Mafia is successful ninety per cent of the time.

But it was not only the farmer and the merchant who felt the weight of the Mafia's New Order. The rich man, drawing his income, perhaps, from investments, could not be allowed to escape the net, and he became increasingly the target of letters of extortion. Such letters are common-place in Sicily, but most of them are composed by novice delinquents who give themselves away by their brusqueness, their semi-literacy, and their habitual decoration with drawings of skulls and crossbones and dripping daggers. Letters of this kind go into the wastepaper basket, or may even be handed over to the police. The genuine Mafia letter-writer is unmistakable in his style, which is likely to have a touch of the nineteenth century about it, with outmoded epistolatory flourishes and protestations. It may even express regret for the inconvenience caused. As no second requests are sent, it is usual for payment to be made promptly.

Some of the rackets sound a trifle fantastic, such as the tax imposed on lovers in Don Vito's day when they went to carry on their courtship in the

Spanish fashion with a girl who sat behind a barred window, and had to pay a Mafia concessionaire 'the price of a candle' for his protection.

More fantastic was the racket – or rather the interlacing series of rackets – built up around religious devotion. The Mafia – always ready to ally itself with the Church as a matter of expediency, in the manner of Don Calogero Vizzini – moved cautiously at first. By the middle of the last century it controlled the confraternities devoted to the cults of the various patron saints, and more important, it directed the standing committees of the cults. It was the standing committees that raised the funds required for the saint's annual feast day; for the processions, the illuminations, and the firework displays. Later a Mafia trust interested itself in the manufacture of devotional candles, and obtained a virtual monopoly. In nearly all Sicilian churches the seats are private property, and it was the Mafia that hired the seats. The Mafia took over the manufacture of religious objects of all kinds, and, being on the whole free of sentimental prejudices, attacked the problems of manufacture and distribution in an entirely dispassionate manner. With the advance of the twentieth century and the streamlining of production, its factories pro-duced statues of saints and madonnas and religious medallions by the million. It employed the most persuasive travelling salesmen, appointed the most go-ahead retail firms as exclusive stockists, awarded bonuses and special quantity discounts, and supplied tasteful window displays to the shops in the bigger cities. Many of the faithful liked to have their religious medallions blessed by a bishop, and the Mafia had no objection to arranging that – and blessed they were, in basketfuls and by the thousand.

Back in the last century the Mafia had turned its attention to the lucrative business of manufacturing relics. The process was a simple one, requiring only the co-operation of the sacred object's custodian – in most cases a village priest. The relic was usually some portion of the body of a saint or a lock of his hair, or occasionally a more fanciful object of devotion such as a miniature urn full of the ashes of Abraham, or a bone from one of the fishes multiplied by Christ in the miracle of the loaves and fishes. All that was necessary to create a second relic having a large portion of the virtue of the original was to bring the new object into contact with it. Although the authorities of the Church frown upon the practice, relics were and are mass-produced by the thousand in this way. The manufacturing process is simplified by the existence of a tremendous number and diversity of saintly remnants upon which local cults are centred. In the course of a recent study of Mafia penetration of devotional practices, the Italian publication *Le Ore* carried out, with remarkable results, a brief numerical survey of the most important of such relics. The paper discovered the existence of seventeen arms attributed to St Andrew, thirteen to St Stephen, twelve to St Philip, and ten each to St Vincent and St Tecla. Sixty fingers belonging to St John the Baptist were in circulation, and forty heads were revered as that of St Julian.

The Mafia seems to have decided that there were profitable pickings to be made in this direction shortly after 1870, when, as a measure of reform, the Italian Government decided to close down a number of religious institutions and the relics they contained were dispersed. Most of these were bought up by the Mafia. A number of extra copies of each were made up from materials furnished by an abandoned cemetery, and duplicates of the original seals of authenticity attached by the Congregation of Rites of the Vatican were assiduously faked. A vigorous overseas market for such spurious articles of devotion – particularly in the Americas – quickly developed. *Le Ore* discovered that in 1962 alone minor sales to the United States made by the organisation they had investigated included twenty suits of armour of Joan of Arc, twenty monastic gowns worn by St Francis of Assisi, fifty rosaries alleged to have belonged to Bernadette, and – as a triumphant culmination of Mafia salesmanship – the wand carried by Moses when he led the Children of Israel into the Promised Land.

Where there was no saint, no holy relic, and consequently no flocking of pilgrims to be fleeced, the Mafia did its best with artificial substitutes. A well-publicised 'miracle', such as the apparition of the Madonna to a child, filled the specially-chartered buses, the shops, and the hotels, and produced an upswing – however short-lived – in the sales-curve for religious merchandise. Thus it was with Padre Pio, the 'stigmatised' monk of San Giovanni Rotondo, whose cult was thought important enough to justify the transfer of a Mafia commando to the Italian mainland itself.

The appearance of a monk whose followers claimed that his hands miraculously reproduced Christ's wounds from the Cross's nails was enough to provoke a delirium of commercial speculation. Within a few years the remote hamlet near Foggia had turned into a sort of embryo Lourdes, with half a dozen prosperous hotels, innumerable boarding-houses, and a hospital with a helicopter landing-stage on its roof, to which rich patients were brought to be exposed to the saintly influence. Books were sold by the hundred thousand, describing Padre Pio's miracles, and records by the million of the father saying mass or at prayer. The photographs of the monk displaying his wounds would not have convinced the hardened sceptic, as the negative had obviously been subjected to crude retouching and the prints daubed all over with a red dye, but they were happily bought by the pilgrims who poured into San Giovanni Rotondo. Such was the clamour to be confessed by Padre Pio (ninety-five per cent of the applicants were women), that confessions had to be booked, and the waiting-list grew so long that pilgrims had to spend days and even weeks in the town's expensive hotels awaiting their turn. By arrangement with the Mafia, however, and on payment of a substantial sum, the queue could be jumped. Mafia agents waited, too, at the bus terminals, ready to carry off new arrivals to be confessed on the spot for sums varying between two and five thousand lire by false Padre Pios who awaited their prey in hastily faked-up backstreet rooms. Most impudent of all was the sale of revolting relics of the monk's 'stigmata' – hundreds of yards of blood-soaked bandages displayed on market stalls outside the convent. Even when in 1960 the newspapers published analyses showing the blood to be that of chickens, the sales did not slacken.

It is this scene of the Mafia presiding over charlatans selling cock's blood and amulets against the evil eye that reminds us how fully the wheel has turned. The Mafia that had come into being as the peasants' refuge against the worst abuses of the Middle Ages now gleefully resuscitated all the bagful of medieval tricks to exploit the peasants' ignorance. The Mafia that had fought feudalism, that had lain in wait on the moonless night for the baron no officer of the law could touch, now elected and manipulated politicians who would guarantee to fight for the survival of the feudal order. But far worse was to come under the absolute rule of Don Calogero Vizzini, General Mafia of Villalba, still known as '*Il Buonanima* – the Good Soul' to the many thousands who cherish his memory. It was Don Calò whose hired killers silenced the voices of protest when the postwar democracy turned out to be a crueller fake than Fascism itself. And when the voices crying in the wilderness of the Sicilian feudal estates swelled into a furious chorus, it was Don Calò and his feudal allies who called in Giuliano, the cleverest and bloodiest bandit in Sicilian history, to fight their battles for them.

3

CALOGERO VIZZINI, the patriarch of Villalba, was born in 1877. His father was a peasant who had been sufficiently astute, as well as personable enough, to marry into a family very slightly more elevated than his own, although still far from middle-class. The Scarlatas owned a few square yards of land – a rare distinction in a feudal community composed almost entirely of day labourers and sharecroppers. They enjoyed, moreover, exceptional prestige in Villalba from the fact that a member of the family had risen to high eminence in the Church.

In defining these matters of social prestige, it has to be remembered that life as lived by the citizens of Villalba is singularly devoid of the incentives and the rewards one takes for granted in a modern community of its size. Most foreigners who have visited Sicily carry with them a mental picture of resorts such as Taormina whose sole purpose is the gratification of the foreign visitor, of the ancient towns of Catania or Syracusa, and of the oriental brilliance and colour of the landscapes squeezed between the volcano Etna's huge paws of lava.

The western Sicily that so few have seen is harsh, lacking in grace, and as utilitarian in its way as the Black Country of England. There are a hundred small and shabby towns like Villalba, possessing – like Villalba – no history, but only a few oppressive memories and nightmarish legends. Their purpose has been to breed and house the labour for the great feudal estates, and to condition the minds and subjugate the bodies of that labour. In such towns as Villalba there is an almost puritanical absence of any of the apparatus of pleasure. Even for the very rich, the only satisfaction is to be derived from the wielding of power. Here, in fact, the feudal order continues astonishingly after a thousand years, rather like a mammoth preserved in ice. The absentee landlord may still rule from his palace in Palermo, through his stewards and armed guards, but more commonly, he will have leased his estate for a number of years to a *gabellotto* – literally a tax collector – who is traditionally mafioso and will not work the land himself but parcel it out between sharecropping small farmers on the most extortionate terms. At the bottom of this social pyramid is the day labourer, to whom the sharecropper passes down as much as he can of his inevitable misery. The only escape for the exceptionally talented boy born into this class has always been the Church, whose intelligent policy it has been to refresh its blood by accepting recruits from all social levels. When a peasant boy is transformed into a priest his old playfellows salute him respectfully – '*bacciamo le mani* – we kiss your hands.' He now shares in the clear-cut four-way division of power with the mayor of the town, the chief of police and the local head of the Mafia.

Don Calò's uncle had been such an exceptional peasant boy, and had had the advantage of not having to force his way out of one of the lowest social levels. He had shot up like a comet through the hierarchy of the Church to become Bishop of Muro Lucana. The rise of a cousin – also on the mother's side – had been even more spectacular, for he became not only Bishop of Noto, but the founder of the monastic order of Maria Santissima del Carmelo. Don Calò's own brother was parish priest of Villalba. As a compensation for his more modest achievement, he had been able to devote more time to side interests, such as running profitable agricultural co-operatives. Such a mingling of spiritual with mundane occupations causes no surprise in western Sicily, where, for example, in 1962 the parish priest of the island's new Mafia capital, Mussomeli, was also chairman of the local credit bank.

The young Calogero Vizzini himself was excluded from the beginning from this traditional outlet by his lack of patience with scholarship of any kind, and a sort of bluff and perverse insistence in remaining a down-to-earth countryman in his general demeanour. Don Calò never confused the shadow with the substance of power, and saw no reason why he should ever be compelled to speak an emasculated Italian rather than the vigorous local dialect. In any case he could never have tolerated the long years of submission to others that would have been demanded of

him as a religious acolyte. As it was, he remained an illiterate all his life –
a state of affairs from which he seemed to derive positive satisfaction,
being inclined in company to boast that he could solve problems in his
head faster than other men could on paper. Although an agnostic, like
most elevated Mafia personalities, he agreed with Napoleon that religion
was good for the people, and when at home he liked to see priests about
the house.

The young Calogero's first trial of strength with the law came at the
age of seventeen, and with it was laid the cornerstone of the edifice of
'respect', which is the prerequisite of high office in the Mafia. Although
even in those days unsentimental in his make-up, he was involved in
some way with the pretty daughter of the well-to-do Solazzo family of
Villalba. It appears that marriage was never contemplated, but none the
less, Calogero imposed his veto on the girl's association with any other
male. When a promising young official from the Magistrates' Court of
Villalba began to pay her attentions, Calogero Vizzini got together a
juvenile gang, burst into the Solazzo home one evening, dragged the
interloper outside, and beat him nearly to death. After this demonstration
the Solazzo heiress was left in peace by all potential suitors, and remained
a spinster until the end of her days. Calogero was arrested and placed on
trial for criminal assault, but through the powerful intercession of his
uncle, the bishop, the Solazzo family agreed to the whole thing's being
hushed up and the case was quashed.

The following year Calogero Vizzini's career began in earnest, with
his choice for a livelihood of the exciting and dangerous profession of
the cancia – which in turn led to his association with a remarkable man.
Practicians of the cancia acted, in effect, as intermediaries between
peasants who wanted their wheat milled into flour, and the mills, located
for the most part in inaccessible places along the coast – in the case of
Villalba, fifty miles away. The mills were controlled by an ancient, highly
specialised and extremely ferocious branch of the Mafia, which refused
to tolerate the building of any competitive mills outside its own area. To
take charge of the grain and get it safely to its destination across roads
unceasingly infested by bandits, called for more than usual toughness

and resource. Calogero Vizzini tackled this problem by coming to an arrangement with the leading bandit of the day, Paolo Varsalona, whose hide-out was, as usual, in the nearby Cammarata mountains.

Varsalona, who was Calogero's mentor in his most impressionable years, was too intelligent a man to have become a bandit other than through circumstances that left him no option. In this case it was a scrupulous regard for the sacred law of vendetta, the fulfilment of which was regarded by most Sicilians of his day as almost an act of piety. Varsalona's brother had been murdered, and at the trial a witness was produced who did his best to provide the men accused of the crime with an alibi. Varsalona felt obliged to blow his head off with a blunderbuss. Once an outlaw, and however reluctant Varsalona may have been to take to the *maquis*, he brought to the problems of banditry the clear vision and the fresh approach of the talented outsider. Up till this time classical Sicilian brigands had organised themselves in mounted bands. They cultivated a fierce appearance, wore outlandish clothing, carried obsolete but impressive blunderbusses, and, in short, placed great reliance on terror. It was the habit, for example, of one of Varsalona's predecessors to ride at the head of his men, carrying by way of a personal standard a skull stuck on a pole. The psychological merits of these old-fashioned tactics were offset by considerable drawbacks. By their very size and the amount of disturbance they created such bands were relatively easy to locate, and were sooner or later destroyed in pitched battles with the police.

The novel strategy invented by Varsalona – for which the bandit Giuliano was later to receive the credit – was simply to arrange for his men to be mobilised and demobilised at will. The Varsalona band went quietly to a planned operation on foot and in their workaday clothes, and when it was over they slipped just as quietly back to their everyday occupations, if they possessed any. With these will-o'-the-wisp tactics Varsalona was outstandingly successful over a number of years, and newspapers got into the habit of calling him 'the bandit phenomenon'. Calogero's admiration for him was such that, while carrying on with the bread-and-butter business of the *cancia*, he decided also to enrol in the Varsalona band. In 1902, after several valuable years of experience gained in this way, Calogero Vizzini found himself standing trial with the rest of the band – which had finally fallen into a trap set by the police – for 'association to commit crime'. He was one of the few to be acquitted. This was the third time he had slipped through the fingers of the law, for at the age of twenty-one he had already been acquitted for 'insufficiency of proof' on a charge of complicity in a murder.

'Insufficiency of proof' is the standard formula under which cases brought against mafiosi are eventually committed to oblivion, and nine times out of ten it covers up the fact that essential witnesses have suddenly decided to retract their damaging evidence. In this case, on-lookers were quick to read the signs. It was probably at about this point in his career that Calogero was invited to become a member of the 'Honoured Society'. By the very nature of that association – the most secret, the most powerful, and the most abiding of all secret societies – the fact that one is a member can never be admitted. At the most a mafioso may allow himself to be described as 'a man of respect', or 'a friend of the friends', or accept – as did Calogero Vizzini at the age of twenty-five – the title of *Zu*, meaning uncle. As for the Mafia, its pretensions were far too lofty to allow of the admission to its association of a common bandit, but its scrutineers may well have recognised in the new acolyte a refined and imaginative criminality that could be turned to the service of the organisation as a whole.

By 1914, and the outbreak of the First World War, Zu Calò was the undisputed head of the Mafia of the Province of Caltanissetta, and as such, in Mafia jargon, a *pezzo di novanta* – a term of honour derived from an unwieldy but impressive piece of siege artillery of the epoch of Garibaldi, firing a shell 90 millimetres in diameter (hence the translated Americanism, 'big shot'). World War One provided Zu Calò with end-less new opportunities for self-enrichment. An Army Commission sent to Sicily and charged with the requisition of horses for the cavalry and artillery suggested to him three separate sources of profit. As a pre-liminary, Zu Calò came to terms with the members of the Commission, who were happy to delegate their responsibilities to him. Thereafter all the infirm and broken-winded nags of the island were collected and sold to the government. Zu Calò then collected a poll-tax on animals whose owners preferred them not to be requisitioned. The third string to his bow was the sale to the Commission of a large number of horses and mules that had been rustled for the occasion and bought from the experts who conducted such operations at the very low prices that stolen animals normally fetched, although resold to the Commission at the top of the market.

A large proportion of the horses and mules supplied by Zu Calò died of glanders, heart disease, pneumonia, malnutrition, or sheer old age before they could be transported to the battle areas, and this *contretemps* was followed by a whispering campaign and then allegations in the Press that the Army had become the largest-scale receiver of stolen property in Italian history.

The Ministry of War instituted an enquiry and a General Moccia was sent to Palermo to investigate. As a result, Calogero Vizzini and a number of his accomplices, both civilian and army, appeared before a military tribunal. What happened at that trial has happened a hundred times before and a hundred times since, and has come to be regarded as the inevitable outcome of all such criminal proceedings when an attempt is made to bring the Mafia to justice. Witnesses, who outside the courtroom had been voluble, were now obstinately silent. Every single person who had made a statement of any kind likely to incriminate the formidable *pezzo di novanta* in any way, forthwith withdrew it. In the course of the brief and frustrating proceedings nine witnesses were condemned and sentenced on the spot for perjury or 'muteness of malice', and it is recorded that the only emotion they showed on hearing their sentences was one of relief.

The defendants were acquitted, to the enormous enlargement of Zu Calò's prestige. The trial had amply shown that he had powerful friends in the Army, the administration, and probably in Parliament itself. Moreover, Sicilians had little stomach for wars that they were involved in by the Italians, and were inclined to throw their caps up in the air when anyone succeeded in making a laughing-stock of the government of Rome.

* * *

It was soon after his discomfiture of the Italian army that Calogero Vizzini, now considered the second Mafia personality of the island and entitled as such to the honorific prefix 'Don', completed a social process that had been going on since 1860 and forms part of the theme of *The Leopard*. The Mafia has at all times delighted in fishing in troubled waters, and has therefore always been ready with its support for any attack on the central government, whether that of Italy or its predecessors. In keeping with this traditional policy, it came to the aid of Garibaldi in his overthrow of the Bourbon kingdom and was properly rewarded for its services. Don Calogero Sedara, Lampedusa's sinister and powerful Mayor, is shown as having made a fortune out of the war and as already overshadowing the Prince of Salina, left defenceless (as the Prince sees it) by his breeding, his gentlemanly scruples, and a somewhat atypical preference for the study of astronomy to the collection of rents. With melancholy resignation Salina foresees the eventual replacement of a class of other-worldly, enlightened aristocrats by one of money-grubbing realists. With allowances for the special angle of the Prince's view, this is roughly the historic process completed by Don Calogero Vizzini sixty years later.

*   *   *

Sicily is not Italy, nor – with the exception of the spas, the palms, and the mimosa of its eastern seaboard – is it even recognisably a Mediterranean country. Scenically as well as sociologically, this country is an archaism. The unbroken, limitless monotony of its interior landscapes has survived from Roman antiquity, when a ground-down multitude of slaves produced nothing but corn for export. A sullen mental climate of those days has not been wholly dispersed. By comparison with the Italy of Rome – above all of Naples – Sicily is morose and withdrawn.

Most Sicilians are peasants who live not in the country, but in small towns. There is only one village in the whole island having less than a thousand inhabitants. This phenomenon – unique in the Mediterranean area – is explained by the chronic and ineradicable banditry with which Sicily has been plagued throughout recorded history, and which itself is an inevitable side-effect of an archaic social system. For this reason, the only isolated houses are the administrative buildings, the granaries, and the warehouses of the great feudal estates – the *latifundia* – which tend to assume a fortress-like character and are defended by armed guards. Much of a peasant's time is taken up in reaching his work in the morning and in returning at night, and the streets of small Sicilian towns come alive long before dawn as long processions of shrouded figures go through, clip-clopping on their mules, towards the distant fields. Some-times, in periods of seasonal urgency, the peasants live temporarily where they work, in an African-looking straw shelter called a *pagliaio* which serves also as a store for tools. An untouchable caste of petty criminals exists which specialises in robbing *pagliai*, and these are hunted down and slaughtered like animals by the Mafia. The men of respect do not tolerate small-scale unorganised crime. A visitor to the latest motel, built by the Italian petroleum company Agip on the outskirts of Milan, is warned not only to lock his car but to remove every article from its interior. This would be unthinkable in Sicily, where a traveller's hotel bills are a little higher, but where, whether he realises it or not, he is under Mafia protection.

Sicilians are delivered up from the all-too-brief respite of work to restlessness and boredom. The narrow, shadeless channel of the main street of a small Sicilian town is full of wandering men. They walk together interminably, displaying their thoughts with small, precise hand-movements, as if assembling delicate machinery. This sombre and solemn human current courses sluggishly up and down the street, into the piazza, and out again. The movement is like a torpid circulation of blood through heart and arteries. There is no trace of the corvine affability, of the companionable noisiness of the southern man. This eternal womanless tramping of the streets is conducted in a glum half-silence only crashingly interrupted by the bells of the church in the piazza, which is usually as big as a cathedral. A stranger meets stares, and is sometimes followed nostalgically, as if for the momentary distraction of his presence from indestructible time. The chronically unemployed are not only labourers who work on average one hundred days a year, but a miscellany of the town's impoverished middle class, whose income is provided in one way or another by the peasant, and who are therefore compelled to share in the peasant's enforced idleness and lack of prosperity. Pacing up and down in this interminable and frustrated perambulation, they are like bored animals behind invisible bars. The street imprisons them, just as their women are imprisoned in their dim harem quarters behind the shuttered windows. The headlines of the newspaper nailed up on the kiosk shout the twentieth century, but the rest of this scene remains the Europe of the Middle Ages.

*   *   *

At the root of the trouble one discovers the extraordinary fact that the feudal system, discarded elsewhere many centuries ago, has managed almost miraculously to survive in this neglected and mountainous corner of the Mediterranean. When the Norman invaders occupied the island, huge corn-growing estates – the largest in antiquity – still survived from Byzantine and Roman times, and the Normans were content to parcel them out without further thought among their followers. Subsequent monarchs regarded Sicily as a colony and ruled from a distance, so that provided the peace was kept and the taxes paid, the barons of Sicily were left to their own devices. Many of these lived outside the country, in Rome or even Paris, and never set foot in their domains. The few who chose to remain in the island were notorious for their detestation of a rustic environment, and preferred to keep to their palaces in Palermo.

Estates were originally administered by all-powerful stewards, who ground the last lira out of the peasants, raised private armies for the defence of their masters' property, and dealt out their own form of justice in the feudal court. Later the *gabellotto* came on the scene. The Italian word means 'tax collector', but the *gabellotto* was more than that. A creeping social indolence had induced the aristocracy to adopt the practice of selling their feudal rights at auction to the highest bidder for a specified number of years. The *gabellotto* was the man who thus bought the lease, and he was usually a member of the Mafia. He in turn leased out the land to sharecropping tenants, who were responsible to overseers and a manager, and the *gabellotto* hired armed guards to see to it that everyone kept his place. The estate normally consisted of huge fields, dedicated in the main to the raising of cereal crops, while the peasants, for reasons of security, would live, not dispersed about the countryside, but in the nearest village, from which they would be obliged to cover immense distances to reach their daily work.

This was feudalism in its simplest form – a rough-and-ready system adapted to the urgent needs of conquest and domination, but unsuited to a settled society. The feudal lord, as in the eleventh and twelfth centuries in England and Germany, finally gave away everything in return for a cash payment. The artificial prolongation of such an order produced not only extreme hardship but grave inefficiencies that would normally have brought about the decay and disintegration of the system. The *gabellotto*, for example, was not encouraged to interest himself in the improvement of the estate when he could only count on a few years' tenure – and the same applied to the sharecropper who worked for him. What he did was to negotiate an extortionate contract with the sharecropper, who was then obliged to deal with his day labourer with equal severity. The outcome of this grinding-down process was the endemic banditry of desperate men who had nothing to lose, plus two or three peasant revolts a century of the kind northern Europe has not known for five hundred years.

Don Calogero Vizzini had no fault to find with the feudal system as such; in fact he was to become its greatest exponent and protector in modern Sicily. What he objected to was the fact that a somnolent and, as the Prince of Salina put it, a 'defenceless' aristocracy should have any part in its benefits. Previously it had become a function of the Mafia to keep a benevolent eye on the feudal estates and to suppress any of the periodical attempts on the part of the peasants to occupy uncultivated land. Now, under Don Calò's leadership, the Mafia proposed to shoulder the barons aside. When, therefore, in 1922, the neighbouring Suora Marchesa estate came under the hammer in the usual way, Don Calò was a bidder, and quite naturally the only bidder, since it was obvious that no other contestant felt like presenting himself at the auction. The estate was knocked down to Don Calò for a derisory figure. The idea quickly spread among the Mafia, and the lease of feudal lands began to fetch a tenth and a twentieth of their normal price. An attempt was made to withdraw lands from the market, but it was hopeless. There was nothing to be done. One or two aristocrats put aside their astral telescopes, bought themselves a farmer's corduroy suit and a pair of top-boots, and appeared on the scene with the intention of organising resistance to this takeover. Within a few days, after they had found a percentage of their grapevines cut down and a few of their livestock with their throats cut, they gave in and went back to their decaying palaces. The Mafia had become the feudal lords of all Sicily.

A further profitable brainwave was Don Calò's last before the cataclysmic advent of Benito Mussolini. In appearance it was a patriotic gesture in favour of the ex-servicemen just returning from the war. There was still a fair amount of uncultivated land about, and Don Calò put forward the idea of forming an agricultural co-operative for the men who had deserved so well of their country. With the government's drugged assent, and the provision by the government of free land and equipment, the co-operative was founded under the presidency of Don Salvatore – Don Calò's brother, the parish priest. When a year or two passed and not a single ex-soldier had been given an acre of land and it was evident that the Vizzinis were working the co-operative for their own benefit, yet another scandal exploded. A charge of fraudulent misappropriation was brought against the whole family. Twenty years later, when the Allies arrived, proceedings were still pending and the case was finally dropped. Three other co-operatives got off to a limping start in the Villalba area in the first years of Fascism, but the members were dogged with incessant ill-luck. Their crops were destroyed by mysterious fires, and their animals sickened and died. The co-operatives appeared to many of the conservatives of Villalba like a malevolent challenge to a system of property backed by divine law, and no one was surprised when all three co-operatives failed and Don Calò took over. Don Calò's overthrow of the co-operatives was his last major coup before the

providential arrival of the Allies. In between stretched the lean years of
the Mussolini dictatorship.

*   *   *

At first Don Calò found it hard to make up his mind about Mussolini. To
the extent that he promised to stop the downhill slide towards socialism,
he was obviously a good thing. But when he began to talk about governing
with a firm hand, the Mafia chieftain was not so sure. Prudently, but
without enthusiasm, Don Calò forked out a handsome subscription for
the march on Rome. What actually saved him from the hurricane to come
was nothing more nor less than a happy chance. In 1922, before Mussolini
was finally in the saddle, the 'Honoured Society' sent Don Calò a young
man, a *squadrista* who had injudiciously murdered a political opponent,
asking Don Calò to look after him until the storm had blown over. This
was done, the fugitive being concealed in the Vizzini house. Later, the
young man became an undersecretary of state, and when the Mussolini
purge against the Mafia was at its height and Don Calò had been
sentenced to five years' *confino*, a letter to his grateful ex-protégé was
enough to procure his release.

4

THE CLASH between Mussolini and the Mafia was inevitable, although each side seems to have underestimated the opponent's strength. Don Calò and the more far-seeing of the Mafia leaders were not the only Sicilians who had thought it advisable to take out an insurance policy by contributing to the Fascist war-chest. The Sicilian nobility also had a paid-up share in Mussolini's revolution, and an anguished chorus of protest against the virtual expropriation of their land was soon heard in Rome.

It was clear enough to Mussolini that the Mafia had always had a vested interest in national weakness and division, and that their support for the revolutionary governments of the past had regularly been followed by a stab in the back. The pattern of obstruction and sabotage seemed about to be repeated. Fascist officials sent down to replace the old corrupt administrators controlled by the Mafia were ignored. Fascist courts trying criminal cases in which members of the Mafia were implicated found it was just as impossible to obtain convictions as it had been for the democratic courts of old. Although the Fascist hierarchs might rub their hands at the sight of a nation marching in step, unity and discipline applied only to the peninsula. In Palermo a member of the Party could be shot dead at midday, in the middle of the crowded Via Maqueda, in the sight of hundreds of people, without a single person being ready to admit to the police that they had even heard the shot. The cudgels-and-castor-oil methods the *squadrista* had used so successfully in northern Italy failed in Sicily against the ancient Mafia defence of silence and vengeance. A carabinieri officer reported: 'Only two kinds of witness exist. The first live in the neighbourhood where a crime has been committed and in no circumstances have ever seen anything, or even heard a shot. The second category are the neighbours of anyone who happens subsequently to be accused of the crime. These have always looked out of their window when the shot was fired, and have noticed the accused person standing peaceably on his balcony a few yards away.'

Disturbing facts came to light as the first enquiries into Mafia activities got under way. It was reported to the Duce that the Mafia had been in complete control of the Sicilian electoral machine, and that the deputies it sent to Parliament spent their time blocking investigations of the Honoured Society's misdeeds, and specialised in the production of speeches attempting to prove that the Mafia did not exist. At this time the incidence of violent crime was ten times higher in Sicily than in the rest of Italy. The case of the small town of Favara was quoted which had suffered 150 Mafia killings in one year and where the Duce was told only one man in the previous decade had died of natural causes and in old age. More displeasing still to Mussolini, with the visions of imperial grandeur and conquest forming in his mind, was the island's unpatriotic performance in time of war. Once again, at the beginning of the 1914–18 war, the Mafia had succeeded in spreading the old rumour that conscripts called up and sent to Italy for training were habitually castrated as soon as they got there. Means of evading service had been made available to those who could afford it, and throughout the war years the island swarmed with deserters who were at once protected and exploited by the Mafia.

Mussolini's anti-Mafia campaign was finally set off by an incident which took place when he visited Sicily in 1924. Having driven through the streets of Palermo, where it was easy enough to stage-manage the display of noisy enthusiasm he had grown accustomed to expect, the Duce suddenly, and to the embarrassment of his retinue, asked to be shown a smaller town in the vicinity. It seemed that at some stage Mussolini had picked up a pamphlet produced for the tourist industry which warmly recommended a visit to Piana dei Greci. This somewhat wretched little township was peopled by the descendants of Albanian refugees from the Turks, who had been given shelter in Sicily, and tourists were often taken there and treated to a programme of folklore by girls dressed in an antiquated Albanian style. It was the only town in Sicily – or in Italy, for that matter – to have a Greek Orthodox Church, with an officiating 'Pope' with a long beard, and high, black hat.

There were two drawbacks to the satisfaction of Mussolini's whim for a Balkan entertainment. The first, and more important, was the security risk involved. By mustering every policeman in Palermo and placing them back to back with loaded rifles at intervals of ten yards all along the Via Maqueda, it had been possible to guarantee the Duce's safety during his flying visit to the capital. But Piana dei Greci, exotic folk-costumes apart, had a reputation with the police as a hive of peasant unrest and for its participation in an insurrectional movement in the 'nineties. The second difficulty arose from the fact that the mayor, Don Ciccio Cuccia, who would officially welcome the Head of the Government, was a Mafia potentate, and one who was notorious for an inflamed sense of his own importance. It was seen that only the most delicate handling of this encounter, should it take place, could prevent an ugly clash of personalities.

Don Ciccio Cuccia, a malevolent frog of a man, was famous for the fantastic exploits in which he was involved by his all-devouring ego, and his traditional Mafia passion for 'winning respect'. The Duce's visit to Piana dei Greci had been preceded a few years before by one by King Vittorio Emanuele. At a certain moment the King – who is said to have been in a thoroughly bad mood, bored by the Albanian dancing, and even distressed by the wild music of the pipes – found himself being led into the church, which was decorated and lit up and redolent of incense for some unfamiliar Greek Orthodox ceremony just about to begin. His Majesty tried to back out, but was artfully separated from his retinue and manoeuvred towards the font. Here, in spite of his protests, he soon found himself holding a bawling infant, with Don Ciccio at his side, and within a few moments had become godfather to Don Ciccio's son.

The prestige gained by this confidence trick played on the King – which had been followed automatically by the arrival of the cross of a Cavalier of the Crown of Italy – may have tempted Ciccio Cuccia to risk some sort of self-publicising exploit with Mussolini. On reaching Piana dei Greci, the Duce's chief of police, who was not at all happy about the security arrangements, suggested that Mussolini should ride in Don Ciccio's car for his tour of the town. The Duce took his seat at the Mayor's side and his motorcycle escort lined up on both sides of the car. At this point Don Ciccio asked in a loud voice, 'Excuse me, Captain, but why all the coppers? Nothing to worry about so long as you're with me. I'm the one who gives the orders round here!' It was then that the Duce at last realised that things had reached such a pass in Sicily that even his own chief of police had thought it advisable to place him, the Head of the Government, under Mafia protection.

Mussolini refused Don Ciccio's suggestion that he should dispense with his escort – a 'lack of respect' which Ciccio Cuccia punished to his own undoing by ordering the town piazza to be emptied when Mussolini made his speech. But where the King had been sulky, Mussolini was grim. As they stood on the balcony of the town hall together, Don Ciccio placed an arm on the Duce's sleeve, bared a row of black fangs, and signalled to the photographers to expose their plates. When Mussolini began his harangue he found himself addressing a group of about twenty village idiots, one-legged beggars, bootblacks, and lottery-ticket sellers specially picked by Don Ciccio to form an audience. The fearful jutting of the Dictator's jaw had not yet become a familiar danger-sign, so Don Ciccio had no warning of what was in store for him. It is unlikely that he even bothered to listen to what Mussolini had to say, although he would have been wiser to have done so, because the Duce's speech amounted to a declaration of war on the Mafia. Weeks later he repeated in substance in the Fascist Parliament what he had said at Piana dei Greci, but by that time Don Ciccio was already in prison.

*   *   *

Of all the bombastic and beribboned figures that strutted on to the Italian stage in the first years of Fascism, none outdid the Prefect Mori, who was given the task of liquidating the Mafia, in terms of pathological delusions of grandeur.

Cesare Mori had come up in thirty years from being a policeman on a beat to the office of Chief of Police, and second only in importance in the hierarchy to the Duce himself. For all that, he remained at heart a simple policeman, who rated success in an operation such as this purely on the basis of the number of arrests he could make.

The Prefect had been present on the fateful occasion of Mussolini's discomfiture at Piana dei Greci, had been physically pushed aside by the preposterous Don Ciccio, and had heard himself referred to as a *sbirro*, a term of opprobrium sometimes applied to policemen in Sicily and roughly the equivalent of the French *vache*.

Mori, a man with a strong sense of the theatre, gave himself the pleasure of carrying out Don Ciccio's arrest in person, calling on him one day with a pressing invitation to cocktails at what turned out to be the Ucciardone prison. Thereafter, armed with the Duce's *carte blanche*, he put into operation what he sometimes jokingly called his 'Plan Attila'. Unimpeded by the legal hair-splittings of democratic justice, Mori arrested suspects by the thousand. Victims of hearsay and denunciation were put in chains and sent off by the shipload to the penal islands. The Mori terror provided a never-equalled opportunity for the settling of old personal feuds and for the elimination of rivals in business and in love. In so far as the Fascist courts administered justice at all it was rough, muddled and perfunctory, and there were many instances of two or even three persons being condemned and imprisoned for the same crime. Mori's descent on a village sometimes meant the arrest and removal of the entire male population, and it was discovered that the only hope of mollifying him when a visit was expected was to erect a triumphal arch bearing the words AVE CAESAR.

The investigating methods favoured by the Prefect were those employed by the Inquisition, and, although illegal for over a century, still practised in secret in the dungeons of the police. Mori is credited with the re-introduction of the *cassetta*, employed in hundreds if not thousands of cases, to extort confessions – both in his day and much later. The *cassetta* was no more than a box, roughly three feet long by two feet wide and eighteen inches deep, and in essence formed a platform to which a human body could be secured while the torturer went to work. As with all such barbarities practised on a large scale, a standardised routine had developed, and had in fact been laid down by an ancient Inquisitional manual for the use of interrogators. Brine having first been poured over the victim's naked torso, he was scourged; it having been found that this system was more painful yet left fewer marks of violence than a normal flogging. If flogging did not produce a confession, the next stages were the forcing into the victim's stomach of huge quantities of salt water, the removal of his fingernails, the removal of strips of skin, and the twisting and crushing of the genitals. The Inquisition had been dealing with dissenters in this way since the days of the Albigenses. Mori merely added a modern touch to the medieval procedure by introducing an electric-shocking machine into the sequence of torment. The *cassetta* often maimed for life.

Mori was the subject of extravagant whims. Once, having heard that many Mafia victims had been killed by shots fired from ambush from behind walls, he ordered every wall in Sicily to be reduced to three feet in height within twenty-four hours. He was capable of striking illogicalities, making it an offence punishable with a long term of imprisonment for a man to carry a stabbing or cutting weapon, but allowing herdsmen, as they had always done, to continue to arm themselves with a weapon like a tomahawk. An epidemic followed of violent deaths caused by this instrument.

In 1927 Mussolini assembled the Fascist Parliament to announce the end of his war against the Mafia. Holding up Mori's arm, and to the tempestuous applause (as it was always called) of his deputies, Mussolini referred to his Prefect as the 'incarnation of the pure white flame of Fascist justice'. The work with the butcher's cleaver in Sicily became 'heroic surgery, performed with a courageous scalpel'. In his enormously prolonged and detailed report of the surgical process it was noticed that the Duce dwelt with particular relish on operations in Piana dei Greci, and with the fate of 'that ineffable Mayor who always took advantage of solemn occasions to have himself photographed'. It was clear that even after three years, Don Ciccio's blow to his vanity still rankled. With well-trained enthusiasm the Press agreed with Mussolini's optimistic forecast for Sicily's future. As the *Resto del Carlino* put it (after a hyperbolical passage of the kind much admired at the time which claimed that 'flowers miraculously bloomed wherever Mori's caravan passed'): 'The extirpation of the Mafia will open the way to the rise of a middle class, based on the modern technical development of Sicily, which feudalism, served by organised crime and its network of political corruption, has always debarred.'

But the effect of the Mori repression could only be temporary, as at best it scythed the heads off a crop of weeds when what was needed was a change in the soil and climate that produced the crop. All the more astute members of the Mafia – professional men, who were largely lawyers or doctors – were clever enough to put themselves beyond Mori's reach by joining the Fascist Party. Other men of influence were allowed to emigrate to the United States; still others to Tunisia – in this case in return for an engagement to stir up what trouble they could for the French in that country. It was the unimportant rank and file of the Honoured Society who went to prison.

Mori's intervention had one important effect: the deprivation of Don Calò and company of the enjoyment of their newly-won feudal privileges. When next the leases of the feudal estates came up for auction, prices reverted sharply to the original level – most of the Mafia chieftains who had escaped the worst effects of the repression having at least judged it better, for the time being, to lie low. From this time on until the coming of the Allies in 1943, the peasants had a better time of it than most of them had ever known before. At least it became possible to argue with a landlord over the terms of a contract without running the risk of being knocked on the head and thrown down some deep fissure in the earth, or into one of those disused mine-shafts favoured by the Mafia for use as a cemetery.

*   *   *

Mori had succeeded in landing one huge fish, and thereby unknowingly advancing Calogero Vizzini to the final pinnacle of authority in the Honoured Society. His catch was Don Vito Cascio Ferro, who had been acknowledged head of the Mafia for twenty-five years and was the most spectacular delinquent in Sicilian history.

Don Vito had emigrated in his youth to the United States, where he had become one of the most active members of the 'Black Hand' – an amalgamation of fugitives from the Mafia, the Camorra of Naples, and a less-known Calabrian criminal society, who had intelligently adapted themselves to the changed social and political conditions of the New World. Quite unlike such roughcast Mafia personalities as Don Ciccio of Piana dei Greci and the slovenly Don Calò Vizzini, Don Vito was always meticulous in his appearance, affecting since his return from the States a dashing anachronism of dress, which included a frock-coat, wide-brimmed fedora, pleated shirt, and flowing cravat. By the time Mori came on the scene, Don Vito had added to the immense dignity of his presence by the possession of a long white beard. He was a favourite of high society who frequented Palermo's most glittering salons. He was in demand to open exhibitions of the saccharine watercolours of the Neapolitan school, romped with dukes and duchesses in party games of musical chairs, listened with reverence to famous actors giving poetry readings from Leopardi, or to the latest long-playing cylinder of *Donauwellen* on Mr Edison's new phonograph, dressed himself fashionably in knickerbockers and Norfolk jacket to shoot thrushes in distinguished company, and joined aristocratic parties to pelt the children of the poor with cakes and sweets on All Souls' Eve. Women of gentle birth spoke of the strange magnetic force with which a room seemed charged when Don Vito was present, and he once administered a severe admonition to his barber for selling the clippings of his hair to a maker of amulets.

Although he had been acquitted of implication in 69 major crimes, twenty of them homicides, Don Vito only admitted to – and indeed boasted of – having taken one man's life. 'My action was a disinterested one,' he used to say, 'and in response to a challenge I could not afford to ignore.' The victim was Jack Petrosino, an American detective engaged on an investigation into the Black Hand. Petrosino's researches in the Chicago underworld had convinced him of a liaison existing between the American secret society and the Mafia, and this induced him in 1909 to volunteer to go to Sicily to study the methods of the most important of the parent organisations on the spot. Petrosino was accompanied by two American criminals, associates of the Black Hand, who had agreed through their Sicilian contacts to assist the detective in his researches, and who probably disclosed his plans to the Mafia in advance.

On the evening of the day that Petrosino's ship docked at Palermo, Don Vito was dining as usual with an influential member of Palerman society, this time a member of parliament. At a certain moment he pretended to have remembered a most important matter that he had forgotten to attend to before leaving home, and asked to be excused for a short time. Borrowing his host's carriage, Don Vito had himself driven to the Piazza Marina, near the port. At about that time Petrosino had left his hotel nearby, clearly to go to a secret rendezvous. A few minutes later the lights of Palermo went out, and Don Vito, who was waiting for the detective, killed him with a single pistol-shot. He then returned to the waiting carriage and was driven back to the house of his friend the member of parliament, arriving in time for the port. When suspicion later fell upon Don Vito, this politician was ready to swear in court that his guest had never left the house on the night of the killing.

The old Mafia leader had to be tried on a trumped-up charge of smuggling. During the greater part of the trial he contented himself with disdainfully ignoring the proceedings of the court. A Mafia exponent of the old school, 'respect' was all that mattered even in this desperate emergency. When a defence counsel appeared to be pleading for lenient treatment, Don Vito rebuked him harshly for adopting tactics 'in conflict with my principles and offensive to my authority'. Before being sentenced, and asked whether he had anything to say, Don Vito replied, 'Gentlemen, as you have been unable to obtain proof of any of my numerous crimes, you have been reduced to condemning me for the only one I have never committed.' This indeed expressed the facts of the case accurately enough.

In prison Don Vito exercised his immense and hardly-trammelled influence in the interests of reform. He organised a kind of welfare scheme by which criminals still at large were obliged to contribute to the maintenance of the families of those in captivity, and he himself, out of his own personal fortune, provided dowries for the marriageable daughters of all his fellow-sufferers. Prisoners took it in turns to clean out his cell and make his bed. Warders whom Don Vito considered overbearing in their manner were discharged when Don Vito mentioned it to the governor. Until recently the motto carved for him in Sicilian dialect (Don Vito was illiterate) on one of the corridor walls was still to be seen, covered with a protective sheet of glass: *Vicaria, malalia e nicisitati, si vidi lu cori di l'amicu* – In prison, in sickness and in want, one discovers the heart of a friend. The streak of sentimentality is the final ingredient that completes the character of this fantastic old criminal.

The cell in the Ucciardone prison occupied by the old man, who died of heart-failure after a short period of incarceration, has always been used since to house prisoners of distinction. In it, Don Calogero Vizzini spent a few days of his five years' sentence before his release through the intervention of the young Fascist he had befriended.

5

IN 1962 a novel appeared on the theme of the mafia from the pen of the distinguished Sicilian author Leonardo Sciascia. In *Il Giorno della Civetta* an interesting passage occurs which suggests the immense success of the Mafia as a *secret* society, showing that its manoeuvrings still remain largely shrouded in a penumbra of uncertainty. It also demonstrates the use of a standard piece of trickery: an attempt to pull the wool over the eyes of the inquisitive by arguing that the whole thing is hardly more than a blown-up piece of newspaper sensationalism.

A politician in the book has taken it upon himself to have a fatherly chat with a carabinieri officer who has actually dared to arrest an important citizen – instead of one of the usual ragged scapegoats – for implication in a Mafia killing.

'I ask you,' says the politician, 'is it possible to conceive of the existence of a criminal association so enormous, so well-organised, so secret, and so powerful that it can do what it likes, not only here, but in the United States? . . . Very well then, put it this way: can you tell me of a single trial that has ever produced the proof of the existence of a criminal association called the Mafia, which actually arranges for and carries out crimes? Has a single document ever been found – I mean real written evidence – any sort of proof, in fact, of a relationship between criminality and the so-called Mafia?'

When Sciascia wrote this in 1961 the answer would have been no, but by the time his book appeared, the missing link in the evidence had at last been found.

For a century the experts had been busy with their arguments. Rival sociological and anthropological schools had even come into being in an attempt to explain 'the Sicilian plague' and powdered the arguments with the dry dust of textbooks. A hundred or so books on the Mafia were written over the century, most of them rich in theory but lacking in focus, due to the fact that so much of the evidence was missing. No one had even been able quite to define just what the Mafia was. How, for example, did one enter the Mafia? Was the Honoured Society organised on a military basis, with ranks, duties, promotions, honours and awards? Were regular meetings held? Did the Mafia possess initiation rites and ceremonies, such as those of the Carbonari and the Freemasons? Was Mafia membership hereditary? Nobody knew, for the simple reason that the fear of certain death prevented the disclosure of secrets of this kind. Meanwhile, all Sicilians could do was to put two and two together and make do with intelligent guesswork.

Little as ordinary Sicilians might know about how the Mafia was put together, they certainly knew just who the mafiosi were. There was something about a mafioso that marked him as indelibly as a facial scar or a harelip. The man who had been admitted to the Mafia saw himself as a member of an élite, of a chivalry of power, and the confidence that this bred oozed from him like a vital current.

Some mafiosi manage to keep this godlike conviction of their superiority under sufficiently close control for it not to be apparent except in cases of exceptional emergency. Renato Candido, a retired carabinieri officer who wrote a book about his experiences with the Mafia, describes an instance where a man well known to him, whom he never suspected of being other than an ordinary law-abiding citizen, gave himself away when he happened to be travelling on a bus that was held up by bandits. The passengers were all hustled out and lined up to have their coats torn off their backs and their pockets turned inside out in the search for objects of value. When it came to the turn of the mafioso, he simply treated the bandit to the celebrated cold stare of the man of respect and said quietly, 'Don't touch me.' The bandit immediately lowered his gun and passed on to the next passenger. One of the victims of this episode told Candido about the singular fellow traveller who could frighten away a gunman with a single look, and Candido put two and two together. Later he went to see the man to try to get a description of the bandits, which none of the passengers had had the courage to supply. It turned out that the mafioso considered the bandits a nuisance. As a man of honour he was prevented by his code from open collaboration with the police, but speaking with such vagueness and recourse to metaphor that what he had to say sounded to Candido more like a parable than a piece of information, he still managed to let drop a hint or two, as a result of which the carabinieri officer was able to arrest the whole band.

The mafioso was recognisable too by his uncanny success in everything he touched. The Mafia doctor got all the patients, and could always find a hospital bed in a hurry. The Mafia advocate had all the briefs he could handle, and his clients usually won their cases. Government contracts always seemed to go to the contractor who was a man of respect, although his tenders were usually the highest and he paid lower wages than the trade union minimum. By tradition, members of the Mafia did not themselves seek election to Parliament, but everybody knew that the political boss who arranged for a candidate's election was a mafioso. The Mafia member was the courteous but laconic stranger who recommended the candidate's opponent not to attempt to hold political meetings in the area. He was the solitary armed horseman riding up and down the boundary of a feudal estate, whose mere presence and power-saturated glance were enough to keep at bay five hundred peasants who had come to claim uncultivated land. The mafioso was also the mayor's right-hand man who handed out all the jobs in the municipality, contributing to the rule of the Mafia not only by fear but by hunger.

*   *   *

Then in 1962 a unique document was published by the Sicilian newspaper *L'Ora*, and instantly the framework in which all these privileged citizens moved and their relationship with one another was filled in. In three long instalments, and with electrifying effect, *L'Ora* published a confession made to the police in 1937 by a certain Doctor Allegra, who had been induced to join the Mafia and eventually been involved in a murder. The doctor told all he knew, revealing a series of new facts about the Honoured Society and its doings. There can be only one explanation of the circumstance that he died peacefully in his bed: that his confession was mislaid in the police record office, probably through being placed by mistake in the file of another Allegra – the name being a not uncommon one. If this supposition is correct, the confession was safely buried in this way until it came to light twenty-four years later and found its way into the newspaper's possession.

It is obvious that on other occasions – particularly during the Mori terror – similar confessions must have been obtained by the police. Such documents would have been quickly got rid of through police collusion with the Mafia. Nothing would have been simpler than for any police official having, say, the equivalent rank of captain, to visit the records office in the Questura, abstract the dossier containing the confession 'for study', and either to remove the confession altogether or to exchange it for some less compromising document. That nothing is easier than such a manoeuvre is demonstrated by the case of Don Calò Vizzini, whose dossier disappeared from the Questura of Palermo within days of his becoming Mayor of Villalba and an honorary colonel in the US Army. Criminologically, the Mafia confession represents an advance in our knowledge as important as the deciphering of a letter in Etruscan script, but up to even twenty years ago no newspaper editor would have dared to look at it. But the offices of *L'Ora* have twice withstood Mafia attacks, the latest in 1958 when the paper started its own investigation of the Mafia and a bomb explosion destroyed part of *L'Ora* building. Since the principal result of these outrages was the great increase in fame and in circulation of the newspaper, it has thereafter lost no opportunity to press home its attacks on the Mafia, which may well realise by now that short of massacring the whole editorial staff, there is very little it can do.

*   *   *

Dr Melchiorre Allegra, the mafioso doctor whose most detailed and largely verifiable confession sheds light on so much of what before was dark, was a medical officer in a military hospital in Palermo when the Mafia approached him. It was 1916, the war was beginning to go badly, and an epidemic of malingering and self-inflicted wounds was occupying far too much of the time of the hospital staff. Some of these simulated pathological conditions were artfully contrived, and Dr Allegra seems to have been amused despite himself by one man who had successfully produced a condition of erysipelas of the knee by injecting himself with a mixture of turpentine and iodine. Allegra threatened to report the man, but within hours, and before he had time to do so, he received the visit of a Giulio D'Agate, whom he instantly recognised from his unmistakable manner as a man of respect. There was nothing of the bully about D'Agate, who merely appealed to the doctor to show mercy to a man who was the father of a large and necessitous family. There was little the doctor could do but fall into line, the mild-mannered Mafia approach being considered potentially even more dangerous than the blustering kind. Allegra cured his patient and got him several months' convalescent leave. In his confession he says that D'Agate later persuaded him to perform another similar favour. This was a time of great Mafia activity on behalf of Sicilians who had lost patience with the First World War.

Some days later Allegra found D'Agate waiting for him outside the hospital. He had two companions, also obviously men of respect. Understandably, the encounter made Allegra feel nervous, but the three men of respect were most friendly and genial, so he decided he had nothing to fear. D'Agate asked him to go with them, as he had something of great importance to tell him. Allegra's attack of the jitters promptly returned, but he says in his statement that he dared not refuse the invitation. He was taken to a fruit shop owned by one of the men, and here, after a fulsome exchange of compliments and after D'Agate had praised him in particular for the 'seriousness of his outlook', other matters were touched upon. 'They explained to me that they belonged to a very important association, which included people in all ranks of society, not excluding the highest; all of whom were called "men of honour". The association was what in fact was known to outsiders as the Mafia, but understood by most people only in a very vague way because only members could really be sure of its existence.' One pictures the three sinister men in the fruit shop explaining these self-evident facts to the fourth (who was also to become a sinister man), while Allegra pretends suitable surprise.

'Continuing their explanation, they told me that infractions of the association's rules were severely punished. Members were not allowed, for example, to commit thefts, but in certain circumstances homicide was permissible, although always by licence of the chiefs. Breaking the rules in this case, that is by taking the law into one's own hands, was punishable by death.' D'Agate hastened to add, by way of encouragement, that when high-level approval for a killing had been secured, a member could call on the assistance of the association, if required, to help him carry it out.

The confession continues with some important new material on Mafia organisation. 'Dealing with the administrative structure, it was explained to me that the association was split up into "families", each one headed by a chief. Usually a family was made up of small groups from neighbouring towns or villages, but when a "family" became too numerous for convenient administration, it was split up into groups of ten, each with its subordinate chief. In the matter of relationship between the different provinces, the rule in the main was independence. However, the provincial heads kept in close touch with each other, and in this way an informal working inter-provincial liaison was maintained. The association had powerful overseas offshoots in both North and South America, Tunisia, and in Marseille.

'Chiefs were elected by the members of their "families" or groups, and they were assisted by counsellors' – this had been quite unheard of – 'who could act as their substitutes in case of absence. In matters of high policy it was absolutely necessary for a chief to consult his counsellor before taking action. They then added that, in general, the association was not interested in politics, but that from time to time a "family" might decide to support the candidature for Parliament of a politician whom they could count on to recompense them by exerting his parliamentary influence to the maximum in their favour. Such protection could take various forms; for example, in the matter of "recommendations" which (from a member of parliament) were very effective with prison officials, the police, the inland revenue authorities, and the administration at all levels, and could be used to obtain firearms permits, bail for prisoners awaiting trial, to smooth out cases arising out of taxation difficulties, and even to obtain passports in delicate circumstances.'

This information was confirmed and amplified in September 1963 in disclosures made to the Italian Press by Nicola Gentile, ex-American gangster and head of the Mafia in Pittsburgh, Cleveland and Kansas City, who had vanished from the United States when about to stand trial on a narcotics charge and turned up in his native Sicily. Gentile described the Mafia organisation as 'very democratic'. Elections were held regularly. The group of ten elected its chief; these in turn elected the head of the family (*capo-famiglia*); and the heads of families, their deputies and counsellors elected the head of all the Mafia, known in Sicily as the *Capo dei Capi*, and in America as the 'King'. The Sicilian and American systems were identical.

Having listened with growing uneasiness to this dangerous information, Allegra says he was now asked for the first time if he would agree to become a member of the association, and he could see that things had already been allowed to go too far for him to draw back. If Allegra was telling the truth, we may assume that the heads of the Mafia 'family' who had approached him urgently needed the permanent services of an intelligent and pliable young doctor, and that Allegra was virtually press-ganged into the Mafia.

'I realised that I was already the recipient of too many secrets to have been allowed to leave that meeting alive, had I refused. My only course was not only to accept on the spot, but to accept with apparent enthusiasm.'

After this the ritual of admission was administered.

'The tip of my middle finger was pierced by a needle, and blood was squeezed from it to soak a small paper image of a saint. The image was burned, and holding the ashes in my hand I was called upon to swear an oath more or less as follows: "I swear to be loyal to my brothers, never to betray them, always to aid them, and if I fail may I burn and be turned to ashes like the ashes of the image." '

This one archaic touch apart, the Mafia showed no interest in mumbo-jumbo. There were no secret hand clasps, signs or passwords. Allegra's sponsors took him on a brisk tour of the neighbourhood of

Palermo and introduced him to anyone in the organisation he needed to know. He might have been a junior sales representative who had just been taken on by a go-ahead firm. Allegra says that he was embarrassed by the fact that most of his new friends seemed to think that he was just the man they had been looking for to concoct some ruse to get a friend out of the army on medical grounds. He met all the Mafia personalities of the day, and among his lists of rank-and-file members one recognises some of the great names to come, the manipulators of power in the era of the Mafia renaissance that was to follow the Allied occupation of Sicily. Of all the names Allegra supplied, perhaps the most surprising is that of a prominent monk – the Father Superior of the Convent of Tagliava: a forerunner of the notorious so-called mafiosi monks of Mazzarino whose trial, lasting three years, was only concluded in 1963.

*   *   *

The social meeting-place of the Mafia élite was the Birreria Italia in Palermo, a café where any Mafia notables who happened to be in the capital often dropped in to talk shop at about eleven in the morning. This is the hour when, after a thousand years, Palermo still turns its face daily towards the East. A baroque façade of dimpled statuary has been built over the wall-eyed old Saracenic town with its pink-domed *kubbas* and its stumps of minarets, but the relaxation of Palermo remains oriental in style. At eleven work peters out for a long interval, while the streets fill up with a pleasantly aimless crowd. The aroma of roasting coffee covers the whole town. Men in darkly discreet clothes file into the cafés and fill them standing, until the only possible movement is that of the hand holding a tiny coffee cup in a cubic foot of space. This is the public display of leisure inherited from turban-wearing ancestors – a dignified setting-aside of the trivial concerns of the day, when every Palerman becomes a pasha for an hour.

Members of the Sicilian aristocracy favoured the *birreria*, going there to ogle the lords of the underworld, so that there were times when every second customer crowded along the counter clutching his minuscule cup was an internationally famous criminal or a duke. Here Allegra saw

Don Ciccio, the absurd and publicity-hungry mayor of Piana dei Greci, shoving his way to the front to talk to the reporters. Don Vito Cascio Ferro, head of all the Mafia in those days, appeared briefly, a prophet dressed up as a Mississippi gambler, to have his hand kissed by the hangers-on. Don Calò Vizzini, now portly from the digestion of his war profits and hardly to be recognised by those who had known the young bandit of Cammarata, put in an appearance. Allegra had lunch with him, and Don Calò brought along a pearl-encrusted mistress, a woman of the old nobility who had persuaded him to make her the first female member of the Mafia. Conversation with the laconic Don Calò seems to have been heavy going.

The doctor had sold his soul to the devil for a fairly good price. He was able to buy a practice in Castelvetrano, and did well enough with it to open his own clinic shortly afterwards, which also prospered exceedingly. Naturally enough, the association expected and got its *quid pro quo*. As this meant helping out from time to time with illegal operations and the clandestine treatment of patients suffering from gunshot wounds, the doctor had some brushes with the law, from all of which, through alibis fabricated by his friends, he escaped unscathed. One attempt, too, was made by the Medical Association to remove his name from the register; but in the case of a man of honour such an attempt could never succeed. Dr Allegra, almost weighed down by now with 'respect', began in the usual way to be more than just the most successful doctor in the community. As an established mafioso, he would be regarded not only as above the law but in some measure as supplanting it, and people would come to him to settle their disputes. He also kept juniors in the association in order, with a sharp reprimand when called for, for wild schemes. 'Cammarata Carmeli, a mafioso of Palermo, came to see me about a baron of the district of Le Madonie who had approached him for help in abducting the fiancée of Professor Stella Pietro. I immediately vetoed this absurd project and it was dropped, so the professor was left in peace.'

*　　*　　*

But amazingly enough, even within the Mafia itself, according to this inside chronicle, things rarely go smoothly for long. A wide rift, not entirely healed to this day, was provoked by a quarrel over payments made to the organisation by the contractors for the development of the port of Palermo. Relations with the Mafia overseas were still close and cordial enough for three separate Mafia Commissions to be sent by the disquieted brothers in New York, Chicago and Kansas City in an attempt to heal the breach. To the American Mafia, the Sicilian parent had always been the '*madre nobile* – the noble mother', custodian of the ancient tradition and fountainhead of doctrinal purity. A request from Sicily to execute the sentence of a Mafia court on a Sicilian who had fled to America would be unhesitatingly carried out – and vice versa. Sicilian emigrants were still handed a clean bill of health by the Honoured Society in Sicily and given the address of the mafioso to whom they should report as soon as arriving in the United States; while leading American Mafia chieftains made frequent sentimental pilgrimages to their home towns back in Sicily. But despite the strength of the ties uniting both organisations, all attempts by the American brothers to bring about a reconciliation failed. Allegra claims to have been disillusioned by the unseemly brawling over the division of loot. It was about this time, too, that his personal interests seemed not to have been fostered by his Mafia connections as well as he would have wished.

In the last free election to be held in Italy before the installation of Fascism, the Mafia, departing from its usual practice of supporting the party most likely to succeed and then getting a stranglehold on it, had decided on a two-way bet. There had been a division of opinion on the Fascists' chances of coming to power, so it was arranged that, with Mafia backing, an equal number of candidates from the democratic and Fascist lists should be returned to Parliament. Allegra had been flattered by the suggestion that he should stand as a democratic candidate, but to his mortification his candidature turned out to be a dummy one, and the full organisational support was given to his Fascist opponent who defeated him with an insultingly large majority.

A worse blow to his prestige was to follow. A vacancy occurred for the post of medical superintendent of a group of hospitals, and Allegra applied to the counsellor of his particular 'family' to assist him in obtaining the appointment. He mentions this in his confession quite flatly, and with almost a kind of innocence. After all, it was taken for granted that such appointments went to the mafioso applicant. Unfortunately for Allegra, there happened to be a second man of honour who had his eye on this particular plum, and although Allegra says that his rival's qualifications were faked to the extent that he did not even have a medical degree, he was senior to Allegra in the Mafia, so he got it.

Allegra's last exploit before he vanishes from sight is an exceptionally grubby one, but it illuminates the limbo into which Sicily fell after Mori had smashed the Mafia, but had failed to substitute law and order for the lopsided Roman peace imposed by the Honoured Society.

The Mafia had never objected to banditry, but had kept it strictly under control, turning it on and off like a tap as Mafia strategy demanded – and, of course, sharing in the profits of the bandits. But the new crop of bandits – coming up like mushrooms in the compost of a social environment which Mussolini had left unchanged – were unmanageable in the Mafia's punch-drunk condition.

A bandit called Ponzio – a petty Giuliano of his day – was terrorising the countryside of Castelvetrano and had even begun to carry out his depredations in the doctor's home town itself. He was a daring fellow, who went about armed to the teeth, and, surrounding himself with a gang of young ruffians, was ready to turn his hand to any form of criminality from sheep-stealing in the streets of Castelvetrano to kidnapping a carabinieri captain. This last achievement brought on unwelcome police reprisals. As Allegra puts it, 'Ponzio was a grave nuisance to people' – such as himself, he suggests – 'who only asked to be allowed to live in peace.'

Ponzio's hide-out was in the neighbouring village of Ghibellina, and Allegra received a visit from a member of the Mafia 'family' of that area, who discussed the problem with him. The trouble was that Prefect Mori had left the 'family' so weakened that there was little it could do about Ponzio – at least without calling in help. The man from Ghibellina mentioned that they had even been bereft of their chief: 'He had retired into private life.' It seems, although Allegra does not say so, that a Mafia court was held in his clinic, at which Ponzio was formally sentenced to death. The question that arose was how the sentence was to be carried out.

Mafia death sentences are normally executed only by the very lowest grades of probationer-members of the association – the *picciotti* (boys) – who gain the 'respect' requisite to their advancement in the society by offering their services for such unpleasant jobs. When no *picciotto* is at hand to kill for honour's sake, the Mafia casts around to find a *sicario*, a hired killer who is a specialist in the use of the sawn-off shotgun, known as the *lupara*. In this case a difficulty arose because Ponzio would normally be in the company of his henchmen, thus making him a difficult and risky target. One of the Ghibellina members had a bright idea. He knew of just the man for the job, a certain Gandolfo, a close friend of Ponzio's, who might be persuaded, for a price, to lead him into a trap.

Gandolfo was called to the clinic and the proposition put to him. Allegra says he seemed very angry at first, but – although Allegra does not say this – pressure must have been brought to bear, because the next day he agreed. Allegra set out for Ghibellina in his Fiat Topolino, with Gandolfo and two other doctors – who were probably brought along as components of a prefabricated alibi – and the *lupara* wedged uncomfortably behind the knees of the two men squatting in the back. At Ghibellina, Gandolfo was left to do his work, while Allegra and his friends called on a patient. Later Gandolfo was picked up again on the outskirts of the village, and Allegra learned, to his anger and disappointment, that nothing had happened. Gandolfo made lame excuses for not having kept his promise, but to Allegra it was clearly a case of cold feet.

It took another week's work on Gandolfo before it seemed quite certain that he had finally swallowed his scruples. To use a Mafia technical expression, 'the spur was applied'. This time, surrounded in Allegra's clinic by the men of honour of Castelvetrano and Ghibellina, Gandolfo was compelled to swear to carry through his mission. In what is described with macabre understatement as the 'usual little speech', Allegra explained to him what happened to those who failed in their obligations to the Mafia. Then the question of the thirty pieces of silver came up again. The Mafia 'brothers' assured Gandolfo that he would be found a job for his pains, and thus be given the means of starting a new life. This time the assassin saw that there was no escape, and he went off to Ghibellina for his last meeting with his friend.

'I never saw him again,' Allegra says. He adds: 'Things had reached such a pitch with the Ponzio nuisance that had we not been able to make this arrangement, it might even have meant breaking the association's rules and turning him over to the police.' Rarely can the mentality of the Mafia have been exhibited so effectively in a single sentence.

6

VILLALBA, classic capital of the Mafia's state-within-a-state, turns out to be a small bleached town, carved from the bone of its own landscape. In winter, rancid water from the cold rains lies in its cobbled streets, and in summer an ochreous bloom of dust covers the stumpy buildings. A few wilted hollyhocks, self-sown in the angles of walls, curl down like flower-decorated shepherds' crooks. Piglets and chickens scuffle among the black refuse piled up in the side-streets. Many of the houses on the outskirts of the town are *bassi*, Neapolitan style, consisting of a single windowless room into which light and air enter only through the door, and in which the members of the family sleep in bunks. Blue paint daubed on door jambs and on window surrounds – when windows exist – testifies that the Moors were here, blue being sacred, the colour of heaven. The name of the feudal estate Villalba was built to serve – Miccichè – derives from the Arabic Mikiken. The town has a saint with a grimacing, anguished face, padlocked into a shrine like an ancient strongbox. In its heyday, twenty years ago, Villalba had a population of about six thousand, a figure now halved by emigration.

The feudal lands that surround Villalba, rolling away to the horizon in all directions, seem un-European. Central Asia must be like this, one imagines. There are no boundaries, hedges, walls, trees, windmills, buildings of any kind. The landscape, green for the weeks of spring and thereafter whitish under the sun, heaves gently like a carpet with the wind under it. Distantly to the north the mountains of Cammarata are traced on the sky, with a faint scar-tissue of forest. Miccichè is sound-less, apart from the dry chatter of bells echoed off some bony hillside and the high-pitched, creaking squeal of falcons. It is a place, too, of unbroken distances, and the peasants who pass down into these empty, vitreous immensities to their work seem to vanish as soon as they leave the town. This feudal estate is dedicated to the cultivation of the lentil.

Danilo Dolci, in his book *Waste*, which is a closely documented study of the social conditions of western Sicily, gives some idea of what it was like to live in such a town five or six years ago. He found that the day labourers composing the majority of the working population were employed on average for ninety days a year. The average pay was 600 lire (seven shillings) per day. Day labourers offered themselves for hire at a kind of human labour auction held each day before dawn, when, as work might be available for only one man out of three, the peasants were encouraged to bid against each other to bring down their terms. Children as young as eight years of age were taken on as labourers for as little as 150 lire a day, and their competition in the labour market further undercut prices. Men who went home without work had to face scolding wives and weeping children. Enormous families were the order. Elsewhere, one reads of visits paid by priests to women who fail to produce a child a year to ask them 'why they are denying souls to God'.

Probing into the threadbare medieval fabric, Dolci describes the uses of the leech, when the cost of calling in a doctor – even if one were to be had – would be unthinkable. After employment the leeches are thriftily 'milked' of the human blood they have gorged, and kept for use again, only being discarded in cases of typhus. The typical small town or village community includes individuals driven by necessity to practise strange livelihoods: gatherers of seasonal foodstuffs such as frogs, snails and wild asparagus. An inevitable ingredient is the big-town usurer's agent, who is of necessity an ex-gaolbird, chosen for his known capacity for violence to intimidate defaulters who fall behind in their one hundred per cent per annum interest payments. Above all, indispensable to this small rustic community, is the *strega*, or witch, who arranges marriages, concocts potions, dabbles a little in black magic, clears up skin conditions, and casts out devils. These witches, since the Inquisition has ceased its drownings and defenestrations, flourish mightily. Since Danilo Dolci carried out his study, a sharp decline in population due to emigration has modified this picture, but the basic misery is little changed.

In 1944, when Don Calogero Vizzini had held the office of mayor for

Danilo Dolci, lone campaigner against the Sicilian evils of the Mafia, poverty, feudalism and fear

eighteen months, the situation in Villalba was desperate indeed. There were many urgent tasks to distract the Mayor from interesting himself in the welfare of his community. Surrounded by his cohort of tried 'anti-Fascists', all of them armed by special licence of the Allied Military Government, Don Calò dedicated himself to a flourishing black market in olive oil. The old interfering police chief of Villalba, Maresciallo Purpi, had been killed off, and his successor knowing what was good for his health, Don Calò's operations could be conducted without concealment. Moreover, the Allies had facilitated his work almost as though the creation of an impregnable black market had been their first consideration after completing their occupation of Sicily.

One of AMGOT's first measures was the freezing of all prices at the level existing when Military Government took over. The measure was unrealistic, because concurrently the lira was devalued to a quarter of its original rate of exchange against the pound and the dollar, and Sicily was flooded with special occupational currency. It became impossible for a citizen, however good his intentions, to avoid dealings with the black market, for the simple reason that the 'white' market ceased to exist. But from Don Calò's point of view the valuable fact was that it existed as a legal fiction, and this permitted him when buying his oil to extort it from its producers at the fixed price of 25 lire per litre, while his selling price on the Naples black market was 500 lire. When it is said that in this way the Mayor of Villalba squeezed Sicily dry of its olive oil, it should be remembered that bread and olive oil were always the staple diet of the Italian peasantry, and that the usual supplement of pasta was at that time unprocurable.

A government official was sent down in an attempt to persuade Don Calò to fall into line. He explained that the legal position was that all oil must go into the government pool.

'The legal position, the laws? . . . What's all this about laws? What laws?' Don Calò finally asked.

'The laws passed by the government,' the official explained.

'But that's just the point, what government?'

The official found this obtuseness puzzling in a man of Don Calò's reputation for shrewdness. 'The Central Government. The Government of Rome.'

Don Calò accompanied his retort, as he often did, with an emphatic ejaculation of spittle. 'Let the Romans keep the laws they make. In this part of the world we have our own way of doing things.'

Don Calò received the loyalist co-operation in these manoeuvres from his friends in AMGOT, who supplied all the passes necessary for his caravans of trucks to travel without impediment up and down the roads of Sicily and Italy. At about that time AMGOT in Sicily had fallen under the sway of its unofficial adviser, Vito Genovese, an American gangster – later named as the head of the Mafia offshoot, Cosa Nostra – who had disappeared after his indictment on a charge of murder and turned up in Italy. Don Calò found Genovese most accommodating. From AMGOT came all the petrol he required, and sometimes, when he ran short of transport for an exceptionally large shipment, his friends helped out with a military vehicle or two. In 1944 I happened to be in the town of Benevento through which Don Calò's black market caravans were obliged to pass on their way northwards, and although at times there were more trucks loaded with Don Calò's oil on the roads of southern Italy than there were army vehicles, there was nothing that could be done to put a stop to this situation. All papers were always in order. Don Calò's friends were powerful, and the only possibility of remonstrance was when one of Don Calò's drivers, or the escorts provided for his merchandise, sometimes got tired of questions and reached for his gun or a hand-grenade.

*   *   *

In those days Don Calò was dividing his time between the black market at Villalba and certain important and most secret discussions that took him frequently to Palermo. At Palermo he occupied his old suite in the Albergo Sole, a remarkable privilege considering that the hotel had been requisitioned by the military authorities, and, with the exception of the Mayor of Villalba, was off-limits to all civilians. The fact is that Don Calò and certain other leading citizens had been called in by the Allied authorities to discuss the future of Sicily. Don Calò and his friends, all of them members of the Sicilian aristocracy, wanted to detach Sicily from Italy. They were divided in their opinion over the form the separate Sicilian state should ideally assume. Some of the nobles were in favour of choosing one of their number to rule as king in the good old-fashioned way, without any nonsense about a parliament. The more moderate voices, supported by the hard-headed Don Calò and the Mafia, were in favour of the country's becoming either a British colony or an American state. All were agreed on the necessity of severing the link with Rome. What was then called 'the wind from the North', a gusty political mistral from the great industrial towns of Lombardy, had begun to blow. The Allies had allowed political parties to register themselves, and Italy north of Rome had immediately and disturbingly swung to the left. Don Calò and his allies remembered, too, that almost every new government from Garibaldi's time on had promised to do something about turning over the uncultivated estates to the Sicilian peasants, and there was always the chance that the one about to be elected in Rome might do just this. The last upheaval in Sicily had followed the end of the First World War when peasants who had fought in the army and rubbed elbows with enlightened northern Italians showed little inclination to buckle down again to the old servitude of the feudal estate. Now, with the forming of the first trade unions in Mafia areas, the outcry for land was louder than ever before and the would-be Separatists, led by the Mafia, asked for the chance to deal with the situation in their own way and without bureaucratic interference from Rome.

There is no doubt that, with their eye on a war situation that was still far from resolved, the Allies encouraged the Separatists – at least for a time. Moreover, Intelligence reports upon the strength of the emergent Italian Communist Party already suggested that this was likely to be the strongest in Western Europe, and that a Socialist-Communist coalition in Italy, should this ever happen, would be able to take over power. Some Allied political observers said quite openly that if when election time came Italy should take a disastrous plunge to the left, it might not be at all a bad thing to know that Sicily, with its excellent naval bases, remained in friendly hands. It is highly unlikely that proof will ever be forthcoming that part of the deal put through with the good offices of Lucky Luciano included a promise of all-out backing for the Separatists (and therefore the Mafia), but this has been widely alleged in the Italian and Sicilian press.

In that troublesome part of the war's aftermath that was the other side of the bright coin of Don Calò's thriving black market, the threat offered by trade unionism may have seemed the most dangerous. In his handling of a prickly situation Don Calò showed, at first, his usual mental pliability. Trade unions were all part of the disease that young Sicilian peasants had picked up by contagion while in the Services. Like a practised judo exponent, Don Calò relaxed his muscles and rolled on the mat with his opponent, while preparing a better hold. To the amazement of the other politically less gifted Mafia leaders, he offered to permit, first the establishment of a trade union centre in Villalba, and later, even, a Communist Party headquarters. The only stipulation he

One of Dolci's protest marches through the streets of Patinico with banners attacking the Mafia – until recently an unheard of defiance

made in each case was that the activities of both these groups should be directed by one of his lieutenants. When both these offers, to his great astonishment, were turned down, he realised – probably with real regret – that a shooting war was inevitable.

After twenty years the gag of Fascism had been removed, and thirty-two political parties, great and small, were almost hysterically preparing for the elections. Some idea of the political temperature of the time can be gathered from the fact that when Don Vanni Sacco, the terrible capo-Mafia of Camporeale, who was subsequently converted to the Christian Democrat cause, announced that largely from sentimental reasons and as a tribute to his father's memory he proposed to see to it that his constituency was represented by a Liberal candidate, the parish priest of Camporeale denounced him from the pulpit for atheism. Don Vanni replied in a letter apparently courteous but so charged with obscure Mafia symbolism that the priest had to have it interpreted by an expert before realising that it contained a threat to hang him from his own church tower. Sicilians were confidently expected to vote *en masse* for the parties of extreme reaction: the Monarchists or the Separatists. The Christian Democrat party had not yet been tailored to fit the needs of the alliance between the Church and the bouncing new capitalism that would shortly be born.

Trade unionists were regarded with a sort of amazed contempt. To the landowner and his supporters there seemed something basically un-Christian – almost diabolical – in the way they corrupted ordinary, decent labourers, *put ideas into their heads*, induced them to extort grossly unfair rewards for their labour by the threat of withholding it altogether. Trade unions had existed in Italy before the coming of Fascism, but down in Sicily, where five men always rushed to offer themselves for every job that was going, it was a distant calamity, something that happened to other people – discussed in the landowners' clubs like some unreal loss of half a million Chinese lives through the flooding of the Yellow River. In the hubbub provoked by the appearance of this sinister organisation of labourers in feudal Sicily itself, there was an echo of England in 1834 and the Tolpuddle Martyrs of Dorset. In Sicily, as in the England of those days, sermons were being preached on the blessedness of poverty, as illustrated in the parable of Lazarus and the rich man, and peasant congregations were being exhorted to render unto Caesar the things that were Caesar's. One remembers the public horror over the 'ingratitude' of the Dorsetshire labourers – the prison chaplain's astonished outburst when he visited the accused men who had organised themselves in such a cowardly fashion, as he saw it, after their wages had been reduced from nine shillings to eight shillings a week. 'Are you then determined to ruin your kind masters, who are worse off than you?' he cried. (Most of the kind masters maintained lavish establishments, including stables of race horses.) Remembering that the Sicily of 1944 was less politically advanced than the England that punished trade unionists with seven years' transportation to the penal colony of Botany Bay, it is not surprising that Sicily's trade union leaders were quietly marked down for elimination.

*　　*　　*

With hostile politicians, and particularly those who dared bring up the matter of the uncultivated estates, Don Calò took direct, immediate, and effective action. On September 16th, 1944, the leaders of the left-wing Popular Front had the temerity to hold a political meeting in the heart of Mafia territory, in the square of Villalba itself. Deceptively mild, Don Calò had agreed to this meeting taking place, but he had imposed his conditions. It was only the second political meeting ever held in Villalba, unless one includes in the category of meetings the periodical rounding-up of peasants for their instructions as to when, where, and for whom to vote. On September 2nd of that year, in fact, Finocchiaro Aprile, the Separatist leader, had come to Villalba and had received what was described as a 'tempestuous ovation'. By virtue of an error, soon discovered, Aprile, the odds-on favourite of the aristocracy and the Mafia, had enjoyed a short-lived popularity with some of the peasants as well. Through a confusion arising over the party's initials – P.S. *Partito Separista* – and Aprile's habit of giving a Churchillian V sign, the Separatists became known as the Party of Spaghetti at Two O'clock, and a legend spread that Aprile's supporters were feasted on pasta at the end of his political jamborees – a considerable inducement at that time to a half-fed peasant. The swing in the opposite direction when the rumour collapsed was inevitable.

For this occasion, when the hope of spaghetti had long been abandoned, several hundred of Villalba's day labourers had been cleaned up and marched into the town square. Aprile described to them the way in which they and their forefathers had been exploited by the Italians, praised them for their new-found Sicilian patriotism, and for their obvious determination, if called upon to do so, to shed their blood for the new Sicily. After this, while the peasants cheered in the somewhat mechanical fashion they had picked up under Fascism, Aprile's helpers went round pinning the Separatist emblem – a star, symbolising the Party's desire for Sicily to become the forty-ninth State of the United States – on all chests present, including that of Don Calò Vizzini.

The atmosphere on September 16th, however, was less congenial. The conditions laid down by Don Calò had included a ban on agricultural workers being allowed to enter the square while the meeting was in progress, and a further veto on the mention by any of the speakers of the vexed questions of agrarian reform. To make quite sure that his stipulations were observed, Don Calò had the side-streets cordoned off, and the only members of the public allowed in the square were his own legally-armed bodyguards, all of them carrying shotguns. Don Calò presided over this singular political reunion, standing in the middle of the square, his Separatist badge pinned on his lapel and a cudgel in his hand.

The opening speech, which was on the historical origins of democracy, provoked no reaction from the Mayor but yawns. Then Girolamo Li Causi, the Sicilian left-wing leader, got up and went straight to the heart of the matter. Li Causi had a very powerful voice, a dramatic oratorical style, and apparently no fear of the Mafia guns, and the peasants began to appear in the windows and the doorways of the nearest houses. Inevitably the forbidden subject was broached. The distant cries of encouragement from the peasants were drowned as the Mafia opened fire. Fourteen members of the Popular Front, including Li Causi himself, dropped to the ground wounded. The meeting was at an end, and with it, all such meetings in the territory of Don Calogero Vizzini. It was fourteen years before the men who fired at Villalba were brought to trial, and although eventually found guilty, they benefited by various political amnesties that had been granted while their cases were being prepared, so that not a single one of the accused men served a day in prison. In the meanwhile some had had the opportunity to commit other important crimes. Not for nothing is the law in Mafia jargon *la sonnambula* – the (female) somnambulist.

* * *

The shooting at Villalba alerted the feudal landowners to the dangers of their position. Laws had been passed under the Fascist régime in 1933, and again in 1940, by which in certain clearly-defined circumstances uncultivated or badly cultivated land could be assigned to the peasants. Nothing had ever been done to enforce these old laws, but they remained on the statute book, and now the reconstituted Board for the Colonisation of Sicilian Landed Estates was receiving demands couched in proper legal form for the long-delayed expropriations to take place.

In March 1945 the Princess of Trabia called Don Calò Vizzini and entrusted to him the management of the estate of Miccichè – the same estate which Don Calò had been able to rent for a negligible annual sum before the coming of Mussolini. This, the first move in the organisation of the defences of feudalism, was the Princess's counter-stroke on learning that her peasantry had formed a co-operative and that the lawyers were busy drawing up their demand for expropriation. By the definition of the Acts of 1933 and 1940, the estate of Miccichè was badly cultivated, and it seemed likely that should the case be allowed to come before the courts, the peasant claimants would win the day. But now, with Don Calò's appearance on the scene, the landowners' spirits revived. The High Commissioner for Sicily himself sent for the papers involved and wrote in red ink across the folder, 'Do not proceed'. Discouraged, but still not quite beaten, the peasants of Villalba sent a deputation to argue their case before a commission that had been set up at Caltanissetta, the provincial capital, to deal with the problem of the assignment of uncultivated or badly cultivated estates. On their return the members of this delegation were seen individually by Don Calò, who recommended them to remember that good health was the greatest blessing this life had to offer, and then advised them to let the matter drop. A few days later, by a unanimous vote, the Co-operative Libertà was dissolved.

Don Calò, however, had a pleasant surprise in store for the ex-members. It turned out that he had decided to console them for the loss of their co-operative by forming one himself, and he not only invited but strongly urged them all to join it. Co-operatives, as run by Don Calò, possessed one main disadvantage as compared with the normal kind, as the peasants had learned by experience back in the 'twenties, which was that members could not expect to share in the proceeds. However, legally Don Calò's communal venture *was* a co-operative, and when, shortly afterwards, the Princess of Trabia handed over to it the whole of her vast estate, this automatically passed outside the scope of the laws governing expropriation.

The other landowners took their cue from the Princess and simply handed over to the Mafia, although there were few Don Calòs about with the intellectual capacity for such manoeuvres as that by which the feudal estate of Miccichè had been transmuted into a co-operative. Many of the other Mafia chieftains were lacking in finesse, men like Vanni Sacco, the Liberal of Camporeale, who got his hands on the Parino estate; the terrible Barbaccia – survivor of the great Barbaccia-Lorello feud – who took the Ficuzza estate under his wing; and the outright gangster Luciano Liggio, who had fallen under the cultural influence of criminals repatriated from America. Even Giuseppe Genco Russo, considered to be the present head of the rural Mafia and the man who personally arrested Colonel Salemi, the commander of the Axis defences at Cammarata, failed to show a lightness of touch comparable to that of Don Calò. Genco Russo became protector of the Polizzello estate, and when a crowd of peasants tried to occupy it they were simply driven out with gunfire. But whether by Don Calò's brand of artfulness or by sheer brute force, the Mafia won this first round in the fight hands down. And in this way the aristocrats whose estates had been given back to them by Mussolini, now withdrew a second time from the Sicilian countryside and left the Mafia once again in possession of their lands.

7

THE PERIOD of the transformation of the Mafia into a kind of beleaguered landed gentry produced some strange episodes. At that time 1944–6 the Mafia could call on five bandit organisations to assist it in its work (there were another twenty-five or so fairly independent bands). One of these had been organised by Salvatore Malta, Mayor of Vallelunga, a particularly inspired nominee of AMGOT dating from the time of Don Calò's original list of recommendations. Imprisoned for banditry and murder, Salvatore had performed the feat – considerable even by Mafia standards – of remaining nominally a registered inmate of the Ucciardone prison while actually being at large and gainfully occupied in the protection of the Tudia estate. In fact, while the authorities believed Malta to be safely in prison, he was engaged in organising another band known as the Capitano, which was employed not only to terrorise the Tudia peasantry laying claim to fifty thousand uncultivated acres, but was also successful in dissuading the peasants belonging to thirteen other feudal estates from pressing any claims for land. The Capitano band installed themselves in the manorial buildings of Tudia, converted into a fortress, in which they remained for two years. They murdered, robbed and kidnapped, but unlike Salvatore Malta they were common bandits, not mafiosi. When eventually they were rounded up and tried, they received life sentences, and for them the gates of the Ucciardone would remain closed. Salvatore Malta was called only as a witness at the trial.

At this stage one or two of the more intelligent bandits even moved in with offers of protection, Mafia style, on their own account. So long as they modestly restricted themselves to the less important estates, the Mafia tolerated the competition. Trabona, leader of the first band organised by Salvatore Malta, was one of these. Known to his friends as

'Rickets', Trabona – like so many bandits, but quite unlike the Mafia – possessed a kind of ingrained and frustrated respect for law and order, and a hankering after respectability. This made him a stickler for legal form, and when he offered to guarantee one of the barons' estates against molestation by troublemakers, he had a proper contract drawn up before a public notary. Being at the time a fugitive from justice, with a considerable price on his head, it would have been unsuitable for Trabona's own name to appear on the document, so his two infant sons, aged four and five, became the beneficiaries of a tenancy contract which gave them one-half of the total revenues of the estate. In consideration of this, Trabona undertook to keep the other sixty-five sharecropping tenants in order and to persuade them to the voluntary renunciation of any claim to a division of the produce on the basis of a new law that had just been passed in Rome.

* * *

Some of the measures of reform hastily put through by the central government in the hope of easing Sicilian tensions proved impossible to carry out in practice, and this was a case in point. Traditionally, the landowner and his tenant had shared on a fifty-fifty basis – or rather, on what was called a fifty-fifty basis, but which, on examination, proves to have been an arrangement heavily weighted in the landowner's favour. While the landowner kept his half-share intact, many deductions were made from that of the tenant. In the first place, he paid for the seed, plus an interest charge on the amount advanced of thirty-two per cent. He was subject to a tribute, dating from Roman times, known as 'the land's dowry' and which amounted to one hundred kilograms of grain for every hectare (2½ acres). Other important deductions were for the maintenance of the armed guards, the upkeep of the roads, the annual feast of St Lucia, the Church, the monks of the local convent, and 'for lighting the landowner's house'. By the time all these levies had been exacted, the tenant's share was possibly as little as one-quarter, or even less.

The new regulation, giving sixty per cent of the produce to the tenant, was intended to compensate him to some extent for these traditional exactions, and they were instantly and successfully opposed by every landowner in Sicily. The method generally adopted for negating the government's efforts was a simple one. When the time came to divide the produce, the tenant would be summoned into the presence of the landowner, who would have with him the local carabinieri officer. The tenant would then be asked if he wanted to make the division 'the way it's always been done or the way the Reds do it'. If the tenant stuck out for his right to take sixty per cent of the produce, the landowner played his next card, which was to give formal notice in the presence of the police officer that he proposed to dispute the claim. It was now the policeman's duty to impound the crop and hold it until a legal decision on the dispute had been reached. As in Italy civil cases take five years on average to settle, and as in any case the costs would have more than swallowed up any advantage the tenant might have gained, he was bound to give in. There were many instances during the six months when this law was theoretically in operation of the tenant being deliberately provoked into losing his temper and thereby committing the serious crime of *oltraggio* – assaulting or even insulting a police officer. In this case he would be hauled off to prison, where he might be locked up for a year or more while awaiting trial. The landowner would see to it that no bail was forthcoming.

Not only was the operation of the agrarian reforms sabotaged by the direct action of the Mafia and the Mafia's hired bandits, but also by bureaucratic delays, many of them undoubtedly arranged by the Mafia at a high political level. Demands that fulfilled every legal prerequisites for the concession of uncultivated lands lay unattended for months and even years in the offices of the special commissions that had been set up. Meanwhile tens of thousands of fertile acres lay abandoned, covered with thistles and scrub. In some instances landowners decided to chasten a rebellious mood by actually reducing the amount of land under cultivation. This kind of reprisal produced calamitous effects in villages where the misery caused by desperate and chronic unemployment had been increased by the draining off of food supplies into the black market.

Then someone had the idea of organising what were called 'caval-cades', which took the form of large parties of peasants 'symbolically' occupying uncultivated estates. Two or three hundred peasants would usually invade the estate, mark out the plots of land they felt that they would like to possess, picnic on the spot, and then, after a certain amount of flag-waving and perhaps a little accordion music, troop off home again. Cavalcades usually started as holiday outings, but only too often ended as near-massacres. Typical of what happened at that time was the symbolical occupation of the estate of Santa Maria del Bosco.

The occasion was, once again, half political demonstration and half picnic, and an outsider would have taken it for one of those cheerful Mediterranean pilgrimages one sometimes sees on its way to the shrine of some local saint. A thousand or more peasants had gathered from three villages, and in their painted carts, or riding horses or mules, with flags flying and religious banners held up, they made a procession half a mile long. The estate had not been cultivated for sixty years, and their first job when they arrived was to clear away the stones laid bare by soil erosion. This was done in light-hearted fashion, singing to the music of accordions and guitars. By nightfall, the symbolical occupation was at an end and everybody went home.

Nothing was easier than to deal with this kind of thing. Next day the police descended on the villages and carried off thirty-five men – their lists were ready – on charges of creating a civil disturbance. The women, as usual, rushed out into the street and did their best to prevent their menfolk's being dragged away. Rifle butts were used, shots were fired, and blood flowed. When eventually the men came up for trial, some of them were sentenced to as little as fifteen days, but they had already spent sixteen months in prison awaiting trial. Ten years later, in 1956, this feudal estate still awaited expropriation, and today in the three villages that had formed the cavalcade it is still only the youngest and strongest who can hope to work a hundred days in a year.

*   *   *

Elsewhere the peasant leaders acted with less obvious and vulnerable enthusiasm, and thus managed to avoid giving the police the excuse to intervene on the side of the landowner and Mafia combination. These were the tactics adopted in Corleone.

In this world one occasionally stumbles upon a place which, in its physical presence and the atmosphere it distils, manages somehow to match its reputation for sinister happenings. Such a town is Corleone. A total of one hundred and fifty-three murders took place in Corleone in the four years between 1944 and 1948 alone, the rate of death by violence in this town with its population of eighteen thousand being probably the highest in the world. Men and women go perpetually in black, worn for old tragedies; for a father, five years; for a brother, three years; for a son, three years; a piled-up account of mourning that can never be settled. Sorrow leaks from these people into the streets. A scurf of old election posters covers the town's walls. Among them appears the astonishing slogan, 'Long live God! Vote Christian Democrat'.

Corleone is built under a lugubrious backdrop of mountains the colour of lead, and its seedy houses are wound round a strange black rocky outcrop jutting up from the middle of the town. Upon this pigmy *mesa* is built the town lockup, and from its summit the crows launch themselves in search of urban carrion. Behind the cliff-shadowed menaced streets of Corleone stretches a savage entranced landscape of rock and grizzled pasture, for centuries the setting of a bloody routine of feuds and ambuscades. A few miles away is the famous wood of Ficuzza, a place of ghosts and legends, over possession of which the two families of Barbaccia and Lorello have been slowly destroying one another since 1918. The problems of the peasants of Corleone are complicated by inheritances from history and prehistory: they are an island of agriculturists in a hostile shepherd sea, and the sayings of the local herdsmen, including such proverbs taken straight from classical Arabic as 'With the plough came in dishonour', enshrine the nomad's detestation of the encroaching farmer. 'They talk about land reform,' a young shepherd says. 'That means there's less and less grazing ground – they take everything away from us poor folk. All us goatherds and shepherds are worried – soon, if they go on parcelling out the fields at this rate, there won't be a blade of grass left for our animals.' The shepherds, then, are on the side of the Mafia. 'We don't hit it off too badly with the mafiosi. The barons haven't robbed us of our pasture-land.'*

The shepherds furnished the Mafia with most of its hired killers.

Another complication in the lives of the peasants of Corleone in the immediate postwar period was the presence of two Mafias. One of these was the classic version, commanded by the town's leading doctor and leading citizen, Michele Navarra. The other, diffusing its schismatic terror, was something quite new at the time: a hybrid between the home product and American-style gangsterism brought back by criminals repatriated to Sicily from the United States. The 'New Mafia', as it came to be called, was represented in Corleone by Luciano Liggio, who at nineteen had become the youngest Mafia chieftain in Sicilian history.

Liggio had made his name as a phenomenally successful cattle thief, and he was without any of the self-delusion of the old-fashioned men of respect. A threadbare vestige of the ancient Mafia tradition of the honourable state-within-a-state still adhered to the power-corrupted persons of Don Vito Cascio Ferro, and his successor Don Calò. Nothing is more certain than that the traditional Mafia chieftains saw themselves not as delinquents but as self-made aristocracy of the intelligence, and as such, at least as much entitled to their privileges as any aristocracy by birth. The old mafioso was jealous of his 'respect', and of the rough justice he dealt out in his own way. He was a man of iron self-control, often an austere man, sometimes – voluntarily, since wealth was his for the taking – a poor man. Liggio, prototype of the New Mafia, was none of these things. The overlord-to-come of Corleone and the most feared and cunning criminal of modern Sicily had modelled his career on a transatlantic pattern and cleansed himself of scruples. In exile in the United States, such mafiosi as Lucky Luciano had forgotten tradition to the extent of making fortunes out of prostitution – an unthinkable vileness to an old-fashioned man of respect – and now on return, and equally to

* Danilo Dolci, *Waste*

Corleone, Mafia stronghold, where one hundred and fifty-three murders took place between 1944–8, dominated by the rock on which is perched the town lock-up.

the horror of the mafioso of the old school, they would set about the organisation of the traffic in narcotics. Liggio and his followers had nothing in common with the organisation presided over by Don Calò but its iron laws of secrecy and the vendetta, and the two Mafias were soon to be at each others' throats.

When, purely as a last sop to the old Mafia tradition, Liggio became a *gabellotto* and the protector of the huge Strasetta estate, his first move was to drive out all the tenants who possessed sharecropping contracts and replace them by cowed day labourers. He did this simply by burning down their houses and cutting the throats of their animals – tactics which would certainly have shocked the warped paternalism of Don Vito. Liggio, whose unprecedented rise to stardom in the new gangsterism had been assisted by material aid supplied by his mistress, a baroness, is shown in photographs of the period as a loose-lipped, smirking, dandified youth, with a slight squint. Apparently the life of a feudal seigneur on the

Strasetta estate soon irked, and he began to widen the scope of his interests. Liggio believed in moving with the times, and he saw that there was ten times more to be made out of seizing control of the supplies of meat to the Palermo market, say, than by growing and selling beans. He threw overboard all the old-fashioned Mafia pretence of reasonableness and persuasion. When anybody crossed Liggio's path, he simply shot him, and he and his strong-arm men, recruited from the nomads of the bitter pastures, filled the streets of Corleone with the dead.

One of Dolci's informants lists a few of the killings of those days, which leaves out of count the many disappearances – men who were spirited away and never seen again, 'so that a vendetta could not be sworn in the presence of the corpse'.

The first of them to be killed after the war was a man called Cianciana, probably for political reasons. It happened right in the middle of the square.

Then there was the man whose father was at Belvedere [a prison]. He was an employee and they were afraid he might talk and so they got him out of the way.

Michelangelo Randisio and the son of Uncle Matteo Capra, the one with the withered hand, both disappeared. Their bones were found later. Donna Calorina Saporita's son had been thrown into the same crevice. They found a whole cart-load of bones there. Angelo Gullota's bones were there too. Ciccio Navarra's brother had also disappeared. This crevice is on Monte Casale.

Then there were Grisi's three brothers. They lived here at Corleone. They found the body of one of them on the railway line. Another brother came home on leave and they bumped him off the very same night near the armourer's. It seems that the one who came home on leave said that the Mafia here were good for nothing but toothpicks. They heard him and killed him the same day. They shot him point-blank in the street.

Then there was a man from Palermo who'd only been living in Corleone a short time. He disappeared. His name was Pietro

Montesanto, and he was a bit of a pansy. He used to wear a velvet suit that must have cost between thirty and thirty-five thousand lire, with kid-leather patches. Someone said to him: 'Lower the flame or you'll burst the pipe.' Meaning, 'Don't show off too much or you'll come to harm.' His mother used to work spells and concoct poisons. The town here is full of people who've been crippled by these spells.

Then there was Pino Orecchione, the road-sweeper's brother. They found him in the hamlet of Frattina with an army rifle slung round his body and his head stove in. He used to go round robbing the shacks to get something for his family, as he was out of work.

Then there was Vito Capra, who was killed in the town here. They guessed who it was that was sending out extorting letters; and they shot him one night.

Then there was another man called Selvaggio who was shot while he was bringing a load of corn into the town. The people say that he was a bit on the haughty side.

A man called Mariano Governale was killed at the second cross-roads in Sant' Elena. They shot him with buckshot and then split his head open with the butt-end of the gun. It was over a question of honour, people say.

Another stranger, who was employed at Madonna di Scala, was found shot dead in front of the Madonna del Mal Passo.

They cut off Mariano Scalisi's hands after they'd shot him in the hamlet of Bingo.

They found another man dead in the hamlet of Pozzillo; but as he didn't come from Corleone, no one took much notice here. Here in Corleone, they shoot people everywhere, wherever they happen to be. There's not a corner of the town where some incident hasn't occurred.

There was Salvatore Amenda. The people called him the 'sheriff' because he was a retired policeman. They shot him with buckshot. Buckshot is less chancy: you've only one bullet with a pistol. They say he was a scoundrel. '*Carnazza successe* – Only good for the slaughter-house,' as they say when a mule's on the ground: by which they mean that it's dead meat.

There's another road in the neighbourhood called Via Vallone. They killed Michele Scuzzulato there; no one knows why.

At Bagarella there was a shooting affray in front of the chapel of St Christopher, as a result of a row over an engagement.

The Government protects the criminals here. Supposing you were to be killed, for example, they'd let your murderer out of prison after ten days. The Government is mad. It's terrible how many people have been murdered here since the war. It's happening all the time. Today, for example, one man will infuriate another, and for one wrong word he'll be bumped off. Or it may be for a dispute over cattle. They take it into their heads to murder the fellow and that's the end of that. One word can get a man murdered, something stupid. It's their mentality. It's habitual here. It makes no more impression on them than killing a goat or an animal. They'll kill you or me to show that they're the masters, always. And after the murder they always expect to get away with it.

Dr Michele Navarra, the leader of the traditional Mafia – and a dependant, as such, of Don Calò's – was a man cast in a more conventional mould. Navarra, like Dr Melchiorre Allegra – whose police confession has already been examined – had passed over his soul to the Mafia and the devil for an excellent price. By a skilful manipulation of the Mafia network of mutual aid and graft the doctor had risen rapidly to become Medical Officer of Health, medical officer for the smallholders' health insurance scheme, Inspector of Health for the area, and chairman of the hospital. Outside his purely medical interests, he was chairman of the local branch of the Christian Democratic Party, and President of the Cultivators' Association of Corleone. He also had a valuable interest in an illicit slaughterhouse, where stolen cattle, kept hidden in the nearby Ficuzza wood, were slaughtered as required. The doctor's photographs show him with a lined forehead and a sensitive, haunted expression, almost as though on the verge of tears over some unhappy memory. Despite the mildness of his appearance, he was given to arrogance – sometimes to impatience as well, as evidenced by his supposed assassination of Dr Nicolosi who preceded him in the various medical posts he held. At a later period he was to make a novel contribution to the science of faking the polls by issuing several hundred certificates of blindness or extreme myopia to the women of Corleone, who were then accompanied by Mafia bullies into the polling booths, to make certain that they voted Christian Democrat.

*   *   *

It was against this composite background of the Middle Ages, and gunplay in the streets, that Placido Rizzotto set about organising the peasantry of Corleone. From the Mafia point of view, it was the story of a promising lad corrupted by army life. Placido had done an acceptable six months in prison in his extreme youth, and he came of satisfactory family. His father had been a low-grade mafioso who had been caught in Prefect Mori's net, sent to *confino*, and thereafter been inactive in the organisation. But years in the army, including a period of fighting with the partisans in northern Italy, had provided Placido with new perspectives and thrown him out of step with the old life back in Corleone. For an ex-army sergeant and a partisan, he seems to have been remarkably gentle in his manner. He was slight in build and is reluctantly admitted by his friends to have been rather girlish in appearance. Placido contrived to see some good in most people, and amazed his fellow trade unionists, whose moral judgments were clear-cut and lacking in in-between shades, by arguing that even the terrible gun-slinging Mafia bullies of Corleone were the products, as well as prisoners, of a tragic environment. One of his frequently-quoted actions was the supply, at a time when paraffin was almost unobtainable, of some of the trade union centre's stock to a Mafia-run farm. When asked to justify this eccentricity, he replied that, having had to do it himself, he knew what it was like to try and run a byre in winter with the butt-end of a candle.

Ingrained in the Sicilian mentality – beaten into it, one might almost say – is the idea that it is respectable to keep oneself strictly to oneself: not to hear the shot fired at night, not to see the figure escaping down the alleyway, to turn back at the sight of the body lying in the gutter ahead, to know nothing of what is going on, to keep one's own counsel, to leave other people to solve their problems in their own way. To the downtrodden Sicilian peasant the parable of the Good Samaritan is almost without meaning, and the conduct of its protagonist irrational. The response to Rizzotto's urgings to unite and organise was slow. The whole conception of peasant unity, of fixing minimum wages, of demanding the division of produce according to the new laws, and of forming a co-operative with the ultimate intention of taking over uncultivated land, was too novel, and with the invisible presence of the Black Knight, Luciano Liggio – too frightening. Moreover, the police were suspicious of trade unionists, and the Church in western Sicily condemned them outright.

Rizzotto went from hovel to hovel convincing the doubters. In his own way he showed a flexibility of character that would have done credit to Don Calò himself. To refute the charge that as a trade union leader he must be an atheist, he took over the organisation of the annual festivities of the patron saint of the town, and provided more coloured bunting, more flowers, and more fireworks for less expenditure. In the end he grew on the people of Corleone, and they were willing to overlook his lack of manly gruffness and his un-Sicilian passion for bothering himself with other people's affairs and for prying into things that didn't concern him. He won over those who hung back from fear of the gunmen by a kind of infective courage. His argument was that only a few dozen out of Corleone's population were members of the Mafia, and that if people got together and faced up to them, then the Mafia would be powerless. In the end Placido had ten thousand peasants behind him. Profiting from the mistakes of others, he gave the police no trouble. There were no rabble-rousing speeches, no symbolical occupation of uncultivated land; just a quiet, steady undermining of the enemy's positions, and always with the law at his back. He worked to such good effect that while the Mafia was busying itself with the immense opportunities for self-enrichment of the postwar period, while Liggio was occupied with marketing his stolen beef, and while Dr Navarra was consolidating his medical monopoly, the citizens of Corleone voted in a left-wing town council.

With the Mafia hold apparently broken, Placido's next move was the

Three women bereaved by Mafia killings

logical one. His co-operative applied to the court in Termini Imerese for the redistribution of the uncultivated land of the Drago estate, and was successful. A few days later a commission was sent from Palermo to inspect the lands that were to be taken over, and Placido showed them round. A mafioso recalling this circumstance said that the only thing that surprised him from the Honoured Society's point of view was that things had ever been allowed to get as far as this, particularly when one remembered that Placido Rizzotto's father had been a man of respect – from which it was to be supposed that his son must be in the possession of dangerous secrets.

On March 10th, 1948, Placido Rizzotto went out for a stroll before supper, telling his parents that he would be back in half an hour. What follows is taken from a signed statement made to an examining magistrate two years later by Pasquale Criscione, a *gaballotto* of the Drago estate that was to be expropriated, and a rank-and-file member of the Mafia. Criscione had begun his statement by saying that he was an old friend of Placido Rizzotto's. They had been born in houses facing each other in the same street, had always played together as children, and in later years 'we used to go around together quite a bit, arguing about one thing and another, just like all the other fellows of our age did – but always in a friendly sort of way.'

> On the evening in question, I'd been out as usual trimming up the vines. I came home, had a clean-up, and decided to take a turn in the square. Just outside the Café Alaimo I noticed a group of three people, two of whom I recognised: Placido Rizzotto and Ludovico Benigno. I went up to them – actually, I was going past them when Benigno pulled out a chair by way of a joke and held me up. Both of them being friends, we started to chat, and the third person went off. We were walking up and down the Via Bentivegna together until about ten o'clock. After that we dropped Benigno near his house by the new bridge, and carried on together towards the Piazza Garibaldi.
>
> Just as we were going by the Café Alaimo again I was called across the road by a certain Luciano Liggio, an acquaintance of mine.

Turning round so that he had his back to Rizzotto, who was still waiting by the café, Liggio said, 'Carry on with Placido as far as the Villa and remember, I'm behind you.' I put up some sort of objection with the idea of getting to know what was behind it, but all he did was to pull up the right side of his jacket and put his hand on a pistol he had in his belt. He then said, 'Do what I say, or I'll kill you.' Being aware of Luciano Liggio's violent character and his reputation as a killer, there was nothing I could do but agree, so I went back to Rizzotto again.

Rizzotto didn't ask me what Liggio wanted, and we started off again in the direction of the Villa. I noticed now that Liggio, having pretended to go off in the other direction, had turned round again and was following us. I made no attempt to put Rizzotto on his guard, and when he wanted to go back to the Piazza Garibaldi I went with him, but then induced him to turn back up the Via Bentivegna again. When we came to the end of the street I made out Liggio standing in the angle of a wall, and he signed to me to turn into the Via Marsala. I then suggested to Rizzotto that we should stroll on up the Via Marsala a bit and to this he raised no objection. We had just reached Triolo's shop when Liggio came up from behind, took Rizzotto under the arm and pointed a gun into his ribs. He said, 'Don't be afraid. I'm not going to shoot you. We're just going to have a quiet chat, and after that you can clear off.'

When Rizzotto saw the gun he was startled and half put his hands up. We went up the street the way Liggio said, and after Triolo's shop we turned into the Via Misericordia and after that the Via Sant' Elena. At the end of the street last mentioned, where the straw shacks are, I saw Vincenzo Collura waiting. As soon as we came up, Collura pulled out a gun and took Rizzotto by his free arm . . . Liggio pointed his pistol at me and told me to go back home. He said that if I ever let a single word drop about what had happened he would finish me off. Knowing he was quite capable of carrying out his threat, I didn't feel like arguing about it. I went back and dropped in at my brother-in-law's house to ask how a sick cow of his was getting on.

In answer to a question, the accused replied:

> After I left them I had a chance to see that Liggio and Collura with Rizzotto in the middle went off up the footpath that leads to Sant'Ippolito. I can't say that I heard any screams. In any case, I'm deaf in the right ear.

Answering a further question, the accused man said:

> Next day, I got up early as usual and went over to Frattina to load up wood. When I got back at about midday, I heard that Rizzotto's father had been looking for me. Later Rizzotto's mother and sister came to ask if I could give them any news of him, as they had heard that we'd been seen together the night before.
>
> Bearing in mind Liggio's warning, I told them I'd parted company with Placido on the previous evening at about quarter-past ten at the corner of the Via Marsala, and that before going off he'd mentioned that he might look in at Coniglio's tailor's shop before going home. I confess that I invented the last detail so as to make my story sound more convincing.

*   *   *

Nearly two years later Criscione and Collura were arrested after Placido's father (once again, a curiously medieval touch) had formally accused them to the assembled citizens of Corleone from the balcony of his house. Collura's confession more or less bore out Criscione's, although he alleged that Liggio had done the actual killing. Rizzotto's body had been thrown into a ninety-feet deep crevice in Corleone's sinister mountain – 'so that the crows would not be attracted by the odour of decay, and give away the place where he lay by circling overhead'. The fire brigade brought up five shoes, a pair of braces, an ankle bone, a piece of overcoat, and a head in their first sack. The head had been lying in the mud and the features had gone, but Placido's father recognised his son's chestnut hair, and also the piece of overcoat. He had only had it made the year before, 'with buttons down the middle, in the new fashion'.

Further searches by the fire brigade produced more sacks full of bones. For many years this had been the hiding-place of bodies of the men of Corleone who had fallen foul of the Mafia.

Inevitably, at the trial, Criscione and Collura withdrew their confessions made before the examining magistrate, alleging that their statements had been obtained by violence used by the police. In addition, Collura – an American repatriate – produced an alibi, a number of witnesses appearing to support his statement that he had not been in Corleone on the day of the killing. The two men and Luciano Liggio were then acquitted for lack of evidence. This more or less is what has happened in the thousand or so Mafia trials (outside the Mussolini period) of which records exist.

Eyewitnesses have supplied a lugubrious account of Rizzotto's abduction and his last minutes on earth. It happened on a fine evening of early spring at about nine o'clock – a time when the Via Bentivegna and the Piazza Garibaldi were crowded with people out for an after-supper stroll before going to bed. Everyone knew what was happening, saw the pointed guns, knew that Placido was being led away like an animal to the slaughterhouse. What took place was a sad Gethsemane sequence of averted eyes and abandonment, of doors quickly closed and lights quickly put out. Within minutes the streets and the square of Corleone were empty, and Placido walked alone with his captors towards the crevice on the mountainside of Casale. As a man present at this scene said, 'He was our hero, and we let him go. All we had to do, every one of us, was to have picked up a single stone from the street, and we'd have been too much for them.'

As to the fashion in which Placido met his end, there will always be a doubt. Collura, in his first statement, said that Liggio shot him three times, but a macabre occurrence that took place immediately after the abduction throws doubt on this. A shepherd boy was brought into Dr Navarra's hospital half-dead from fright. He said that he had been on the mountainside and had seen two 'bandits' hang another man from a tree. Dr Navarra listened sympathetically and then administered a 'sedative' injection. Soon after, the boy was dead. At that time Liggio and Navarra were good friends, and it was to be exactly ten years before it was Navarra's turn to die from a burst from Liggio's sub-machine-gun.

After the loss of Placido, the peasants of Corleone gave in. All idea of a co-operative was given up, and in 1963, fifteen years later, the feudal land they had been allocated remained covered with brambles and stones. Placido Rizzotto turned out to be one of the first of a series of thirty-nine trade union leaders assassinated more or less in this way. The Mafia regarded them not so much as a real danger, but as a nuisance that might grow into a danger, and their elimination was seen as a tactical success. The great Mafia strategic offensive was directed elsewhere – having as its first target a Separatist Sicily, and when that failed, the demolition of the peasants' Popular Front and its threat to the political party the Mafia supported. For this it enlisted its own private army, and as its commander-in-chief it chose the bandit Salvatore Giuliano, who now comes on the scene.

8

THE CONDITION of Sicily at the end of the last war is hardly imaginable by anyone who has not assisted at the spectacle of a country prostrated by defeat and occupied by alien troops.

In the towns, basically honest citizens lived empty preoccupied existences full of the petty manoeuvres and shifts necessary to keep body and soul together when all commerce and industry lay in ruins and the value of the lira had dropped to a point where a small employee's wages were worth a couple of packets of cigarettes a week. A large proportion of the feminine population supplied the family's income, or were compelled to supplement it, by sporadic prostitution with Allied soldiers. Every Sicilian, in order to live, had been driven to become a black marketeer in his own small way, and was liable, as such, to constant harrying by the police. But immune from interference of any kind, Don Calogero's private black market, that leech with a thousand mouths, sucked steadily at the country's lifeblood.

In the countryside these problems were aggravated by a total collapse of security. Thirty armed bands – at least one of them led by an AMGOT-appointed mafioso mayor – were at large. Their numbers had been swollen by six hundred criminals who had escaped from Sicilian gaols damaged by Allied bombing, numerous army deserters, and a contingent of convicts – all of them lifers – who had succeeded in breaking out of the Volterra prison during the battle for the town, and had taken refuge in Sicily. The bandits were abundantly armed with weapons collected on the battlefields. They staged innumerable highway robberies, held up trains, drove off the peasants' flocks, kidnapped rich men by the hundred and held them for ransom, and even laid siege to the police in their barracks. The Sicilian barons had managed to come to terms with them, paid them protection money and allowed them to hide out on their estates – sometimes even to use their granaries and warehouses as headquarters. The Mafia, despite its deep distaste for uncontrolled crime, was busy with its own organisational problems, and being able to do little or nothing to straighten out the chaos, was content to watch and wait. Sooner or later it was bound to occur to someone that these roaring gangs of freebooters might be usefully harnessed to the cause of the Sicilian Separatists, and in due course this expedient was suggested at an extraordinary congress of the movement held in September 1945 at a nobleman's villa on the outskirts of Palermo.

Present at this gathering was the Duca di Carcaci, regarded as the head of the Separatists (and a likely candidate for the throne, were a Sicilian monarchy ever to be established), as well as a miscellany of barons. Present also was Don Calò Vizzini, *éminence grise* of the movement since its beginnings in 1941. Don Calò, never avid for personal publicity, was known only by reputation to some of this central committee, and his rumpled suit and insistence on expressing himself in a peasant dialect which – rich in vivid metaphor and salty allusion as it was – could hardly be understood by a patrician, probably caused some surprise. However, the little that Don Calò had to say was, as usual, very much to the point, and he was soon able to impose his view at this most fateful moment in the party's history.

The purpose of this meeting was to work out a revised plan for an armed insurrection originally scheduled to take place later in the same month. The movement had recently been thrown into severe disarray by the loss of Antonio Canepa, the man who had been the brains of the organisation, as well as its military strategist. He personally had organised activist cells throughout Sicily, and he had seen to it that there would be real mass support for the insurrection when it came. While Canepa had been there to lead them, the Separatists had felt themselves invincible. But now there were doubts and divided counsels, and it took all the weight of Don Calò's singular authority to work out a final agreement on the course to be taken.

Like most revolutionary organisations, the Sicilian Separatist movement had brought together some strangely assorted bedfellows. In the forefront, in the full glow of the footlights, was the Duke himself and his supporting barons, all of whom hankered after an unqualified return to the Middle Ages, and who were absolutely certain that the only way to prevent Sicily from being overrun by Communist hordes was to detach it from Italy. Behind this façade of aristocrats was – for the moment – the Mafia; but only for the moment, and while it suited the Mafia's purposes. For the rest, the movement was largely composed of young idealists and romantics who looked forward to a war of liberation from the 'Italian Oppressors'. Each of these groups mistrusted the motives of the others, and each was quite certain of its ability to seize power as soon as separation from Italy became a fact.

Canepa was the hero of the romantic-idealist faction, as well as of such of the peasantry as had been attracted to the aims of Separatism. He was an ardent anti-Fascist as well as a Separatist, and for this reason was always viewed with some reserve by the aristocratic right wing of the movement, which on the whole had no reason to complain of the epoch of Mussolini. Canepa's history had been an astonishing one. In 1933, when a university professor of economics and still in his late twenties, he had been seized with the implausible idea of descending with his brother and a party of student disciples on the tiny mountain state of San Marino, of declaring it an anti-Fascist Italian Republic, and holding out at least long enough to show the world that not all Italians had bowed their necks to Mussolini's yoke. Betrayed by a police spy in his organisation, he was arrested, certified as insane, and locked up in a lunatic asylum. By 1943, he was back again in Sicily, now in the employ of British Intelligence. Early in that year he carried out a totally successful sabotage mission against the German-held airfield of Gerbini, near Syracusa, and was then para-chuted into northern Italy to organise the partisans around Florence. Sixteen guerilla formations of the so-called Canepa Brigade awaited his order in July 1945 to raise the yellow Separatist flag throughout Sicily. The police showed him nothing but benevolent neutrality. The Allies had – so far – been discreetly favourable to his cause. Then the unthinkable happened. It was revealed that Canepa was a secret Communist.

One can imagine the explosion of horror in Sicilian baronial circles when they were confronted with the nightmarish fact that the war chief they relied upon to establish a feudal monarchy in Sicily had turned out to be an advocate of the dictatorship of the proletariat. An unsigned pamphlet was discovered, popularly attributed to Canepa, in which he seemed to be explaining to his Communist supporters the reasons for his dubious associations with such bloodsuckers as the baronial clique. 'For the moment,' the pamphlet ended, 'we are content to follow a parallel course, but the time will come when they will give us their land or their heads.' Canepa's communism was unorthodox, as his support for the Separatists was in direct conflict with the Party line. The Italian Communist Party believed that a separate Sicily would inevitably be dominated by the Allies, and would therefore be anti-Communist and anti-Russian. So persuasive, however, had Canepa been in arguing his position with the Party leaders, that his relationship with them continued to remain cordial.

How was it that the barons were finally informed of the secret nature of the viper they had been nurturing in their bosoms? How can they have been provided in such detail with the account of Canepa's conferences with Communist Party officials in northern Italy? This is where speculation comes up against the higher cynicism of international politics – the obscure treacheries and amoralities of actions taken for reasons of State. The time had come when many interests would be served by the elimination of the brilliant but complicated Canepa, and eliminated Canepa was.

The thing was not well done by the standards of political assassination, and the lack of professionalism – of careful attention to details – suggests that Don Calò had no hand in the planning. The operation was carried out by a patrol of nervous young carabinieri who panicked as soon as their task was completed. Canepa had been caught returning in a truck with his bodyguard from some night excursion and riddled with bullets by the previously well-disposed police manning a road checkpoint. The ambuscade was bungled, as two of Canepa's companions were able to escape and later furnished an account of what had happened; nevertheless, the distracted carabinieri still went ahead with the second part of the plan, now rendered meaningless by the incompleteness of the execution.

It was clearly intended that Canepa should quietly disappear from the face of the earth, but he did not do so. That same night, in the small hours, the custodian of the cemetery of the village of Giarre – thirty kilometres from where the shooting had taken place – was awakened by the police who carried in four coffins. These they tried to persuade him to bury immediately. Their explanation was that they contained the bodies of bandits killed in a battle, but their evident nervousness and their inexplicable insistence that the burials should take place there and then, excited the custodian's suspicions. When asked for the death certificates, the carabinieri said that they had none and that they were acting 'on higher orders'. At this point the custodian, who seems to have been both an obstinate and indomitable fellow, insisted on prising open the coffins. Being himself a Separatist, he instantly recognised the corpse of Canepa. One of the four encoffined men turned out to be still alive, and actually survived the experience.

Thus all hope of disposing discreetly of Canepa, the man and the legend, failed through the officiousness of a village sexton, and with it failed the cause of Sicilian Separatism. Canepa's death – by treachery, as was popularly supposed – split the organisation. His sixteen guerilla formations, left abandoned and without direction, dissolved themselves. The barons and the Mafia were left with their plans for an armed rising but with nobody to carry them out – and for that matter, no insurrectionists.

*   *   *

The Separatists, barons and mafiosi who now foregathered with some anxiety in the villa of the Palerman nobleman, had chosen as their new captain Concetto Gallo, a lawyer and small landowner from the east of the island. Gallo was not the man that Canepa had been, but he possessed all Canepa's almost insane courage and was a gifted orator, who at a moment's notice could unleash a rhetorical flood, behind which an absence of original thought passed unnoticed. Physically he bore a strange resemblance to Lord Kitchener, with his drooping *mustachios*, his severe gaze, and even – in the way of the Kitchener of the famous recruiting poster – his habit of shooting out an admonishing finger at the half-hypnotised victims of his harangues. Gallo showed none of the defunct Canepa's inclination to tinker with the established order. At the meeting he outlined his strategic plan for the 'tactical utilisation' of the outlaw bands. He was particularly eager to enlist the bands of Giuliano in the west, and a heterogeneous collection of brigands led by a notorious murderer called Rizzo who operated in the east. In this way the forces of the Italian State could be harried on two widely separated fronts. One or two of the less violently reactionary delegates voiced some alarm at this proposed open association of the Separatist cause with common criminals, but were shouted down. The vice-president of the organisation, Lucio Tasca, intervened to point out, with telling effect, that even Garibaldi had consented to align himself temporarily and for the best possible motives, with the underworld of his day.

Tasca was the Mayor of Palermo, an elderly and capricious mafioso whose appointment had confirmed Sicilians in their belief that the Allies were not only dedicated to the rehabilitation of the Mafia, but also solidly behind the Separatists. Like so many aristocrats, he was a devout believer in the divine mission of the aristocracy, and he had even elaborated his social philosophy in a treatise entitled *In Praise of the Latifundia*. In this he set out to show that the special spiritual qualities possessed, as he saw it, by the Sicilian peasantry – their innate nobility of soul – could be quite simply extended to Italy, and in due course to the rest of the world, if only humanity could be induced to return to primitive forms of agriculture. Tasca recommended that every tractor in the world should be scrapped in favour of the 'nail plough', an archaic instrument of husbandry in use in Roman times. For the tillers of the soil he advocated a low diet of maize gruel, early rising, early marriage, and prayer. They would revert to the wearing of short homespun tunics, which would both proclaim their condition and ensure the freedom of the limbs so desirable for their work. As of old, the patrician would be distinguished by his flowing robes. Agricultural production was to be improved by converting Sicilian peasant women to the Indian squaw's method of working, more or less uninterruptedly, with her baby bound on her back. In short, the moral regeneration of mankind – with the exception of the aristocracy, who were not in need of it – was to be achieved by turning as many people as possible into peasants working under a paternal feudalism he proceeded to describe. Tasca was a great admirer of Don Calò Vizzini, and had sent him a handsome tribute of black-market grain on the occasion of the head of the Mafia's elevation to the dignity of Mayor of Villalba. He was now to be rewarded by Don Calò's massive and incontrovertible support.

Sweeping aside the objections of the few liberals left in the movement, Don Calò stated his absolute confidence in the success of the revolt. However, he recommended that the old Canepa idea of a popular revolution be thrown overboard. Who could say where a real insurrection would stop, and how could anybody be sure that it could be kept under control? Don Calò offered the delegates his guarantee that he in person would assume the indirect leadership of the outlaw bands. What he proposed in effect was a bogus insurrection. The bandits could be disguised as Sicilian patriots, and where necessary their numbers could be bolstered by enthusiastic university students and lads of good family with a spirit of adventure. In this way the Italian authorities could be harried quite as effectively as by an undependable rabble that might at any moment pick up the Communist virus and start to help itself to other people's property.

It was a suggestion that found ready acceptance. Machiavelli would have been delighted by some of the realistic political thinking that found expression on this occasion – certainly by the subsequent performance of his star pupil, Don Calò, who went straight from the meeting to an appointment with Messana, Chief Inspector of Police. To Messana, Don Calò gave a detailed report of all that had taken place, omitting only the small matter of his own enthusiastic vote in favour of enlisting the bandits. In this way, and in perfect Mafia style, the ground was prepared for certain delicate and profitable manipulations, which Don Calò, as holder of the balance of power, expected to perform. He also made himself as indispensable to the police as he was to the barons, and as he shortly would be to the bandits.

A few days later the Duca di Carcaci sent a message to the bandit Giuliano, inviting him to come to Catania for consultations. Giuliano's reply was brief but characteristic: 'I slip on asphalt.' Mahomet was therefore obliged to go to the mountain, and the meeting finally took place in the warehouse of one of the feudal estates, within a few miles of Giuliano's mountain stronghold of Montelepre. Here Concetto Gallo, the commander-in-chief of the Separatists, formally offered Giuliano the command of the Separatist guerilla forces in western Sicily. In return, Giuliano was promised a free pardon for his now imposing list of crimes, plus a high government post in the new Sicilian State. Giuliano accepted and was commissioned on the spot as colonel. Gallo handed him a Separatist battle standard, and a badge showing a map of Italy and America and two American soldiers, one in the act of cutting the chain linking Sicily with Italy and the other chaining Sicily to the United States. This had been hastily confected by the 'Bureau of Psychological Warfare' of the organisation, in deference to Giuliano's known belief that Separatism could not win without American military aid. It is probable that he was persuaded that this aid was about to be given.

*   *   *

Already, at the age of twenty-three, Salvatore Giuliano ranked as the most famous Sicilian bandit of all times, and was by then usually referred to by the Italian Press as 'The King of Montelepre'. Montelepre is a small, mean, poverty-stricken town, lodged like the cells of a cancer in the flanks of the mountains of northwest Sicily, less than fifteen miles as the crow flies from Palermo. Behind it are the desert acres – a bony, sun-corroded African landscape of spectral peaks and whining siroccos. Below, between Montelepre and the sea, stretches the great glistening plain of Partinico. Here the civilisation of antiquity drove back the desert and filled the landscape with a brilliant filigree of gardens. There is no place in the world that reeks more strongly of the remote past than this. Any house that is more than a hovel is the ghost of a Roman villa, displaying the wasted grandeur of massive portico, cracked arch, and vaulted, sounding interior. All around, the orange orchards spread their magnificent gloom, through which the peasants move almost with stealth. Water – now the prey of the Mafia – gurgles everywhere through a complex of ancient conduits, splashing and cascading from the jaws of stone pythons into moss-rimmed cisterns and ditches. Through Partinico's scent of dust and oranges strikes coldly a rank odour of marshes. In this plain, and to create this miraculous fertility, the voracious colonisation of antiquity consumed slaves by the thousand. They worked in chains, were housed underground, and in three years a man's lifetime was used up by labour. The few that escaped took to the mountains behind Montelepre, and were instantly lost to their pursuers in the chalky dazzle of the rock-maze and among the ramparts of gesticulating cactus. In bad times there have always been bandits above Montelepre.

Giuliano had become a bandit two years previous to his encounter with the Separatist leaders. Two carabinieri, patrolling the mountains on the lookout for petty black-market operators, had caught him with a sack of contraband flour. It was a period when, as revealed in the memoirs of the carabinieri NCO in command of the Montelepre station at that time, the police were actually employed as escorts for large-scale transportation of black-market provisions up and down the roads of Sicily, but when such small offenders as Giuliano were vigorously prosecuted. Resisting arrest, Giuliano shot one carabiniere dead, and was himself wounded by the other. He took to the *maquis*, and as soon as his wound had healed, began a series of audacious coups, the first being the liberation of a number of criminals from the gaol at Monreale. It has been suggested that this operation was planned for him by the Mafia, who had already estimated his potential usefulness in any armed showdown with the peasants that it might be necessary to stage. The escaped prisoners formed the nucleus of his band. By way of reprisal for this humiliation, the police organised a mass roundup of suspects in the town of Montelepre. As the arrested persons were being led away in chains, Giuliano made a dramatic appearance in the town square and opened fire on the police escort, killing another carabiniere. Giuliano's exploits were carried out with a feeling for the theatre that endeared him to newspapermen, and constantly provided the subject of special editions of Italian papers. On one occasion he materialised suddenly in the path of two carabinieri who were supposed to be looking for him and deprived them of their weapons and their boots. As this performance was held to reflect grave discredit upon the carabinieri as a whole, some effort was made to hush it up, and the Mayor of Montelepre, who happened to be Giuliano's uncle, used his good offices to persuade Giuliano to return the confiscated property. However, the restitution was accompanied by the maximum publicity – to the enormous increase of Giuliano's prestige and the disparagement of that of the police.

The King of Montelepre showed, at the age of twenty-one, a quite extraordinary capacity for leadership and organisation. He soon involved the whole countryside in a kind of conspiratorial network to safeguard him from being taken unawares. A warning system was worked out by which the presence in the mountains not only of a policeman, but of any stranger to the neighbourhood, was immediately signalled to him by shepherds who could transmit a simple message by whistling from one to the other from hilltop to hilltop. Like all the bandits remembered by history, he was careful to cultivate the Robin Hood tradition of robbing the rich to give to the poor. To this conventional source of popularity he added another and specifically Sicilian qualification for the people's esteem by declaring against the Mafia – which turned on him its reptilian smile and simply bided its time. In one way or another he succeeded in winning over not only the whole of the civil population of Montelepre, but a number of its authorities as well. Giuliano had the intellectual raw material of a political thinker, and although he was handicapped by his limited education and knowledge of the world, he was a master – out of sheer natural genius – of the art of guerilla warfare. He was a far abler strategist, too, than Concetto Gallo, the Separatists' commander-in-chief. It was inevitable that his fame should go to his head. He was courted by journalists and film producers; received the diplomatic visits of such celebrities as Vito Genovese, the American gangster who was unofficial adviser to the Allied Military Government; was wined and dined in secret by politicians and high

*The twenty-three-year-old bandit, Salvatore Giuliano, 'the King of Montelepre',
with his mother. Giuliano began by opposing the Mafia and ended as its tool.*

officials of the Italian police. He became a letter-writer, explaining and justifying his actions to the Press, the police, and members of parliament, in letters couched in vigorous style that had also the ring of proclamations and often began: 'My name is Giuliano' in the manner of Ozymandias, King of Kings.

The photographs of the Giuliano of the period show him as an athletic stripling with the kind of good looks a Northerner can understand and appreciate. He was a man of what in the old days used to be called an open countenance, with a good forehead, a firm mouth, and a certain directness of expression. Giuliano had the face of a Latin, but not that of a Mediterranean man of the deep south. His appearance, indeed, was in striking contrast with that of his henchmen – in particular Pisciotta, his egregious second-in-command, whose almond eyes and long thin nose with recurving nostrils belong to the face on an Etruscan vase, or even a Persian bas-relief.

For formal occasions, or for one of his incognito visits to the city, Giuliano dressed with the sober dignity of a true Sicilian – 'better than a professor or lawyer', as Cicciu Busacca, the troubadour, puts it in his 'Ballad of Giuliano, King of the Brigands'. The touches of luxury he permitted himself were discreet: a calendar wristwatch, a golden belt-buckle, and a diamond solitaire ring which he had taken in person from the finger of the Duchess of Pratameno on the occasion when he obtained admission to her house by a trick, having arranged for a member of the band to be employed as her doorkeeper. His dramatic announcement, 'I am Giuliano,' appears to have fallen flat. One version has it that the Duchess took him for a rather brash young relation of one of her domestics, and, although startled by the intrusion, recovered herself to murmur politely, 'How nice of you to come.' In the end Giuliano convinced her that in spite of his exceedingly bourgeois appearance, he really was an outlaw, and indeed compelled her to hand over her jewels by threatening to kill her nephew. Otherwise the interview was conducted on his side with courtesy, and even gallantry. It was at the moment of leave-taking when he bent over the Duchess's hand to kiss it that he noticed the famous ring. This episode has been made much of by the folk-singers of Sicily, and it was vivaciously described in Cicciu Busacca's ballad – which, by the way, got him into trouble with the authorities as late as 1962, when he was placed on trial for 'apology for crime'.

At the most, Giuliano saw himself as reduced to expedients of this kind through the force of circumstances. He would probably have admitted that – through no fault of his own – he was temporarily an outlaw, but it would have shocked him to hear himself described as a bandit. He was desperately eager for the excuse, presented in due course by the Duca di Carcaci and company, to describe himself as a political fighter. Even before the Separatists made their offer, there is evidence that Giuliano had some amorphous vision of himself as a potent force for the reshaping of the new Sicily that was bound to emerge eventually from the disorders of the day. Giuliano was no cynic. He had his own definition of righteousness. Like every one of the fantastic plotters he was to serve as cat's-paw, he managed to equate the furtherance of his own ends with the ultimate benefit of his country. Giuliano's Sicilian Utopia was far from the slaughtered Canepa's Marxist state, or the medieval paradise of Tasca, the Mayor of Palermo, where the peasants were to be ennobled by endlessly scratching with their wooden implements in the soil of the feudal *latifundia*. But Giuliano's Utopia had a real existence in his own mind. Its starting-point was justice for those like himself, whom he saw as having been wronged by a corrupt society, and after that he would have cleared away all the oppressors of the poor, beginning with the police and ending with the Mafia.

*　　*　　*

Giuliano, the reformer, gave the people of Montelepre a foretaste of the stern but paternalistic régime he had in mind. Common criminals, i.e., robbers who were not members of his band, were caught and executed by firing squad. Members of his own band were sometimes liquidated too; one for assaulting a woman, another for requisitioning a poor farmer's cattle, and a third – who had stolen two barrels of wine – for 'disrespect to the poor'. Petty dishonesty infuriated the King of Montelepre, who said on one occasion, 'A rich man no more misses a million lire than he would his hat, but if you take a sack of wheat from a peasant, you leave him in misery.'

Having licked his own band into shape morally, Giuliano next decided to clean up some of the civic wrongdoers of his home town, and a post-office employee was promptly executed for stealing the mail, and a shopkeeper for oppressive usury. It had been the shopkeeper's misfortune to give credit to Giuliano's sister. When possible, executions were carried out with proper formality in the town itself, while the police cowered in their barracks. The condemned man was given time – in fact urged – to say a prayer before the volley was fired, and afterwards his body would be exposed in a prominent place bearing a notice such as 'Giuliano Does Not Steal From the Poor', in indication of the reason for the execution.

The Giuliano despotism, however, was not all repression. In a capricious and erratic way the bandit did succeed in distributing a fair amount of his loot among the neediest of the peasants of the area. Once he descended like a fairy godfather with a wad of bank-notes in hand on an old woman who was about to be evicted from her house, and there are many instances where he is known to have contributed from his war-chest to alleviate suffering that had been reported to him. The real trouble was that, like so many of the contenders for power in the Sicily of the immediate postwar period, Giuliano found himself obliged to make alliances of convenience with the oppressors of the poor whose protector he claimed to be. Determined as he was to strike at the Mafia when the moment came, he listened too long to the siren voice of its whispered promptings. The end, Giuliano assured himself, justified the means. But the end as seen in Giuliano's naïve vision never came about, and before the Mafia had finished with him it had turned him into a marionette with a machine-gun, who killed mindlessly, and strictly to its order.

Already, at this early stage of his career, there was something not altogether explicable in Giuliano's unbroken run of success. Maresciallo Calandra, who took over command of the twelve badly armed and somewhat demoralised carabinieri of the Montelepre detachment, while far from underrating the bandit's intelligence and intuition, began to be puzzled by the fact that Giuliano seemed not only to be aware of all the police's moves, but also of their intentions. These sinister powers of augury enabled Giuliano to move his men across the mountains into position to ambush a police convoy, not merely as soon as the trucks were sighted on the road, but even *before* they had left police head-quarters in Palermo. How also could the bandit have known in advance of an occasion when Calandra was obliged to go to Partinico on official business? Giuliano had let it be known that he proposed to be revenged on the Maresciallo for compelling his mother to come to the police station at Montelepre and then treating her with insufficient respect. At the last moment Calandra decided to go to Palermo that day and sent his sergeant to Partinico in his place. The sergeant was ambushed with his men and only narrowly escaped, and Giuliano, calling on him to surrender as the sergeant lay concealed behind a rock, hailed him as 'Maresciallo' – making it quite plain that it was Calandra who had been expected.

Calandra's memoirs, entitled *I Could Have Captured the Bandit Giuliano*, were published seventeen years later, in 1961, when the Maresciallo was in retirement and felt himself able to dispense with some of the reticence expected of a serving noncommissioned officer. Looking back, he has the sensation that even in those early days Giuliano was being protected; that he may have been marked down to be held in reserve for the execution of some occult task, the nature of which might some day be hinted at, but never stated.

The Maresciallo's situation in Montelepre was an uneasy one. He found himself isolated with his men by the total hostility of the local population, and the victim of pronounced logistic difficulties. There were no beds for the men, and no change of clothing when they came in from patrols carried out in the freezing winter rain. Somewhat more remarkably there were no more than six pairs of boots among the twelve, so that only half the contingent – wearing boots which fitted them only roughly – could leave the barracks at a time, while the others waited in their socks. The disparity in fire power between the bandits and the carabinieri was notable. Giuliano's band was equipped with up-to-date machine-guns, German P60 automatic pistols, American rifles, and hand-grenades. Calandra's men carried antique Italian revolvers based on an 1889 version of the Colt, and Italian army rifles, model 891, which to an outsider look more like a well-made toy than a weapon of offence.

Calandra's first attempt to round up the band came within a few weeks of taking over the command of the station. It was a fiasco. He had completed his investigations and applied for one hundred and fifty warrants for the arrest of members or accomplices of the band. At that time many of the bandits, including Giuliano, frequently slept in their own houses in Montelepre, and Calandra, who had laid his plans on the basis of information supplied by police confidants in the civil population, expected to catch a large number by surprise. The arrest warrants were applied for on November 4th, 1944, a few extra pairs of boots were begged or borrowed from somewhere, and the twelve excited carabinieri awaited Calandra's signal to pounce. But that very night, without any warning to Calandra, a large body of ordinary police – the Pubblica Sicurezza – descended on the town, provoking a mass stampede of wanted persons to the mountains. All the bandits were, of course, able to slip away in the rumpus. This was only the first of many frustrations to be endured by the Maresciallo in his one-sided battle with the bandit, which was to be terminated so abruptly, at the very moment when he felt victory to be within his reach, by his transfer to another part of Sicily.

9

A SERIES of discussions was arranged between Giuliano and Sicilian Separatist emissaries in an effort to work out some necessarily hasty plan of action for the projected rising. In the end, Giuliano demanded a meeting with the Separatist leaders themselves to settle the final arrangements. This encounter took place on the Sagana bridge on the Palermo highway, and only fifteen minutes from the centre of the city. Giuliano, still apparently not entirely convinced of the *bona fides* of the people he had to deal with, had chosen a position where the road crawled through a naked amphitheatre of rock, and the approaches to the bridge could be kept under observation for miles.

The whole central executive of the Separatist party put in an appearance on this occasion, and, leaning on the parapet of this bridge while his bodyguard sauntered up and down, fingers on the triggers of their tommy-guns, Giuliano more or less dictated his conditions.

Concetto Gallo, the Separatists' commander-in-chief, had come in the hope of convincing Giuliano of the strategic necessity of moving his whole band right across Sicily to the Caltagirone district in the southeast of the island. The reason for this switch in Gallo's plans was that, since the opening of negotiations with Giuliano, the Separatists had been successful in enrolling an important complex of outlaw bands operating in this area – which, by the way, was Gallo's home country. These were known collectively as the Niscemesi. For a year or two they had been organised in small groups of ten or a dozen men and had plagued a wide area of roadless countryside centring on the small town of Niscemi, to the south of Caltagirone. More recently they had come together in a loose confederation. There were a lot of them, and Gallo seemed to think that, properly fed, armed, and disciplined, they could be turned into

125

passable soldiers. The Niscemesi were to be joined, when the moment came, by several hundred young enthusiasts Gallo had enlisted in the towns of eastern Sicily. Now, if only Giuliano could be induced to make the move, the Separatists would possess a real army. The main force, dispersed through the wooded mountains round Niscemi, would fight a classic guerilla war of attrition with the government forces, and in the meanwhile the carabinieri, parcelled out in tiny groups of two, three, and four men in towns and villages all over Sicily would be pinned down by a series of attacks on their barracks.

The Gallo plan was turned down emphatically. Giuliano quite simply refused to budge from the mountains of Montelepre. He proposed that his contribution to the revolt should be massive attacks on the various carabinieri headquarters in his own area, synchronised with the action planned by Gallo in eastern Sicily, in such a way as to confront the authorities virtually with a second front. He showed himself determined not to budge from this decision, and in the end the Separatists could do nothing but agree. And now the question of financing Giuliano's campaign in western Sicily came up, and this called forth some strange proposals. An Italian White Paper, *Armed Bands of the E.V.I.S. (Voluntary Army for Sicilian Independence) and their Criminal Activities*, gives an account of what was said.

> . . . Giuliano asked for a payment of ten million lire to be enabled to put his plan into action, but the Duca di Carcaci, Baron La Motta, and Gallo showed themselves somewhat perplexed and undecided over this. Their friend Franzone intervened with the suggestion that it would be possible to raise the necessary funds by kidnapping wealthy persons and holding them to ransom. The suggestion was well received by Carcaci, Gallo and La Motta, the last-named offering to point out suitable victims chosen from people of his acquaintance. Giuliano, however, rejected the proposal with disdain. At this point La Motta undertook to hand over to Giuliano the sum of one million lire.

One result of Giuliano's refusal to move from Montelepre was that the date of the insurrection had to be put back so as to give Gallo time to enlist more volunteers for his eastern front. Most of these were students left at a loose end by the closing down of the universities, and young white-collared employees who were without work as a result of the postwar chaos. Recruiting went on all through October and November, and the volunteers arriving by train and bus in Caltagirone paraded the streets wearing Separatist armbands and singing patriotic songs. From Caltagirone they were taken to the Separatists' camp in a wood on the top of the nearby mountain San Mauro, on Concetto Gallo's estate. Here they were fitted out with uniforms and given guns. By comparison with the police, they were extremely well-armed. Baron La Motta had helped himself to a small arsenal left on his land by the retreating Italian forces at the time of the invasion, and these arms were duly distributed among his followers.

At the San Mauro camp, the volunteers met for the first time the bandits who were to be their companions in arms, and their high spirits were a little chilled. Unlike the stalwart malefactors who formed the hard core of the Giuliano band, and in spite of their fearsome reputation, the Niscemesi were on the whole a scarecrow collection. Most of them were ex-day labourers or drovers who had committed some petty offence and had taken to the *maquis* to avoid the certainty of spending two or three years in prison while awaiting trial. Since then they had become of necessity robbers, but very few had committed a murder. There was little that was warlike in the appearance of the Niscemesi, but much that was pitiful and ridiculous. One man had a huge, clownish head, and bandy legs; another was quite bald and toothless; a third looked like the early Charlie Chaplin; yet another suffered from St Vitus's dance. Their absurd names, in translation, are straight out of *Henry IV*: Muckrake, Tasty, Shuffle and Chewed-Nose. Concetto Gallo explained to the disconcerted townsmen that these men had all given an undertaking to desist henceforth from criminality and to repay their debt to society by dedicating their lives to the liberation of their country.

There was no foofah about democracy in these transactions. The gentlemen volunteers were housed and fed separately and considered themselves officers, and the bandits cleaned up and ran errands for them, carrying out their orders with almost servile alacrity. Much as some of the young volunteers might have wanted to have their blood curdled with stories of desperate deeds, they soon found that this subject was taboo in bandit circles, and that all the Niscemesi really wanted to talk about was the families they had been driven to abandon, for whom they felt an extreme nostalgia. Most of them refused even to admit that they were criminals, and argued that any temporary irregularities of conduct should be blamed on the abnormal times. Above all, they longed to regain their respectability. As the White Paper puts it: 'Persuaded and inflamed by Concetto Gallo's diabolical suggestive powers, these men sought to camouflage a loss of moral virginity by sacrifice to an ideal.' One thought constantly troubled them. Having in most cases robbed only, they would now be expected to kill. Taking the measure of the young city gentlemen, on whom they waited at table and whose soiled underlinen they washed, they realised that it was they, the Niscemesi, who would do most of the fighting when the time came. The army commander, Concetto Gallo, had assured them that they were now regular combatants, and whereas before it had been absolutely wrong, for example, to steal sheep to keep from starving to death, it would now be right and commendable to shoot down carabinieri from ambush for a political cause. The trouble was, what was to happen if things did, after all, go wrong? The bandits' instinct told them that the lads from good families would be let off lightly and regarded as misguided rather than vicious; but should the worst happen, they knew that they themselves need expect no mercy.

*   *   *

October, November, and most of December passed; time hung heavy and morale began to wilt. Concetto Gallo was expecting more volunteers to bring his force up to a minimum of a thousand; more weapons, including artillery; and especially more money. Nothing of this arrived. Recruiting declined to a trickle. A tank hidden in a cowshed on one of the barons' estates was to have furnished at least a symbol of armoured might, but this could not be started. Rats had found their way into the engine and gnawed the insulation off the electrical wiring – an echo of the quandary of Sennacherib's expedition against Israel, immobilised by bow-string-devouring field mice. Gallo did his best to combat the gathering dejection by tightening up discipline. One of the bandits, an ex-army NCO, undertook to drill the volunteers, and many otherwise unfruitful hours were used up in sloping, ordering and presenting arms. As for the bandits, they were kept busy scrubbing the floors of the farm buildings converted into barracks. When nothing else could be found for them to do, Gallo had them marched round and round the base of the mountain San Mauro, swinging their arms and shouting 'Left-right! Left-right!' until they croaked with fatigue.

The niggardliness that Giuliano had encountered when he had asked for funds was much in evidence here too, and had a paralysing effect on the liberation army's activities. Some of the volunteers had undoubtedly been attracted to the Separatists' standard by the promise that they would be paid 400 lire a day – at that time about equal to the pay of a general in the Italian Army. But not a single recruit had received any money at all, and it was obvious that the news of this breakdown in the Separatists' financial arrangements had reached the ears of many of those who had intended joining the movement, and caused them to change their minds. It began to look as though the multimillionaires who had organised the revolt expected to get their rebellion without having to pay for it. Two hundred volunteers who had been enlisted at Caltanissetta cried off at about this time, when their demand for pay in advance could not be met.

Soon even food supplies began to run short, and now the time came when the bandits were to be called upon to place their special aptitudes at the service of the cause. For three months they had led a quiet and self-respecting life composed largely of guard duties and domestic chores. Now they listened unhappily while their leader, Gallo, assured them that to ransack farmhouses and carry off cattle could not be classed as banditry so long as they were provided with proper requisition orders signed by him. Thus exhorted, but still dubious, the bandits were dispatched to resume their reign of terror through the countryside. When they returned with the looted sacks of corn and the cows they had driven off, they thoughtfully brought a few women with them, and some of these, dazzled with the picture painted for them of their future in a free and joyously independent Sicily, were persuaded to remain.

The difficulty was that hardly any of the volunteers, being townsmen, could ride, and the distances that had to be covered in this largely roadless countryside, across the swarthy mountains between one isolated farmhouse and the next, were too large to be attempted on foot. This meant that either the bandits had to be allowed a free hand, or that Gallo, their commander, had to accompany them in person and keep an eye on what went on. On one such occasion he was recognised by two of his neighbours, dressed in a city suit and unsuitably mounted on a recently purloined racehorse, at the head of a company of ten or eleven bandits, all of them dressed in black-market American uniforms.

A full account of this singular expedition was later made public. It was undertaken at a time when the need for money to pay the waverers, as well as for rations to feed the half-starved men – reduced to a diet of American dried milk and salted horseflesh – had become crucial. The targets of the raid were rich landowners who had been ready to pay lip-service to the cause, but now could not be induced to part with a single lira. At the first call, the party drew an emphatic blank. Two previous frustrations had been experienced here. On the occasion of their first visit Gallo and his bandits had imposed a patriotic contribution of two million lire on the proprietor of the estate, and when four days later the money had not been forthcoming, the landowner had been fined an additional three million lire, and the bandits had ridden round smashing up a few agricultural machines by way of a warning. Such farmhouses – which in the case of one of the large estates would consist of a complex of administrative buildings, barns, and warehouses – would be as a matter of course defended by armed guards, traditionally recruited from the Mafia. On the third visit the band met with the same headshakes and bleak mafioso stares as before. The mafiosi were too few in numbers to fight off an armed band, but their refusal to knuckle under to Gallo's threats showed that they believed that time was on their side. This time the bandits wrecked the outhouse where the landowner kept his wine, smashed up the wine barrels, and doused petrol over the floor. One of them then aimed a flame-thrower through the window. The result was an explosion which blew out the walls and brought the building down, burying the bandit with the flame-thrower under the ruins.

The home journey proved to be almost equally unfruitful. The rich landowners let it be known through their guards that they had no intention of paying up. The bandits punished the first one by shooting all the cattle in sight, and from the second farm they carried off three horses. This was the day's one success, but to offset it, they had failed to add a single lira to their funds, a member of the band had been killed, and they were now faced with the implacable hostility of the whole countryside.

The Duca di Carcaci appeared on a morale-boosting visit, effusively embraced Gallo, wrung the officers' hands, and pinned on medals. Like Gallo, he was an excellent and inspiring speaker. He congratulated the volunteers on their many sacrifices, and the bandits on their progress along the road to moral regeneration, but he had no money to give them. Another distinguished visitor to the camp was Giuliano, who inspected the troops, kept his thoughts to himself, and hastily departed. Introducing the great ally from the west, Gallo told his men: 'Patience. In a few days we shall occupy Caltagirone.'

But as the days became weeks and the possibility of action seemed to become even more remote, scepticism began to corrode the spirits of Gallo's army. A more vigorous discipline, the posting of sentries, and the surrounding of the barracks with barbed wire, giving it the appearance of a prison camp, failed to prevent the desertions. By the beginning of December the Separatist army of eastern Sicily numbered fifty-eight men. At about this time two loiterers captured in the vicinity of the camp were presumed to be carabinieri in disguise, and a plan was conceived by which the suspects, if indeed they were members of the police, should carry a false report of the Separatist strength back to their superiors. The guards who led them blindfold about the camp, were instructed to let drop casual remarks about tanks and artillery hidden in the wood. In one way the trick was effective. The Italian military authorities were indeed misled into the belief that the Separatist force was much stronger and well equipped than it actually was. But their reaction was not to call off their projected attack, but enormously to strengthen the units employed to carry it out. By the end of December, Monte San Mauro was surrounded by five thousand troops with full armoured and artillery support. This imposing force was commanded by three generals. On the mountain top the 58 men of the Separatist army waited for battle to be joined.

*   *   *

The guiding principle of the battle that followed was caution, and this was adhered to by both sides. The attack on the Separatists' positions began soon after dawn, and by ten o'clock a spirited exchange of fire was continuing. The tanks lumbered into position, but as so often happens, turned out to be useless in rugged and wooded terrain and were withdrawn, leaving the artillery to pound away somewhat vaguely in the general direction of the enemy. There was a prodigious expenditure of ammunition on both sides. The Separatists made use of the cover given by a network of irrigation ditches on the mountain's lower slopes continually to shift the position of their machine-guns – a tactic which served to confirm the three generals in command of the attack in their pessimistic evaluation of the strength of the force opposing them. An infantry attack was tried and then hastily called off when a fusillade of bullets whistled round the ears of the attackers, and the army settled down to mortar the Separatists' positions for the next few hours. Several of the defenders' machine-guns jammed as a result of the almost uninterrupted fire they kept up in reaction to this treatment, but by nightfall, when action was suspended, they appear to have suffered no losses.

Next morning brought a brisk renewal of mortar fire from the government side plus a cannonade from anti-tank guns that had been manoeuvred into position during the night. The first newspaper reports of the conflict appeared. One of them described the mountain of San Mauro as being honeycombed, in the manner of the Maginot line, with reinforced concrete passages leading to a number of strong points, all of them linked to a main fortress on the summit of the mountain, which had been constructed in conformity with 'the most up-to-date theories of defensive military technique'.

Whatever his defects may have been as a tactician, Gallo at least believed that a commander ought to lead his troops in action. Accordingly he had taken up his position in a hole in the ground on the lower slopes, and here he remained all day long blazing away enthusiastically for hour after hour, until his machine-gun, too, jammed. He then gave the order to the two volunteers with him to withdraw, and there was a tense and heroic moment when they refused to do so and Gallo drew his pistol and brandished it at them. As even this gesture had no effect on their determination to stay where they were and fight it out to the last round of rifle ammunition, all three men embraced in an emotional leave-taking and the fight went on. Eventually when the defenders' last shot had been fired, Gallo was knocked out by the blast of a hand-grenade, and all three men were then captured. After a few months in prison, Gallo was amnestied.

Night fell again, and with it came the end of the battle. In two full days of fighting hundreds of shells had been fired from artillery pieces of all kinds, and tens of thousands of bullets had been discharged from pistols, rifles and machine-guns. The desperate and bloody resistance described by the newspapers had cost the Separatists six wounded, while the government forces had sustained six casualties too, one man being killed. With the loss of Gallo, the Separatists accepted the impossibility of continuing an organised resistance from their mountain redoubt, and placing themselves temporarily under the orders of a bandit leader who possessed a professional knowledge of local topography, they were able to filter safely through the cordon of surrounding troops and make their escape under cover of darkness. Three of their wounded were in a dangerous condition, and through a prearranged system of liaison they were able to get these away safely by car to the Duca di Carcaci's villa in Catania, where it was expected they would be well looked after. The presence of three wounded rebels in his house, however, seems to have caused the Duke grave embarrassment, and the men were shuffled hastily, and without medical treatment beyond doses of aspirin, from hiding-place to hiding-place until one died. The unfortunate rebel's naked body was tied on the back of a mule, taken up a mountainside, and thrown into a ravine. It was clear that by now the Separatist leaders had got cold feet.

The remnants of their eastern army dragged themselves miserably about the mountains throughout the bitter months of winter, chased from pillar to post by enormous bodies of soldiers and carabinieri. By early April their numbers were reduced by sickness and desertion to eight bandits and twelve volunteers. Some of the volunteers suggested calling the whole thing off, but the bandits always refused. While the volunteers stayed with them the bandits could still believe in the myth that they were the soldiers of a defeated army, with at least the possibility, when the end came, of being treated as such. Clinging to this straw of hope, the bandits refused to let the young townsmen out of their sight. Then five broken-spirited men laid down their arms, prepared even to brave the fury of the diehards rather than go on. There was a moment when the bandits surrounded them, guns in hand, and their lives seemed to hang by a thread, and then the remaining seven volunteers joined in and persuaded the bandits to let them go.

And now all contact with the headquarters of the movement in Palermo was broken. Always before, in the months of hardship spent wandering through the mountains, the handful of Separatists had been occasionally revived by a message from their chiefs assuring them that their sufferings would soon be at an end, that help was coming, that new insurrections would be announced at any moment, and that in the west Giuliano's guerilla band had the army and the police at its mercy. But now they were encased in silence. The cold weeping mists of winter in the Sicilian mountains were behind them, spring – compressed into a single month – had come and was nearly gone, and not far ahead a burning and atrocious summer threatened. By the end of the month the remaining volunteers slipped quietly away, leaving the bandits as they had always dreaded they would be left – alone in the mountains. By the end of that year, all but two were dead.

*   *   *

Meanwhile, from the wings, Don Calogero Vizzini had been watching the comedy. Of the tiny handful of those who manipulated the Separatist movement from behind the scenes, he was probably the first to lose confidence in Separatism. Close as he was to the secret counsels of the Allies, this supreme realist must have realised that the Americans and the British had lost interest in this sickly political infant, and that without their succour it would never survive. It was becoming clear, also, that with Separatism gone by the board, the political party of the Right that stood the best chance in the battles ahead was the Christian Democrats, now vigorously supported by the Catholic Church. Preparing himself for a political conversion, Don Calò saw no reason to prolong the Separatists' agony. The trifling fact that he himself was deeply compromised with them, and with what were seen at that time as their crimes, hardly troubled him in view of his intimate friendship with Messana. Now, to cement his friendship with the Chief of Police, Don Calò betrayed to him the Separatists' plan of action for western Sicily, where, as arranged, Giuliano was engaged in attacking the carabinieri barracks. Nothing was farther from Don Calò's intention than to bring about Giuliano's annihilation, but he preferred him, the way things had gone, to be kept in check. When, therefore, Giuliano next attacked a police-station, he found that he was expected, and suffered a sharp reverse.

Following Don Calò's furtive abandonment of their cause, the dukes and barons flocked back like prodigal sons to make their peace with the Italian Government. If nothing else, the faked-up popular revolt, nine-tenths of which had been banditry, had succeeded as a piece of blackmail. Meanwhile the storm clouds of real rebellion had gathered and muttered on the horizon. At Lentini and at Carletini infuriated peasants broke into the granaries of the feudal estates where corn was being hoarded against a rise in prices, and carried it away. The time had clearly arrived for conciliation and the peace of compromise.

In the negotiations that followed, the principle naturally enough was that the leading figures of the Separatist movement were to go scot-free. Writing to the Italian Premier, De Gasperi, the carabinieri commanding officer in Sicily, General Branca, said of such of the leaders as Tasca and

Don Calò Vizzini: 'There is no evidence of their direct participation in the organisation of armed bands, and certainly insufficient proof to warrant their arrest.' De Gasperi laid down the policy to be followed in a letter to his high commissioner. Everything possible was to be done to restore normality in Sicily. He was to show 'benevolent discrimination in the case of those who had been misled by others and who now wished to draw back from the dangerous position in which they found themselves.' However, it was clear that somebody had to pay the penalty for the loss of life and property, so common malefactors who had exploited the emergency to commit crimes were to be prosecuted with the utmost rigour of the law. It was hastily agreed that Sicily should be granted autonomy within the framework of the Italian State. The Central Government recognised the very special social structure of the island. In other words, there would be no land reforms pressed through over the heads of the feudal landowners. To sum up, the barons were given almost everything they had almost had to fight to get. In return, they believed themselves able to guarantee that Sicily would remain a perpetual reservoir of voters for the Right.

Against this background of fraternal hugs, misty-eyed reconciliation, and the popping of champagne corks in honour of the new autonomous Sicily, Giuliano, Colonel of the Separatist Army, still carried on what was now a meaningless private war. His coups were increasingly audacious, bloody and successful. He blew up carabinieri barracks, massacred soldiers and policemen from ambush, disrupted all traffic by road or rail in western Sicily, and was even almost successful in an attempt to take over the Palermo radio station. Until May 1946, when Sicilian autonomy was officially announced, he managed to see himself as a soldier legitimately killing the enemy. But with the declaration of autonomy and the turning of the Separatist barons' backs on their unruly past, he was a criminal once again. There was to be no amnesty for Giuliano, and the violences he had been induced to commit as a result of his association with the Separatists enormously diminished any hope he may have had of eventual rehabilitation.

But even as a bandit there was still a use to be found for Giuliano's services. De Gasperi, the Premier, had ordered that normality should be restored in Sicily without delay, but the men in his service on the spot, the army and police chiefs, asked themselves how the head of the government supposed that his orders could be carried out, with the thirty armed bands still at large, and – with the exception of the Niscemesi, who had borne the brunt of the campaign against Gallo at San Mauro – still as active as ever.

The problem was solved with brilliant economy by Don Calò himself, who, having facilitated and come to terms with the Allied occupation of his country in such a way that western Sicily at least was spared from becoming a battlefield, now took it upon himself to tidy up the litter of the war's aftermath.

A certain Cavalier Santo Fleres, a dependent of Don Calò's and head of the Mafia 'family' of Partinico – a man who had grown so fat in his latter years that he could walk only with the aid of a couple of lesser men of respect propping him up on each side – met Giuliano and put a proposition to him. Giuliano was to persuade the electorate in the area under his control to vote Christian Democrat, and he was to go to work immediately to eliminate all the rival bands within his reach. In return, the Mafia would use its influence through its tame representatives in Parliament to obtain a pardon for him and his men. By this time the Honoured Society felt itself strong enough to add a stipulation: Giuliano was to cease his depredations in country areas and leave landowners alone. In future his tribute-raising activities were to be confined to the towns.

Giuliano went to work with speed and silence. After the months and years of half-hearted footslogging across the mountains by thousands of soldiers and carabinieri, the huge encirclements that closed in on nothing, the massive cannonadings that claimed no victims, what now happened was murder reduced to clean surgery. Working in unholy trinity, Inspector-General of Public Security Messana, Don Calò and Giuliano not only cleaned up the country but deftly removed most of the unpleasant traces of what had happened.

It was a task undertaken in traditional Sicilian fashion without publicity. A handful of the condemned bandits actually met their deaths, gun in hand, in the open, but in nearly all cases they were the victims of cold-blooded betrayals by those whom they believed to be their friends. Don Calò suspended the code of *omertà* and death made its approach in many unexpected disguises. It was in the changed smile of the mistress waiting to signal from the window of a room where a worn-out fugitive sprawled on the bed, and in the hand clasp that become a grip from which a man could not tear himself free, while a knife struck down from behind. A new gun, the gift of an old friend, exploded in a man's face the first time he tried it. A car crashed mysteriously into a wall, killing its driver, when the steering unaccountably failed. One simple-minded swashbuckler, grateful to receive an invitation to the house of a mafioso, was drugged with luminal tablets dropped into his wine, then carried outside and shot. Bandits were induced to come out of hiding by faked appeals from their families, or by promises that clandestine emigration had been arranged, and were then mown down from ambush. The Mafia showed no loyalty or fair play to the 'trash'. All that counted was expediency. What had to be done was best got over with quickly.

Men who had been called to protect manorial property from the demands of land-hungry peasants were told that their services were no longer required. 'Rickets' Trabona, the brigand who had a legal contract drawn up by which his two infant sons received a half-share in the produce of an estate he 'protected', now found himself obliged to hide out in a *pagliaio* straw shelter, and in this he was shot dead in his sleep. The nights of Sicily were full of the stealthy comings and goings of the executioners.

Mafia orders were that none of the bandit leaders, burdened as they were with compromising secrets, were to be taken alive. Obsessed, almost, with security, the men of respect put themselves to trouble to prevent their victims' identification, and there were hideous discoveries of assortments of corpses charred beyond recognition in country shacks destroyed by fire. Sometimes a carabinieri officer would manage to secure a recognisable body and have himself photographed beside it like a hunter with his trophy, but the dead man had always been dispatched elsewhere, and in circumstances that would have done little credit to the law. The demoralised and leaderless rank and file of the bands were now rounded up by the police. At the 'Trial of the Rags' as it was called, by contemptuous allusion to the prisoners' quality, two hundred and ninety-two obscure criminals stood in the dock, round which had been built an enormous cage. Among them there was only one notable figure. This was Salvatore Malta, the man who had performed the singular feat of being on the register of the Ucciardone prison while actually at large and engaged in terrorising the peasantry of the Tudia estate. Most of the prisoners received life sentences, but Inspector Messana, Don Calò's friend and head of Public Security, as well as three other senior police officers, spoke in Malta's defence and he was acquitted.

*   *   *

This trial marked the end of the period of postwar anarchy. By the end of 1946 order returned to five-sixths of Sicily. Only one band remained, but it was as active, as numerous and as apparently invulnerable as it had ever been. This was the band of Giuliano, and as the retired policemen publish their memoirs and the grains of evidence accumulate over the years, the fantastic reason why becomes plain.

Maresciallo Calandra in charge of the carabinieri of Montelepre tells us that he could have captured Giuliano at the beginning of the bandit's career *but was not allowed to*. Giuliano, he says, always seemed to know in advance when any attack on his hiding-place was contemplated. Later we read from official Italian sources of Inspector-General Verdiani of the Public Security exchanging an affectionate correspondence with the bandit, and once joining him for an intimate little meal *en famille*, with sweet cakes and wine. Meanwhile, and at a time when carabinieri, public security agents and soldiers were dying in ambuscades staged by the Giuliano band, Pisciotta – Giulano's second-in-command – was out shopping for silk shirts in Palermo, accompanied by a carabinieri captain. Pisciotta carried in his pocket two genuine police passes, one permitting him to move about freely, and the other to carry arms. One of these bore the signature, whether forged or not, of Mario Scelba, Minister of the Interior.

The fact is that there was no desire whatever to destroy the Giuliano band. On the contrary, the evidence is that it was kept in readiness; an instrument to be used in a final emergency for the performance of a grim task. On May 1st, 1947, Giuliano and his men, having at last received their orders, moved to the attack – not this time on the police, but on a great multitude of peasant holidaymakers. Italian politics have never recovered from the effect of the deed that was done that day.

10

To AN OBSERVER of the Italian – and Sicilian – political scene in the immediate postwar period, a swing to the Left seemed certain as soon as parliamentary democracy could be established. Allied Intelligence agencies were surprised, and in some cases disturbed, at the strength and vitality of the emergent Left-wing parties at a moment when, in many places, it was felt necessary to confront the Communist Eastern bloc with an undivided and anti-Communist West.

The Italian drift to the Left was the foreseeable and indeed inevitable reaction from twenty years of government by a clownish dictatorship which had finally succeeded in dragging the nation after it to disaster. The weary disgust of nearly all Italians for the Mussolini régime was extended to embrace those many ex-Fascists, or Fascist collaborators, who now offered themselves under various labels as candidates for democratic election. The only parties harbouring none of these damaged reputations or political turncoats were those of the Left, and many Socialist and Communist leaders could speak of years spent in Fascist prisons in support of their political good faith. In so far as the Left attracted the Italian middle classes, it was because it promised a reversal of everything Fascism had stood for. In the Italian deep south and in Sicily, the Socialists' and Communists' appeal was based on their promise to assuage the peasants' centuries-old hunger for the land. Peasants everywhere know little of and care less for the doctrinal concepts of Communism. If they are landless, and if there is uncultivated land within their reach, they will follow whoever shows them how that land can be occupied.

By 1947 the Sicilian peasantry were licking the very dregs of misery. The sparse and wretchedly-paid labour given them on the feudal estates provided hardly enough food to keep body and soul together, and they were mocked by the bitter vision of the weeds growing high on the uncultivated land that had become theirs by a law which was seemingly never to be put into force. Where they had tried to stand up for their rights, the Mafia or hired bandits had quickly browbeaten them back into submission. Killers had been hired to assassinate their leaders. Occasional mass demonstrations which had been too strong for the Mafia to break up had been dealt with by police riot-squads with tear-gas and machine-guns. It began, in fact, to look as though autonomous Sicily was to be quite indistinguishable from a peasant's angle from the feudal paradise the Separatist barons had planned for themselves.

Then the Right made a psychological blunder. A referendum was held to decide the fate of King Umberto II, and the Monarchists adopted as their campaigning slogan, 'Whoever votes Republican votes for the Communists'. The slogan acted as a boomerang, because by this time Don Calò Vizzini himself had become a Republican and a Christian Democrat. Umberto then appealed to the American gangster Nick Gentile, who was erroneously believed by some to have replaced Don Calò as the head of the Honoured Society, and the esteem shown this gangster chieftain by Allied Military Government was exceeded only by that accorded to Don Calò himself. The ex-American capo-Mafia discusses his cosy relationship with the occupation authorities in his autobiography, published in Italy in November 1963. AMGOT, he says, found him indispensable in his home town, Raffadali. 'One might say that Major Monroe and I formed an administration, a government of the territory.' Unfortunately the British moved in and took over the whole province, and a British general sent both Gentile and the Major to gaol. But he was soon at liberty again, and this time provided with a more powerful ally, a Colonel Max Brod. It was the Colonel who begged Gentile to exert what he calls his persuasive labours in favour of the royal cause. Gentile agreed, and suggested that the Freemasons be roped in, and in due course he and his friend the Grand Master were received in audience by Umberto. The King asked Gentile for the Mafia's support 'for a last glorious victory for the scutcheon of the House of Savoy'. 'Our talk was carried on in very affectionate terms,' Gentile writes, 'and when I told the King that all Sicilians were behind him, he was deeply moved.'

An admiral and a general were ordered to work with him, and we are told of their sincere and single-minded collaboration with this dark captain of the Western underworld.

Yet despite the power of the Mafia, and the secret labours of the service chiefs and the Freemasons, the House of Savoy was to founder, and to the peasants' enormous astonishment, Umberto seen by them as the patron and ally of the feudal landowner – was – sent packing. The figurehead of an invincible order had been thrown down. Suddenly the peasants understood that there were weaknesses in what they had previously supposed to be the undivided ranks of their betters, and that their position at the bottom of the feudal pyramid was not necessarily preordained. Some of them certainly took the King's word for it that the Republicans were Communists, and gave the Communists the credit for the demolition of the Royal House. There was some point, after all, in fighting for their rights.

The peasants took heart again. With the exception of Sicily's north-western corner, where Giuliano still reigned unchallenged in the mountains that look down on Palermo, the bandits were gone. Despite the Mafia bullies and the police who seized on any excuse to intervene that presented itself, the occupation of the uncultivated estates began again. In September 1946 the Prefect of Caltanissetta finally gave in to peasant pressure to enforce the law and signed the document by which five uncultivated estates were handed over, and within the next few weeks fourteen more estates were occupied, cleared of stones and brambles and put under the plough. When in one case a gang of ruffians was hastily organised in an attempt to drive the peasants out, a general strike was called throughout Sicily. At Sciara, when land due for legal expropriation was held back, the peasants thoroughly scared the authorities by arriving on horseback, six thousand strong, to protest at the town hall. To the Sicilian landowners, it must have seemed as though their gloomiest prophecies about the Red tidal wave that would eventually engulf the country if abandoned to irresponsible democracy were about to be fulfilled.

*   *   *

This was the stage-setting for the elections to the Sicilian Regional Parliament which took place on April 20th, 1947. The Separatist and Monarchist Parties had faded out of the picture now, and the real contenders for power were the Christian Democrats – which had absorbed the members of the two defunct parties of the Right – and the Popular Front amalgam of the parties of the Left: Independents, Socialists and Communists. The Christian Democratic Party supported by the Church and by the feudal landowners was considered a certain winner. A strong majority in the Regional Parliament was essential to the landowners at this strategic moment, because once they were in full control of local government, nothing would have been simpler than to neutralise the irksome measures of reform enacted from time to time by the central Italian government in Rome.

The electoral proceedings were conducted in the usual atmosphere of cajolery, intimidation and sheer violence. It was no longer possible, as it had been in 1900, to administer a thorough beating to the elector before allowing him to enter the polling booth, but many and varied were the forms of psychological coercion applied. The Church, more politically-minded possibly in Sicily than anywhere else on earth, electioneered in energetic fashion. On the Sunday preceding the voting a sermon was preached, by order, from every pulpit in the country extolling the benefits of Christian Democracy, and warning churchgoers against the atheism, licence and depravity of the state in which the ideals of the Popular Front were allowed to prevail. The usual inducements were held out to those whose votes could be cheaply acquired. To turn to the evidence of Danilo Dolci (*To Feed the Hungry*):

> ... The Sisters came to every house in Petralia with presents of food and 1,000-lira notes. ... 'I'll give you a kilo of pasta,' they say, 'if you vote for our party. ... ' They bribe people to vote by giving them presents and promising them this and that ... Yes, the vote's bought, all right – with packets of pasta.

And then there was the other side of the medal. 'Vote for our party, and you can keep your land – if you don't you'll be kicked off,

Communist electioneering in a village near Corleone

double quick!' ... Just before the election the landowner sends for the tenant and says: 'Vote for me, otherwise out you go!' ... 'Put your mark against No. 1 and No. 8,' the master says to them, and they daren't do otherwise for fear they'd lose their jobs. The scrutineers check the slips as they come in, so they know whether you've voted for their party or not.

That was the worst risk of all – the risk of losing one's job in a country in which, as Dolci's informants told him, most people couldn't even be sure that the ballot was secret. And there was not only the risk of losing a job that one had, but the fear of never being able to get a job again if one voted for the wrong party. No one in Sicily would ever think of presenting himself for employment without a 'recommendation' from either a priest or a politician (in 1963, 35,000 such recommendations were received by a petroleum company at Gela which had advertised eight hundred vacancies). It was unlikely that a recommendation would be forthcoming in the case of a man known to have voted for the Popular Front.

The final guarantee – or so one would have imagined – of a triumph by the Christian Democrats – was that Don Calò, in accordance with the Honoured Society's tradition of supporting and then endeavouring to control the strongest political party, had ordered all the mafiosi of Sicily to back the party of the landowners and the Church. Popular Front political meetings were outlawed in Mafia territory, and when election day came, gun-slinging thugs hung about the polling stations to remind the voters where they were expected to put their cross. In these circumstances it seemed almost incredible that the Christian Democrats could have been defeated – but defeated they were, and by a substantial majority. At the very moment, in fact, when the feudal landlords and their allies believed that at last they were going to be able to put their house in order, this catastrophe – all the more terrible because so unexpected – confronted them with the spectre of the howling revolutionary mob, and Red ruin.

*   *   *

Seven days later occurred the turning-point in the bandit Giuliano's criminal career when his brother-in-law, Pasquale Sciortino, reached his headquarters with what seems to have been a long-awaited letter. Several members of the band were present, but Giuliano and the brother-in-law went aside to read the letter, after which it was carefully burned. Giuliano seemed greatly excited by its contents. At the mass trial of the Giuliano band in 1950 for the massacre of the peasants at Portella della Ginestra, the judge said of this letter: 'That it had some bearing on the crime that was to be committed a few days later by Giuliano and his band, there can be no doubt whatever.'

The judge's opinion was based on a description of what took place by Giovanni Genovese, given to the examining magistrate at Palermo, and the inevitable conclusion is that the letter did in fact contain the order to carry out the massacre.

On April 27th, 1947, in the morning at Saraceno near Montelepre, Salvatore Giuliano came to see me, with the brothers Pianelli, and

Salvatore Ferreri, so-called 'Fra Diavolo'. They had something to eat in my croft, and then stayed to chat a bit. About three o'clock Pasquale Sciortino showed up. He had a letter for Giuliano and called him on one side. The two of them went to sit down behind the wall, where they read the letter and discussed it. It must have been an important document, seeing that after reading it, Giuliano burned it with a match. After that Sciortino went off. Giuliano came over to me and asked me where my brother was. I said he was probably in town, because he was suffering from a boil. Then Giuliano said to me, 'The hour of our liberation has come.' I asked, 'How's that?' Giuliano said, 'We have to go into action against the Communists; we've got to go and shoot them up on May 1st, at Portella della Ginestra.'

It is here that Giuliano's obsession with liberation from his predicament is revealed. The muddled romanticism of the Robin Hood has been driven out by a bitter realism. Giuliano no longer thinks of punishing the Mafia, avenging the poor, or of ruling in a brigands' cloud-cuckoo-land – a kind of police-free Sicilian Valhalla. What he craves now is simply 'to go free' at any price. The sterile liberty of the fugitive is no longer freedom, and the vast, silent amphitheatre of mountains has closed in on him to become a prison cell. Eighteen months before this Giuliano had treated on equal terms with the nobility of the country, who had promised to repay him for his support with high office in the government of a Separatist Sicily. Then, when Giuliano had agreed to assist in refurbishing the lost lustre of kingship, there had been more promises. But despite the bandit's massive influence with voters at the time of the referendum, the King had gone, and Giuliano still trudged the prison corridors of his empty mountains. Now he dropped his price. All he asked was to be allowed to escape with his men – if the worst came to the worst, even to Brazil. The only political party in a position now to do business with him – or even to pretend to do business – was the Christian Democrats, who were in power in Rome but had suffered their unpredictable setback in the Sicilian elections. Giuliano had already followed Don Calò and the Mafia into Christian Democracy, and now for the third time a bargain was made, but this time the terms were cruelly high. At the great trial of the bandits held at Viterbo, Pisciotta, Giuliano's lieutenant, summarised these occult transactions.

> I don't hide the fact that I was a member of the Giuliano band at the time when it formed part of the Separatist army, and Baron La Motta, the Duca di Carcaci, the Honourable Finocchiaro Aprile, and the Honourable Gallo told us that we were fighting for the freedom of Sicily. That was the first deception. With Separatism over and done with, I thought that everything was finished for us, but the Christian Democrats and the Monarchy got interested, and managed to swindle Giuliano into fighting for them. The Monarchists and the Christian Democrats promised us that if they won the election we should go free, and that if they lost it, it would be fixed up for us to emigrate to Brazil, on the property Prince Alliata has there. I didn't share Giuliano's opinion when he tied himself up with these two parties, and I told him so one day. 'Watch what you're doing,' I said, 'this lot will let you down just like the Separatists did.' But Giuliano said it was none of my business. I was too sick to go with him on that bloody job at Portella, or to attack the various Communist headquarters, or when they massacred the carabinieri. Anyway, those who made us all the promises were Bernardo Mattarella, Prince Alliata, the Monarchist Deputy Marchesano, and also Scelba [Scelba was Minister of the Interior at this time]. The first three used the Honourable Cusumano Geloso as their go-between. I was present at the meetings with this gentleman, but the instigators didn't put much faith in me. It was Marchesano, Prince Alliata and Bernardo Mattarella who ordered the massacre at Portella della Ginestra. Before the massacre they had a meeting with Giuliano.

II

THE SMALL TOWN of Piana dei Greci differs principally from the other small towns of western Sicily in being a tourist attraction – which the others emphatically are not. Piana dei Greci has colour and folklore to offer, although it is supplied strictly to order. The girls still possess the Albanian-Greek national costumes handed down by their great–great-grandmothers, and these are charmingly illustrated in leaflets produced by the Sicilian Office of Tourism. The drive out to Piana dei Greci takes only an hour and gives the visitor a chance to see some of Southern Europe's most eerily impressive mountain scenery. Palermo's leading hotels are happy to arrange such an excursion, and if the party is large enough to make it worth while, a dance can be arranged. This, after four and a half centuries of transplantation from its native Albanian soil, still remains curiously oriental in feeling. It will be remembered that King Vittorio Emanuele was bored by an entertainment of this kind when he allowed himself to be persuaded to pay a visit to Piana dei Greci and was subsequently tricked by its mafioso mayor, Don Ciccio Cuccia, into becoming the godfather of Don Ciccio's son.

After these brief eruptions of organised gaiety, Piana dei Greci relapses into the brooding calm of its everyday existence. Life is monotonous, and too often divided between huge surfeits of enforced leisure and brief spells of crushing labour. The men of Piana dei Greci are yoked to the cruel and complacent fertility of the feudal estates, and their town lies on the frontier between the ancient corn-lands and a sun-flayed mountain wilderness that is the colour of leprous skin. Two desolate and fateful peaks that look as though they were made from ashes rear up behind the town. A wind bickers ceaselessly in the streets, tears at the sails of a half-dismantled windmill, puffs white grit into the eyes, and ruffles the festoons of washing into a brisk, scudding sea. Most of the citizens of

Piana dei Greci go in black, speak in low voices, and use the gestures of a tragic resignation.

In 1959 Professor Silvio Pampiglione of the University of Rome investigated the lives of six hundred families living in such a town and produced a report which startled the Italian conscience, although it did little to modify the conditions the Professor described. The six hundred families, the Professor found, lived in a total of seven hundred rooms – 4.86 persons to a room – two hundred and sixteen of which possessed no window. (In most other cases the 'window' was nothing better than an opening in the wall, hardly ever covered with glass.) Only fifty-two houses possessed a water supply and eighty-two a lavatory – which in only three cases was anything more than a hole in the floor in the corner of a room. A quarter of the houses possessed floors of beaten earth or of bare rock.

The acute shortage of living-space invoked other problems. Every family was obliged to supplement its minute income by keeping a variety of animals, and as there were no pens or outhouses in which these valuable possessions could be enclosed, they had to be brought in to sleep with the family at night. Thus, sharing the seven hundred rooms with 3,404 humans were 5,085 animals, among them goats, pigs, donkeys, horses and mules. On one occasion the Professor was hospitably offered a glass of goat's milk. 'Where does the goat sleep at night?' he asked. 'Under the bed,' was the reply. 'But doesn't the stink of it kill you?' 'You get used to it, like everything else, in time.' The hygienic implications were clearly catastrophic, because there were ten bakeries in the area embraced by the Professor's enquiries, and in every case the inevitable animals were lodged and slept in the bakery – often a single room – along with the baker and his family. In one case there were the man and wife, seven children, a nanny-goat, four hens and a dog. In another the dough was prepared and loaves finally produced in a cavern which sheltered three humans, a donkey, a mule, four goats and twelve hens. As one newspaper summed up, with bitter humour, 'This kind of thing could never happen in England. The Society for the Prevention of Cruelty to Animals would see to that.'

The town investigated by Professor Pampiglione was Palma di Montechiaro – which incidentally contains one of *The Leopard*'s splendid baroque palaces – but it might as well have been Piana dei Greci, or any other of fifty or so small towns of western Sicily. Each town wears the same kind of misery like a threadbare reach-me-down suit. Where Piana dei Greci differs perhaps, apart from its astutely commercialised folklore, is in its tradition of resistance, which has given it a bad name with the authorities for a hundred years or more. Not even the Mafia has been able to beat this germ of defiance out of existence. In the early 'nineties Piana dei Greci was involved in the agitations of the peasant leagues known as the *Fasci*, and shared in their violent suppression. When Mussolini visited the town in 1924 the memory of those turbulent days was still sufficiently fresh for his secret police to place the distinguished visitor under the protection of Piana dei Greci's ridiculous mafioso mayor, Don Ciccio Cuccia – an experience which convinced the Dictator of the necessity of crushing the Mafia.

In spite of this mute but persistent spirit of rebellion, it would be an error to believe that in the days of the fateful elections of 1947 more than the tiniest proportion of the people of Piana dei Greci were either Socialists or Communists. Their lack of education, if no other reason, would have prevented them from grasping more than a few homespun economic facts. The traditions of such communities are Tolstoyan, pacifist, and puritanical – government is seen at best as useless, and at worst as an evil fraud: a conspiracy of visibly corrupt politicians, lawyers and policemen, abetted where necessary by criminals, by which the land – stolen from its cultivators in an unremembered past – is to be kept for ever beyond their reach.

In April 1947, Piana dei Greci went to the polls. Despite the appeals to their conscience, the 'electoral spaghetti', as it is called, the threats of punitive unemployment, and the gunmen lurking outside the polling stations, their hands on their pistol-butts, the Popular Front combination of the parties of the Left, Socialists, Communists and Independents, gained an astonishing and quite unexpected victory. But what the citizens of Piana dei Greci had really voted for was not

Socialism nor Communism, since neither of these terms possessed any clear-cut meaning for them, but the right to wipe out the agonising spectacle of land being allowed to go to waste.

*   *   *

It had been the custom, never abandoned even in the severe days of the Mussolini dictatorship, for the people of Piana dei Greci to join forces with those of San Giuseppe Jato for the celebration of the First of May. San Giuseppe Jato is on the other side of a low mountain pass, about seven miles from Piana dei Greci, and the arrangement had always been for the festivities to take place on a conveniently open place at the top of the pass roughly equidistant from both towns. This spot had the additional advantage of being furnished with a large flat rock which served as a rostrum. As May 1st is observed in Sicily – apart from any political significance it possesses – as the religious feast of Santa Crocefisso, it was difficult for the Fascists to prohibit these gatherings, and the anti-Fascists of the two towns managed to work out a technique by which they could disparage the régime in their May Day speeches, not so much by direct attack, but by sly references.

Often the serious purpose in demonstrations of this kind tends to be engulfed in the holiday spirit. A small responsible minority of males listen to the speeches, and do their best to shush the rest into a respectful silence, but for the majority – for the women, and for the innumerable children – this is the outing of the year, and to be enjoyed as such. Immense time and thought, therefore, go into the preparations; into the sprucing-up of holiday clothes, into the refurbishing of conveyances of all kinds, and into the baking of special feast-day bread and its moulding into decorative shapes. The men who possess them will ride their horses and mules with bells specially attached to their harness, and many of the families will travel in those extraordinary Sicilian carts, every foot of which is covered with paintings of the bloody passages of knight-errantry – scenes from the Epic of Roland, or the crusading adventures of Roger the Norman. When they arrive at their destination, stalls selling sweets will be set up, and there will almost certainly be a phrenologist,

Sciara, a village in the grip of the Mafia and virtually depopulated by murder and emigration

and a ballad-singer standing with his guitar in front of a kind of giant cartoon peopled with the stiff and grimacing figures his song will bring to life. For such an occasion the Sicilian is ready to allow himself to be coaxed out of his habit of silence into an almost noisy sociability. After the speechifying comes the picnic, the holiday bread, and the sausage, and the thick new wine. The women will publicly and proudly suckle their babies. There will be card-playing and perhaps horse-racing, and then naps in the shade, where it can be found, before starting home.

This was more or less the way May Day at Portella della Ginestra had always gone, but this time the people of the two towns really had something to celebrate. Incredibly, they had beaten the seemingly invincible combination of landowner and Mafia, and now, their leaders assured them, there was no power on earth that could stop them from taking over the uncultivated land. True, the Mafia had issued its official and public warning at San Cipirrello, at an election meeting, when a mafioso called Celeste had said, 'Vote for the Communists, and we'll leave you without father or mother.' But nothing had happened, and it was only later that a woman of San Giuseppe Jato remembered that early that same morning a rich citizen of the town had not been able to restrain himself from croaking at a flag-waving party of peasants as they passed, 'Just you wait until you see how things go today.'

But there had been no interference of any kind with the groups of peasants coming singing and playing their guitars up the winding mountain road to Portella, and by half past nine of that tranquil and brilliant morning over two thousand people, more than two-thirds of them children, had reached the open place where the celebrations would be held. At ten o'clock the first speaker, the secretary of the Popular Front, climbed on to the rock platform, and stood waiting while the stewards went off after a group of youths who were fooling with some horses, and others tried to rope in a number of women who were already boiling water for the pasta. Behind the speaker the floor of the pass sloped gently up to a white muddle of rocks topped by the ashen pinnacle of Pizzuta, and facing him, pencilled in on the grey heat mist, were the ridges and stark cliffs of the mountain Cumeta. By ten-fifteen a reasonable audience had been rounded up, the secretary held up his hand, and began his speech.

At that moment a distant popping was heard, an unimportant sound described by those present as resembling that of rockets exploding at a great height. The speaker hesitated and turned his head, distracted, went on, and then stopped again. Francesco Liotta, a seventy-year-old peasant who was standing close to the rostrum, felt his wife tug his sleeve. 'They're letting off fireworks for the *festa*, Francesco,' she said. But then, suddenly, she shrieked and fell down. At the same moment ten-year-old Rigotta Castrense held up her hand to her father, the fingers hanging by bloody ligaments, while her thirteen-year-old friend sprawled suddenly, the lower part of her face carried away. The speaker jumped down from the rostrum as the crowd broke into a babbling confusion, some parents throwing themselves across their children on the ground, others snatching them up to run, hardly knowing from what they were trying to escape, or where to run for shelter. Animals were screaming and kicking and spraying their blood over those who rushed to secure them. In this dolorous, keening commotion, Filippo di Salvo, pointing to something he saw on the slopes of Pizzuta, was caught in the mouth, and dropped dying. Beppino Muchetta, a boy who had been looking after the family cart, came with the news that the horse was dead. 'We've something more than that to weep about, my boy,' his father said, and then Beppino saw his mother and sister lying on the ground, his mother dead and the sister screaming in agony. Celestina Alotta, aged eleven, separated from her parents, was carried along on a human panic-wave almost to safety, when a random bullet tore through her back. A father with his dead son in his arms, running first one way and then the other, said years later, 'All I wanted to do was to shield him from being hurt again. I didn't realise that he was dead all the time.' Bullets ricocheting off the rocks inflicted atrocious wounds. Sixteen years after the event a participant in this apocalyptic moment recalled the spectacle of an old man staggering past him, both hands pressed over his abdomen to push back the entrails. In ten minutes the shooting was over.

*   *   *

Down in Piana dei Greci, Lieutenant Ragusa, a straightforward young infantry officer, commanded a special anti-bandit squad of thirty-three men. Curiously enough, Lieutenant Ragusa took his orders from the senior carabinieri NCO at Piana, Maresciallo Porchera, and on the previous evening when the Lieutenant had asked whether he should make arrangements for security measures to be taken at the Portella meeting, the police NCO had put him off by saying that such measures were inadvisable. Ragusa, however, was well aware of the fact that demonstrations of any kind in this particular zone were liable to give rise to serious incidents, so, acting on his own initiative, he took what precautions he could by cancelling all leave and confining his men to barracks.

Shortly after ten o'clock on the fateful day, the Lieutenant was coming out of the barber's when he heard the crackle of distant small-arms fire. Running to the Piazza where he could get an unobstructed view of Portella, he soon saw a sight 'just like something you see in a film. An

enormous crowd of people was pouring down the road from the mountain. Even at that distance you could hear the women screaming. I tried
without success to contact the police. There was only one carabiniere and
a duty clerk at the station . . . The carabiniere told me about the massacre,
and I got on the telephone to the Inspectorate-General of Public Security
at Palermo, to Carabinieri Headquarters, and to my own company
commander to ask them to cordon off the whole of the Portella area.' It
was twenty minutes by fast car from Palermo to Piana dei Greci, but five
hours before any of the reinforcements requested by Lieutenant Ragusa
arrived on the scene.

And in the meanwhile, in the absence of ambulances, the dead and
the desperately wounded were being brought down on the backs of
mules by volunteers who never knew when the assassins they believed to
be still hidden among the rocks might choose to fire again. A father who
had been absent from the meeting went up with them to look for his
missing son and found him dead. Coming up to the pass, he remembers
a chilling sound that warned him of what was to come. Swollen in the
harsh acoustics of the rock-vaulted wilderness was a moaning that
sounded as though thousands of doves had perched themselves among
the crevices and ledges. It was the groans of the wounded lying among the
bodies of humans and animals scattered everywhere in that narrow place.

*   *   *

Having carried out his orders, Giuliano made haste to withdraw from
the position on the slopes of Mount Pizzuta, where he and his men had
lain in waiting since shortly after dawn. Three young men who had
decided to spend the holiday in their own way by taking a prostitute with
them on a mountain expedition had a lucky escape. 'We were going to
the meeting,' they said later, 'but decided to call it off because we had an
Englishwoman with us.' ('Englishwoman' is the Sicilian euphemism for
a whore.) Hearing the shooting, they hid themselves in a fissure among
the rocks, and soon after saw twelve armed men come down the
mountainside, eleven of them in American uniforms, and the twelfth –
Giuliano – in a white raincoat. An estate guard who ran into the bandits

The May Day procession to Portella della Ginestra, where in 1947 eleven people were killed and fifty-five wounded in a massacre carried out by Giuliano at the instigation of the Mafia, after the peasants had voted overwhelmingly for land reform

a few minutes later was less lucky, despite the fact that he was a well-known mafioso. He was made to turn out his pockets, and among the contents was a note from some minor police official, inviting him to call at headquarters that same evening. The man's body was found in a ravine forty days later.

Four other men passed through the edge of the shadow of death that day. These were peasants from Piana dei Greci who had decided to play truant from the demonstration at Portella della Ginestra, and were setting snares for rabbits on the slopes of Pizzuta shortly after dawn. Suddenly they found themselves confronted by a youth who covered them with a sub-machine-gun. He asked whether they were Communists, and on receiving their energetic denial, said, 'Lucky you. We'd have finished you off if you were.' Other members of the band then appeared, and the hunters were marched off to a cave where one of the bandits was left to guard them, while the others went off. The bandits left their captives in no doubt about the reason for their presence on the mountain, and one man who had two sons playing in the band at the celebration begged that their lives should be spared. To this he received the reply, 'They want the land, and we're going to give it to them – six feet of it apiece.'

This literally seems to have been the bandits' intention. The massacre at Portella, in which only eleven people were killed on the spot and fifty-five wounded (some died later), was certainly a less bloody act of terror than had been planned. As a military operation the thing was a near-failure. In addition to Giuliano and his nucleus of machine-gunners on Pizzuta, an unknown number of men lay in wait on the mountain Cumeta across the pass. The plan was to catch the crowd between two fires. But when the stampede took place from the fusillades poured down from the Pizzuta, the fire which was to have taken the peasant crowd in the rear was slight and ineffective. There is a theory that many of the marksmen placed on Cumeta were shepherds who had been conscripted for a task for which they felt little enthusiasm – particularly as some of them had relations in the crowd – and that their aim was intentionally ragged. The three men and the girl who had hidden in the crevice as the bandits came down the mountainside reported that they had been arguing with each other in angry tones about something that had gone wrong.

Next day the conscientious Lieutenant Ragusa searched the mountainsides and found a position from which a Breda .38 machine-gun had been fired. Some eight hundred empty cartridge cases were strewn about the ground. The Lieutenant thought that the range – about half a mile – was too great for accurate shooting, and to decide whether this was so, he fired a machine-gun of the same type from the same position and found it difficult even to hit the large rock from which the speaker had addressed the crowd. He carefully collected up the empty shells, believing that they might prove useful as evidence, but a few days later they were spirited away.

For days Ragusa and the police authorities occupied in carrying out investigations on the spot followed a false scent. A woman of San Giuseppe Jato had been taunted on the morning of the massacre by a mafioso landowner, and from this it was assumed that the Mafia had carried out the crime. No one seems at first to have thought of Giuliano. But Ettore Messana, head of the Public Security Police for Sicily, knew better. On the day of the shooting of the peasants, Messana sent a telegram to the Minister for Home Affairs, Mario Scelba, informing him that Giuliano was the author of the massacre. To many at the time it seemed strange that the Inspector-General should have known with such certainty a fact that was only discovered independently by his subordinates after much investigatory labour. It seemed less strange four years later at the Viterbo trial of those who had fired on the peasants, when it became known that Messana had a 'confidant' among the bandits who kept him aware of their intentions!

*　　*　　*

The next few weeks were filled with intense activity for Giuliano and his band. A few days after the massacre at Portella, Giuliano gave one of his many journalistic interviews. This time it was to an American, Michael Stern, who went to a rendezvous with the bandit dressed in an American officer's uniform. Giuliano handed Stern a letter for President Truman:

a masterpiece of self-apology and persuasion, which it is unlikely he could have concocted himself. Giuliano pleaded for the President's 'moral support' for his struggle to wipe out Communism in Sicily. 'Because with a lost war we find ourselves in a hopeless state, and will easily fall a prey to foreigners – especially the Russians, who long to appear in the Mediterranean Sea. The consequences, if this should happen, would be of the greatest importance, and you know it.' Thereafter Stern and Giuliano kept up correspondence for some time, Stern writing quite openly to Giuliano, care of his parents at Montelepre. One letter Giuliano sent back fell into the police's hands when they captured the courier carrying it down to Montelepre. In it, Giuliano spoke of 'the circle closing round him', and said that he could no longer carry on with light arms, but must have mortars and artillery. This letter has formed the basis for a belief, widespread in Italy, that Stern was something rather more than a mere scoop-hunting journalist.

On June 22nd, trade union centres and Communist Party headquarters were attacked simultaneously in many towns in the province of Palermo. Hand-grenades, dynamite and Molotov cocktails were used to demolish the buildings, and their occupants were machine-gunned by the bandits as they ran from the flames. Militarily the operation was on this occasion irreproachable, and as a piece of terrorism it was a masterpiece. With Giuliano's gunmen now actively entering the fight on the feudal landowners' side, few people were inclined to give much for the peasants' chances of pressing home their claim to the uncultivated land. The imminent collapse of the Popular Front was generally predicted. In a year's time there would be more elections, and for another year Giuliano was to remain indispensable, and to prosper accordingly.

The mortars and the artillery were never forthcoming, but the band was otherwise splendidly and abundantly equipped for the extermination of unarmed enemies. Much of Giuliano's funds was derived from kidnappings carried out by an efficient specialised squad led by a foundation member of the band, Frank Mannino. The obscure mafiosi who now manipulated Giuliano and his band as confidently as if they had been marionettes dangling from strings, designated the most promising victims. It was the Mafia, too, that negotiated the ransoms, arranged for their payment, and saw to the kidnapped men's safe return to their families. Sometimes the Mafia found it desirable to temper the zeal of some young police official by doing him a favour, and in this case the policeman might be allowed to take the credit for the release. This happened in the famous case of the abduction of Baron Agnello, who was finally turned loose after a record thirty million lire had been paid over. A police commissioner called Tandoy – a northerner who had hitherto shown himself unreceptive to the special Sicilian atmosphere – was softened-up in this way. He got the credit for reducing Giuliano's original demands from ninety million lire to the sum finally paid, and thereafter, one supposes out of gratitude, remained notably quiescent for ten years. After this period of total inactivity he gave trouble again, and was shot one day while strolling with his wife in the streets of Agrigento.

Agnello, like so many of the rich men kidnapped by Giuliano, seems on the whole to have been stimulated by the experience. He was taken in broad daylight in the middle of Palermo while leaving his mistress's house, and carried off in a taxi which immediately broke down with a mild case of engine trouble, and then, when restarted, developed a flat tyre. The Baron, whose Sicilian aristocratic tradition compelled him to abstain from displays of vulgar emotion, sat imperturbable while the repairs were being effected. He spent several weeks with the bandits, shared their lodgings and provender, was forced to accompany them in all weathers on enormous marches, and sometimes – to his disgust – to eat rabbit. They looked after him as well as they could, and he was charmed with Giuliano – a *gentiluomo* – but found the rest of the band unattractive, and lacking in the social graces.

Another nobleman described how, the morning after his abduction, he found himself in a decent room with a bowl of fruit at his bedside. The bandits kept out of sight, but about midday a voice was heard through the shuttered window, 'What will it be for lunch, your lordship?' 'Spaghetti and fried fish,' was the reply. 'Will you be taking beer or wine, sir?' 'Beer, I think.' Shortly afterwards the guard was back. 'Be so good as to face the wall, your lordship.' The baron complied, and the bandit came in with the tray of food. A few days later the kidnapped man had stomach trouble. He was visited by a doctor who, remaining unseen, asked him to describe his symptoms and then prescribed an efficacious remedy. Later, when confidence grew between the bandits and their captive, they tried to make him see that the money they proposed to extort from his family would be expended in the best possible of causes – Giuliano's personal war on the Reds. 'Don't fret, your lordship. Just leave it to us. We'll finish the Communists off for you.'

Some of the victims seem to have accepted Giuliano's assurances that they were getting value for their money, for they remained on friendly terms and in contact with him after their release. Giuliano's popularity in certain quarters was, in fact, never greater than in the twelve months that followed Portella and his attacks on the trade unionists and the Communists. But in 1948 there was another election, and as had been foreseen, the Popular Front was routed. Giuliano had done his work almost too well. Now there was no further use for him. He was merely a nuisance to be disposed of as soon as it could be conveniently done. Giuliano was undoubtedly pressing his claim for payment for his service. As the bandit Terranova testified at the Viterbo trial: 'After the elections of April 18th, 1948, I saw Giuliano and asked him to keep his promises. Our orders had been to make people vote for the Christian Democrats, and we had carried them out. In return he had promised us our liberty. Giuliano replied that the instigators of the massacre had refused to carry out their side of the bargain, and they wanted to make us emigrate to Brazil. Giuliano wanted to stay in Sicily, and said to me: "We must compel these gentlemen to carry out their undertakings. Go to Castellamare del Golfo and kidnap the Honourable Bernardino Mattarella and his family." '

*   *   *

The situation was taking an ugly turn and drastic remedies were called for. The Cavalier of the Crown of Italy, Santo Flores, capo-Mafia of Partinico, who had been responsible for bringing Giuliano and the Christian Democrats together, proposed quite simply to resolve the predicament by betraying the bandit to the police. But for once something went wrong with Mafia planning. Giuliano got wind of the trap that had been set for him and took his revenge. Both the mafioso Santo Flores and the secretary of the Christian Democratic Party of Alcamo who had negotiated with Giuliano on behalf of the Party were shot dead. Some indication of the other personalities Giuliano believed to be involved in this deal, which was now quite clearly to be repudiated, is afforded by the names of those whom Giuliano, in his rage, ordered his men to abduct.

They included, as was revealed at the bandits' trial, Monsignor Filippi, Archbishop of Monreale, and Don Calò Vizzini, the acknowledged head of the Mafia. But in believing that he could touch men of this calibre, Giuliano showed a loss of touch with reality. 'Fra Diavolo', the police spy placed by Inspector Messana in the band, was the safety valve that operated in this kind of emergency, and the intended victims received their warning. Don Calò took Giuliano's threat seriously enough to shut himself up in the Albergo Sole in Palermo – the corridors and public rooms of which were filled with his men-at-arms – until he judged that the danger had blown over. When urgent business called him back to Villalba, he travelled hidden among the vegetable crates on a local market gardener's truck, so that when the bandits stopped his car they captured only his chauffeur and a friend of the chauffeur's who had begged a ride. It was months, too, before the Archbishop left the safety of his palace.

Abandoned by the Christian Democrats, just as he had been as soon as he had served their purpose by the Separatists and Monarchists in turn, Giuliano now hit on an ingenious method of staving off the fate that had overtaken so many bandit chieftains in Sicily since the end of the war. In 1946 Maresciallo Calandra of Montelepre – the local police chief whose twelve men shared six pairs of boots between them – had found that he was not to be permitted to arrest Giuliano, and when he insisted and went to his chief with a cast-iron scheme for rounding up the whole band, he was hastily transferred to another district. The problem for Giuliano was to extend this kind of immunity which he had enjoyed in his politically useful days to a time when every politician in Italy would have been delighted to hear that he was dead. He did it by capitalising on the guilty secrets of the massacre of Portella; composing a memorial, of which several copies were kept, in which the political motives of the massacre were revealed and its instigators named. One copy of the memorial was given into the keeping of his brother-in-law, Pasquale Sciortino, who was smuggled safely away to America. Thus, for fear of the deadly secrets in Giuliano's possession, he could not be captured alive, nor – until it was certain that the various copies of the incriminating memorial were in safe hands – could he be killed. In the meanwhile the daily butchery went on of ordinary policemen and army conscripts engaged in farcical drives against a bandit it was never intended should be caught.

*   *   *

It was the public outcry that followed the slaughter of eight carabinieri in an ambush and the wounding of thirteen more that brought about the dissolution of the special Public Security organisation under Inspector Ciro Verdiani, hitherto – at least in theory – engaged in the prosecution of the war against Giuliano. This was now replaced by the Force for the Repression of Banditry, led by the carabinieri Colonel Ugo Luca. Clearly as it was realised in high places that in the present situation Giuliano himself must remain untouchable, Luca seems, at first, not to have been made aware of this. The Colonel's task was to be complicated by numerous difficulties, not the least being the fact that the Public Security Police and carabinieri viewed each other, at that time, with undisguised hatred.

The antipathy was a traditional one, and had been very obvious to Allied Army officials who were brought into touch with the Italian police during the war. It stemmed from the carabinieri's pride in their status as a military organisation, and a contempt – not unsullied by envy – for a rival force that was not exposed to military discipline, and had, as the carabinieri saw it, a relatively soft time. It had proved quite impossible to draw a clear line between the functions of the two forces, so that over-lapping took place constantly, and wherever it happened, bitter friction was engendered. The furious hostility shown by one brand of Italian policeman for another was a source of constant astonishment to the judge trying the bandits two years later at Viterbo. When Colonel Luca arrived in Palermo to take up his duties, he made the discouraging discovery that the documents relating to the Giuliano band, and all the evidence gathered about their activities over three years, had been made to disappear. This meant he had to start from scratch with his investigations. It was the first blow struck in the private war between the carabinieri colonel and the inspector of Public Security.

Although Inspector Verdiani should have ceased at this stage to interest himself in any way in the Giuliano 'affair', he remained in fact in close contact with the bandit through the Miceli family, who were important mafiosi of Monreale. One of the Micelis flew to Rome to meet the Inspector there to hammer out a plan for forestalling any action Luca might be proposing to take to settle the Giuliano problem. A result of Luca's preliminary drive in the Giuliano zone had been the arrest of several hundred of the people of Montelepre, including Giuliano's mother and sister. Mother-attachment has been observed to be characteristic of every bandit, as well as the one human weakness of almost all mafiosi, and Giuliano seemed ready to agree to anything to secure his mother's release. Verdiani offered to use his influence to arrange this in return for the bandit's undertaking to call off the war against the police. The second part of the bargain was that Giuliano would be allowed to emigrate. Miceli made another trip to Rome to discuss how this was to be done, and soon afterwards Giuliano left the safety of his mountains to go down to Castelvetrano. It was proposed that he should be smuggled out of the country in a military plane from the airport of this town. While these negotiations were proceeding, Verdiani and Giuliano exchanged letters couched in terms of brotherly affection. Later Verdiani travelled from Rome to meet Giuliano in a farmhouse near Castelvetrano. The two men hugged each other, and then the Chief Inspector sat down with an intimate little gathering of bandits and mafiosi to dispose of the sweet cakes and wine that he had thoughtfully brought along in his car. At this meeting Verdiani warned his protégé that Pisciotta, Giuliano's second-in-command, had been drawn into the orbit of Colonel Luca and might be planning some treachery. By now Giuliano was virtually the prisoner of the Mafia, and not only Verdiani, but even the members of the band could contact him only through the good offices of the men of respect.

Meanwhile Colonel Luca had set to work to liquidate the band, a task facilitated, as it happened, by Verdiani's manoeuvrings, which had virtually brought to an end Giuliano's bloodily successful campaign against the police. Italian public opinion wanted action at all costs, so with the enthusiastic co-operation of an imaginative Press, it was fed with stories of last-ditch stands by trapped desperadoes against bodies of hand-picked troops supported by parachutists, reconnaissance planes, and helicopters. Behind this stage-scenery, painted with fictitious violence, Luca tackled the problem in his own singular fashion, and under the sardonic eye of his exceedingly down-to-earth senior NCO, who, in later years, furnished a description of the events of those days which was much at variance with the official story.

Colonel Luca had spent many years in Intelligence duties in the Middle East, a circumstance which inevitably encouraged the newspapers to call him the 'Italian Lawrence of Arabia'. He was deeply imbued with the attitudes of cloak-and-dagger fiction, and some of his actions almost parody the most improbable doings of Somerset Maugham's secret agent, Ashenden. Luca had the idea of importing a professional assassin from Constantinople; a hairless-Mexican sort of character, known as 'the Turk'. The Turk was about forty-five years of age, tough, thickset and dumpy, and a little ridiculous in appearance; his fingers were covered in rings, and he habitually wore shorts and a khaki desert forage-cap with neck protector. This imported specialist in violent death was a shy and taciturn man, who sat for hours eating enormous quantities of spaghetti, and swilling down strong Sicilian wine. He lived by himself in a room in the carabinieri barracks, and when not eating, tinkered end-lessly with a great collection of professional equipment he had brought with him, including pistols, guns and knives of all sorts and descriptions. On the rare occasions when he strolled outside the barracks, he was never without a small leather case intended for a musical instrument but which actually housed a tiny sub-machine-gun of British manufacture which had been fitted with a silencer, and which enchanted all the men. Whenever the presence of Giuliano was notified in a particular area, the Turk was hastily taken there by night and left with his arsenal, seemingly in the remote hope that Giuliano might accidentally run into him. However the hard-bitten policemen of Luca's command may have viewed this project, one thing about the Turk staggered them all. This was his immense resistance to fatigue. They would leave him propped in the angle of a wall with some dried emergency rations and a gallon of wine, and there he would stay day and night without moving, sometimes for as long as three or four days at a time, waiting for Giuliano to pass that way. However, the opportunity never arose for him to prove his worth as a one-man army, and in the end, he was packed off back to Constantinople.

Outside the boisterous legends concocted by the Press and the improbably heroic scenes drawn by the cover-artist of the *Corriere della Serra*, there were few armed conflicts in Sicily in those days, but there were many betrayals. Material for a macabre window-display of corpses was furnished by more than one bandit who had surrendered peaceably enough. Rosario Candela, who had managed to get away to Tunisia with several other leading lights of the band, was arrested by Interpol and handed over to the Italian police, and although the news of his arrest in Tunisia had been published, this was cynically ignored and he was 'killed in a terrific battle' in the Sicilian mountains. The newspapers published photographs of him lying armed to the teeth, a grenade still clenched in his hand, much, as Gavin Maxwell put it, as the weapons of the dead warriors of the past were placed round them for burial.

Torture was automatically the fate of any captured man, and one of them, Giuseppe Sapienza, in his torment let slip the fearful truths of political instigation behind the massacre of Portella della Ginestra. The report of this interrogation had to be hurriedly destroyed. Astonishing facts came to light at the Viterbo trial, when the President of the Court asked the bandit Terranova how this could have happened.

TERRANOVA: Giuliano told me personally that he had had the statement destroyed. He knew that Sapienza had talked, and told me that the confession had to be destroyed before it got into the hands of the examining magistrate.

PRESIDENT: It seems strange to me that Giuliano could have been in a position to arrange for evidence to be destroyed.

TERRANOVA: Giuliano had his confidants in the police, just as they had theirs in the band.

PRESIDENT: But how could Giuliano have known that Sapienza had confessed?

TERRANOVA: I don't know. He was in direct contact with the police. I don't know how he managed it.

12

MARESCIALLO LO BIANCO was the most active member of Luca's special force, and years later, after his retirement, he supplied a newspaper with a disenchanted account of the goings-on of those days. The lack of a university education had prevented the Maresciallo from rising to commissioned rank, but like many senior carabinieri NCOs, he possessed real power. At the Viterbo trial he made a great impression, wearing his authority easily, like his dapper check suit. Most witnesses travelled by train, but the Maresciallo was flown to the trial, kept the court waiting half the morning on the day he was to appear, and when he finally arrived, had a carabiniere trotting at his heels to carry his briefcase.

Lo Bianco soon fell foul of the Machiavellian Inspector Verdiani, who was doing everything he possibly could to hamper, discredit, and cast ridicule upon Colonel Luca and the operations of his Force for the Repression of Banditry. While, for example, the two thousand men of the new special force were chasing phantom outlaws in the mountains, Giuliano was giving interviews to newspapermen whose visits had been arranged by Verdiani with the co-operation of the Mafia, and even taking a week off to make a documentary film, *A Day in the Life of Giuliano*. All Lo Bianco's coups were based upon information supplied by confidants whom he arranged to meet in his father's photographic studio in Palermo, so one of Verdiani's first moves was to try to seduce these informers away. 'A thing,' Lo Bianco says, 'he should have realised it was quite impossible to do. The most junior agent in his force could have told him that a confidant is like an honest woman – absolutely faithful to one man only.' Verdiani went a step further and had one of Lo Bianco's best informers arrested. 'I had been cultivating him for three years.' The man was held in a dungeon for a week, and was warned before being released that in future he must work for nobody but the Public Security Police.

'This, of course, was quite out of the question, for the reason I have already given.'

The wrangle over the loyalty of this informer ended in a public scandal. In due course he was re-arrested by the Public Security, and induced by some agent, lacking in – as Lo Bianco put it – 'intelligence and serenity', to produce a statement which named a number of dignitaries, among them none other than the Cardinal of Palermo and the Archbishop of Monreale as accomplices of Giuliano. Horrified senior police officials immediately suppressed this document, but not before someone had been able to spirit it away for photographic copies to be made. These, in due course, fell into the hands of the Princes of the Church involved, as well as those of the Minister of the Interior, who in a fury called Verdiani to his office and hauled him over the coals. Assuming that the copies had been made in the Lo Bianco studio, the Inspector counter-attacked by having his men ransack the place and arrest Lo Bianco senior. This episode produced a sarcastic letter of condolence addressed to Lo Bianco from Giuliano, which was published in a local newspaper. It was one of the last of such letters to appear. Giuliano had been a compulsive writer to the Press, and up till then several letters had sometimes been published in a single week, but now Colonel Luca made an order cutting off this form of publicity.

*   *   *

While Inspector Verdiani intrigued with the mafioso Miceli, his rival Lo Bianco had succeeded in persuading someone to present him to Don Nitto Minasola, also of Monreale, and in fact the head of the Honoured Society in that small Mafia-ridden town with its stupendous Norman cathedral on the hilltop at the back of Palermo. There was never a more remarkable possessor of the not fully explicable power of the mafioso than Don Nitto, whose name could not even be mentioned in association with any of these events until twelve years later when he was safely dead – assassinated in the sombre main street of San Giuseppe Jato at high noon, while looking over the animals in a horse fair.

Minasola had started life as a poor shepherd, but he had always possessed all the qualities demanded of a man of respect, and inevitably he became one. He was patient, self-controlled, intelligent, full of the knowledge of men, and implacable. Had he been born, say, in Milan, the son of a comfortable family, nothing could have prevented his becoming an outstanding politician, or at least a millionaire. But Minasola's father had left him two scrawny goats, and he had never set foot inside a school. Lo Bianco says he was still a poor man at the time he knew him at the age of fifty-two, although greatly feared. A lifetime's habit of guarding his expression had given his face an oriental quality, a mandarin's impassivity, which Lo Bianco found disconcerting. The Maresciallo told him straightaway that he wanted his help to capture Giuliano, and Minasola shot him one of his penetrating and enigmatic looks, followed by an almost frightening smile, and said, 'You ask me for Giuliano in the same way as one asks a friend for a cup of coffee.'

However, it turned out that Minasola was disposed to collaborate. To mafiosi such as this man, the bandits were a contemptible rabble. They were the Brownshirts of a bypassed revolution, and now that the Mafia was finally back in the saddle, a quiet and economical version of the Night of the Long Knives had to be arranged. Besides, Minasola had a special dislike of the flamboyant Giuliano, with his press conferences, his letter-writing, and his obvious taste for self-advertisement, all of which was distasteful to a true man of respect. In spite of his high authority in the Mafia, Minasola still looked after his own sheep, and more than once members of the Giuliano band, taking him for just another shepherd, had tried to bully him and had refused to be warned in time by Minasola's cold mafioso stare. Now, the shepherd capo-Mafia of Monreale was induced to suggest to Maresciallo Lo Bianco how Giuliano could best be taken.

When Luca had first come on the scene with a special force of two thousand men at his back, Giuliano and the hard core of his band had prudently withdrawn into the province of Trapani in the far western corner of the island, where he was under the protection of Mafia 'families' described by Minasola as 'unfaithful' – in other words, they showed poor response to Don Calò Vizzini's central authority. Minasola's opinion was that it was necessary to entice Giuliano back to the Monreale area, thereby bringing him under the sway of the 'faithful' Mafia again – himself included. To achieve this, the first thing that had to be done was to move out all the police operating in the Monreale area. This was done, and the task of elimination proceeded smoothly enough according to Don Nitto Minasola's plan.

At some time in the past when the Giuliano band had been a valuable military asset to powerful men, it had been reorganised by an expert in guerilla warfare and divided into a number of self-contained cells. The intention was to prevent the secret dispositions of the whole band being given away through the capture or defection of a small number of its components, or even of a single member. In practice, the Giuliano band became a total dependant of the Mafia at this point, because the Mafia volunteered to effect the liaison between the different groups, and thus the functioning of the plan became conditional upon Mafia goodwill. In the mountains the bandits were independent and self-supporting, but as soon as they were obliged for any reason to come down into the towns, it was to the local mafiosi that they were obliged to go for shelter. Also, when any bandit who had been sent on a mission wanted to return to Giuliano's constantly shifting headquarters, he was passed from one man of respect to the next until the new hide-out could first be located, and then reached.

It was this crippling involvement with the Mafia that made Minasola's task so easy once he had set his mind to it. The next step in his plan was to suggest to Giuliano, through one of Minasola's relations who was a member of the band, a suitable victim for extortion living in the Monreale district.

After a long period of inactivity Giuliano's funds were running low, and Minasola managed to whet his appetite with the description of an immensely rich and defenceless landowner, guaranteed to disgorge millions of lire at the mere sight of Giuliano's well-known signature at the bottom of a letter of extortion. Giuliano took the bait. The letter was sent off, and the landowner, who was in the plot, ignored it, as instructed. Minasola had been of the opinion that such a rare act of defiance would bring Giuliano himself on the scene, but instead Giuliano sent a member of his general staff, Frank Mannino. Mannino, as foreseen, was forced to contact Minasola, who invited him to a meeting of Mafia notabilities at the Villa Carolina, the property of the Archbishop of Monreale, just outside the town. '*Salutiamo gli amici*,' was Mannino's Mafia-style greeting as he advanced with hand outstretched towards 'Don Peppino', Minasola's guest of honour. But Don Peppino turned out to be Maresciallo Lo Bianco in plain clothes, and Mannino's hand was seized and not released, while police agents rushed in from the next room with levelled guns.

A few days later two more of the key personalities of the band, Madonia and Badalamenti, fell into the trap. A military truck had been converted into an imitation fruiterer's van, and Madonia and Balda-menti, who wanted to get back to Giuliano, were invited to enter this and to conceal themselves among the piled-up fruit baskets. They were then driven, not to Giuliano's hide-out, but to the police barracks at Calatafimi. Nino Miceli, the mafioso who had collaborated so far only with Inspector Verdiani, was dragged – most reluctantly – into this adventure. He had given way in the end to a combination of Lo Bianco's threats of sending him to *confino*, and Minasola's pressure as his superior in the hierarchy of the Honoured Society. Miceli admitted that the principal objection hitherto to his collaboration had been the eighty million lire promised him by Inspector Verdiani as soon as Giuliano had been smuggled, safe and sound, out of the country.

These were the great names of the Giuliano organisation, and they had been known for years to every Italian, but in addition many lesser figures were removed from circulation by the Minasola-Lo Bianco combination. With a single exception, all these men claimed to have been diabolically tortured by the *cassetta*. One, Francesco Caglia, told the judge at his trial that he had lost a testicle as a result, and Frank Mannino was roped up in an excruciating position and kept like this for a hundred and ten days after his arrest. The only man to escape the torture-chamber was the single mafioso in the band, a low-grade mem-ber of the Honoured Society, who was removed from prison by an order from the Ministry of the Interior in Rome and sent to the more comfortable confinement of the criminal lunatic asylum at Barcellona. The Press was not informed of these captures made by arrangement with the Mafia, so for a while Giuliano too remained in the dark about what was happening to his men. It was considered of the utmost importance not to arouse his suspicions while the Mafia's trap was still doing its work. One day the special squad guarding the house of the landowner-decoy were amazed to see a young bandit drive up in a brand-new car with a final ultimatum from Giuliano. They were obliged to arrest him, but then thought better of it, and after having devised some method of making him serve the police's interests in future, he was released and sent back to his chief.

*　　*　　*

In the meanwhile, the rival cause of the Public Security Police had suffered a crippling blow through the loss of a confidant planted on Giuliano since the very first days of the band's inception. This was Salvatore Ferreri, known as 'Fra Diavolo', a murderer who had been about to begin a life sentence when Inspector-General Messana – Don Calò Vizzini's bosom friend – had released him with orders to join the band. On reaching Giuliano's mountain headquarters, then near Montelepre, Ferreri had made no bones about the realities of the situation. Giuliano, for his part, had accepted him as a useful liaison with the police, who, through Ferreri, could be told just as much as he proposed they should know. Trapped by Luca's men, and wounded into the bargain, Ferreri made the fatal mistake of disclosing his link-up with the Public Security and demanding to be taken to Inspector-General Messana, whose secret pass allowing him to move freely about Sicily he produced in support of his claim. There are conflicting reports as to what happened next. Officially Ferreri was killed in a gun battle that broke out in the police barracks, but most people believe that, having listened to his story, the carabinieri NCO in charge telephoned for instructions to one of his superiors, and then simply finished him off.

There was an unwelcome moment of distraction for Lo Bianco and

Minasola from the job in hand, when a certain Father Biondi made a dramatic appearance at Monreale. This silver-haired and golden-tongued priest had been able to persuade someone at the Ministry of the Interior to allow him to undertake a one-man hunt for Giuliano. In his pocket he carried a postdated letter of credit for fifty million lire, drawn on the Bank of Italy, which was to be his if he succeeded in his mission.

Father Biondi's bungling amateurism caused Don Nitto Minasola the most acute distress and embarrassment and almost upset the delicately balanced mechanisms of deceit that it had taken so long to assemble. Quite clearly convinced that the most direct way to Giuliano's hiding-place was through the Archbishop's palace, Father Biondi went straight there and offered to split the fifty million with the Archbishop's secretary, the Reverend di Giovanni, in return for his help. The proposition proved acceptable, the secretary making it clear that he intended to devote his share of the proceeds to the betterment of the condition of the poor of Monreale. Unfortunately his contact in the Giuliano band happened to be the relation of Minasola already referred to, and naturally this man went to the capo-Mafia for advice. Minasola sternly warned his relative, to keep away from this kind of dirty business – 'out of consideration for the family honour', as Maresciallo Lo Bianco puts it. Meanwhile, some-one had warned Giuliano of the mission of the Roman priest and the machinations at the Archbishop's palace and he had fallen into a terrible rage. Only three months before Monsignor Filippi's name had had to be publicly cleansed of scandalous imputations of complicity with Giuliano, and the strange rumours current at that time were only just dying down. Now the Archbishop was compelled to find some means of making it clear to the bandit that he was not a party to any plot against him that may have been hatched in his palace. Yet another most secret meeting took place in the Archbishop's villa at Monreale – so frequently the scene of the councils and the stratagems of the Mafia. 'To this was called, besides the Archbishop's secretary, Inspector Verdiani and a member of the Mafia in Giuliano's confidence, to clear up the facts of the case and above all to make quite clear to the bandit that he, Monsignor Filippi, had nothing whatever to do with the affair.'

However, Giuliano was dissatisfied with this explanation. 'He ordered the suppression of both the Archbishop and his secretary, and from that time, neither of them was able to visit the country, while Monsignor Filippi had to be given a strong bodyguard.' Father Biondi, the cause of all this trouble, was quickly induced to go back to Rome. Some time later he was arrested for a spectacular fraud in the matter of company promotion, and eventually received a sentence of three years.

At this point Lo Bianco interrupts his chronicle to exclaim plaintively, 'How many intrigues and what extraordinary happenings!'

There are times when one discovers defects in the carpentry of Lo Bianco's narrative. There are too many unexplained gaps in the sequence of events, too many anonymous faces, and even after twelve years, too much has to be left unsaid.

Giuliano was now alone with his lieutenant, Pisciotta. Nothing more is said about traps being set for him. In fact, he seems to come and go much as he pleases, and even pays unmolested visits to Monreale, where he is recognised in the streets. Lo Bianco paints an unconvincing picture of the wounded tiger at bay, as cunning, as ferocious and as unapproachable as ever. His colleague Maresciallo Calandra in his memoirs entitled *I Could Have Captured the Bandit Giuliano* presents a different view. He speaks of the first months of 1950 when the obscure manoeuvrings of Lo Bianco and Minasola seem no longer to have been producing results.

> Now only Pisciotta remained at Giuliano's side, and he had decided to betray him. But even if Pisciotta had not decided on this betrayal, it would have been child's play to capture Giuliano. And if so much time had to be taken over it, this was probably from the necessity of carrying out to the very end a plan that had been pre-arranged with the Mafia. At this period, in fact, a squad of men and an officer would have been all that was necessary to capture the two bandits that remained.

There is a hint here at the true facts, which were that the last moves in this tragic farce had to be continually postponed until it was quite certain that the bandit's elimination could be carried out without fear of damage to men in high political places. Two circumstances made it possible for the order finally to be given for the winding up of the Giuliano affair. One was that Inspector Verdiani persuaded Giuliano to give him a statement in which he took upon himself full responsibility for the massacre at Portella della Ginestra and denied that instigators had ever existed. The other was the news of the FBI's arrest of Giuliano's brother-in-law, Pasquale Sciortino, who had got away to the States with a copy of the famous memorial upon which Giuliano believed his security depended. It has always been supposed that this news was accompanied by some message of reassurance as to the fate of this document.

On one of his visits to Monreale, Giuliano ran into the uncle of Madonia – one of the two bandits who had been carried off to police headquarters in the spurious fruiterer's van. After the usual exchange of courtesies, this man asked for news of his nephew, whom he had not heard from since the day he had seen him go off with Minasola – in theory to be conducted to Giuliano's headquarters. It was then that Giuliano realised what had been the fate of all the men who had disappeared. In the early hours of next morning Miceli and Minasola were dragged from their beds by Giuliano and his lieutenant and forced to confess. They were hidden in a house in Monreale and Pisciotta was left to guard them while Giuliano went off to kidnap three more mafiosi who had been named in the confession. These, together with Miceli and Minasola, were to be publicly executed in the main square of the town. It seems that Giuliano was still able to conscript 'occasionals', as they were called, when an operation of this kind was projected. Minasola received permission to prepare a will, and somebody wrote it out for him on a sheet of squared-off paper from a child's exercise book and took it to his wife. In it Minasola told her to sell off all the goats, which would otherwise be killed in the vendetta which was now certain to start.

Meanwhile, Giuliano's absence gave him the opportunity to work on Pisciotta, and for seven clear days the twenty-five-year-old bandit was left alone at the mercy of the acute native intelligence and the suggestive power of the head of one of the most prominent Mafia 'families'. It was inevitable that by playing constantly upon Pisciotta's vanity, his fears, and his obvious obsession with 'freedom', Minasola should win him over to his side and prepare the ground for his betrayal of his chief. In the end Pisciotta released both mafiosi, and when Giuliano got back, made the excuse that he had been worn out from guarding them night and day, and that they had got away in his sleep. Minasola later told Maresciallo Lo Bianco that Pisciotta had asked him for all the details of the capture of Madonia and Badalamenti in the fruit van, and had appeared highly amused.

Within a few days a meeting was arranged between Pisciotta and Colonel Luca, at which some haggling went on about the price of the treason Pisciotta was to be induced to commit. Broadly, Pisciotta was offered a half of the price – fifty million lire – on Giuliano's head (the other half was to go to Minasola), and a passport under a false name. This, unfortunately for Pisciotta, did not satisfy him, and he preferred to renounce the blood money but stuck out for a pardon, which was to be granted 'in recognition of his special services to the State'. This, even Luca was not in a position to agree to. There was some humming and hawing, but the reward finally agreed upon has never been made clear.

While awaiting his moment of truth, Pisciotta remained at liberty and tasted a kind of freedom he had never known even in his palmiest days, before the commission of his first crime had turned him into a bandit. At a superficial level he was probably a likeable man. One's mental image of the criminal tends perhaps to be influenced by the cretinous psychopaths represented in gangster films, but many of the Giuliano band were handsome, and Pisciotta strikingly so in his dark Asiatic way. He could counterfeit a sincerity of manner that deluded most people, had a bold wit, and made full play with his sardonic sense of humour. Pisciotta and the police got along together swimmingly.

The president of the court at Viterbo was to express his horrified amazement once again at the descriptions of this brief but exuberant phase of Pisciotta's career. He was given a safe conduct from the Ministry of the Interior bearing Minister Mario Scelba's signature (Lo Bianco coolly confides in his readers that this was forged), as well as a permit to carry firearms. When in Palermo, he stayed as an honoured guest in the flat of Captain Perenze of Colonel Luca's special force, who went on shopping expeditions with him and took him to a clinic to arrange for treatment of a pulmonary complaint. A famous lawyer arrived from Rome to discuss with him his defence, should he elect to remain in the country and to stand trial. As the president of the court pointed out, the Italian Government footed the bill for all this expenditure.

Pisciotta was kept thus in readiness for about three weeks. There was a period of tension when Colonel Luca became briefly obsessed with the idea that this co-operation was part of an incredibly elaborate plot concocted with Giuliano and Inspector Verdiani, by which he, Luca, was to be kidnapped, but in the end this was resolved, and the awaited signal was received. At the end of June 1950 the last phase of the operation was prepared. Until this moment Maresciallo Lo Bianco says that he had remained unaware that it had been decided that Giuliano was not to be taken alive. His immediate superior, Colonel Paolantonio, too, showed himself scandalised at this new turn in events, and so from then on an attempt was made to keep both men in the dark about what was going on. Giuliano was at that time receiving shelter in the house of a mafioso lawyer, De Maria, in the town of Castelvetrano, where he had lived off and on for several months while the negotiations for his expatriation had been going on. Now it was arranged that Pisciotta should go to him.

On the night of July 4th, Colonel Luca gave orders that all carabinieri of his special anti-bandit force were to be withdrawn from Castelvetrano, and Pisciotta, accompanied by Captain Perenze and several picked carabinieri, set out on their mission. Lo Bianco and Colonel Paolantonio were to have met and joined forces with this expedition, and they had hired a taxi and were on their way to the meeting-place when Paolantonio suddenly suffered a *crise de conscience*, and told the driver to stop.

'Lo Bianco,' he said, 'there's no risk or glory awaiting us at the end of this trip down to Castelvetrano. It's just a killing rigged up with the help of a bandit. The affair's taken a bad turning, but there's nothing you or I can do to change the course of events, so let's go home.'

And this, so far as Lo Bianco was concerned, was the anticlimax that came at the end of the adventure. 'I affirm,' he says in his memoirs, 'that we could have captured both Giuliano and Pisciotta. The plan for such an operation involved only a minimum of risk . . . Later it was said, "What does it matter how he died? The important thing is that he's out of the way. With Giuliano in the dock with the others, certain things would have come out at the Viterbo trial." ' As a rueful afterthought, the Maresciallo adds; 'And even if he was destined to die, surely the thing could have been done with more propriety, and without all those fantastic stories that they put about.'

*   *   *

Castelvetrano lies fifty miles to the south of Palermo across the bare mountains. Its population has always been dependent upon the fertility of the high districts surrounding it, the property for centuries of the Dukes of Pignatelli-Monteleone. The dukes spent their revenues on palaces and parks and religious foundations elsewhere. Ten centuries after its foundation, Castelvetrano remains hardly more than a great dung-bespattered Arab village of the Middle Atlas, a mugger of walled lanes, blinkered houses, and secret courtyards, full of the dour odour of confined animals, with a single European high street driven right through its middle. It was here that the mafioso Dr Allegra had his clinic; the town where, after Mussolini had weakened the ability of the Mafia to curb petty criminality, the outlaw Ponzio came in broad daylight to seize sheep in the market, and was later tried and sentenced to death by Dr Allegra's Mafia court.

On the night of July 4th, 1950, Pisciotta reached Castelvetrano just after nine o'clock. He told his carabinieri driver to stop about one hundred and fifty yards from De Maria's house in the Via Mannone, walked the rest of the distance, and after being kept waiting at the door while De Maria questioned him through the keyhole, was eventually admitted. Going up to the room which he and Giuliano had often shared, he met with a cold reception from his chief. 'What are you doing here?' Giuliano asked him. Since their last meeting Verdiani had warned him that Pisciotta was now working for Luca. A violent argument took place, Pisciotta vigorously refuting Giuliano's accusations and bringing all his natural endowment of plausibility into action in the attempt to disperse Giuliano's suspicions. It took several hours before Giuliano could be convinced of Pisciotta's sincerity, and then the two men went to bed, but more time was spent in discussing future plans. Even when the conversation finally flagged and broke off, 'action was held up' – as Pisciotta put it – because Giuliano kept twisting and turning in a restless half-sleep.

Meanwhile, Pisciotta's driver and Captain Perenze in the second car, parked a little farther down the street, had been waiting for nearly six hours. Perenze was becoming nervous. It was now just past three o'clock, with signs of the sky's paling in the east; with the bakers – the town's earliest risers – lighting up their ovens, and the first of the peasants starting out for the day's work. Perenze's men had to be mobilised to keep the street free from such unwelcome intruders. At nineteen minutes past three two muffled shots were heard, and a few moments later Pisciotta burst into the street. He was half-naked, agitated to the point of hysteria, carried a shoe in one hand and was waving a pistol in the other. Pushing his driver away from the steering-wheel, Pisciotta jumped into the car and drove off at great speed.

Perenze and his two carabinieri now ran to beat on De Maria's door, and once again there was some delay before De Maria thought it advisable to let them in. The three policemen rushed up the stairs and found Giuliano lying dead on the bed, with two bullet holes under his left armpit. They dressed him with frantic haste, and as no jacket could be found, one of the carabinieri, who was in plain clothes, took off his own jacket, and this – although ridiculously small – was put on the corpse. The maid was roused, ordered to wash the bed linen, and to clean the blood from the floor of the room. The carabinieri then dragged the body downstairs and pitched it face downwards in De Maria's courtyard, where Captain Perenze fired two bursts at it from his sub-machine-gun. Insufficient blood issued from these wounds, so one of De Maria's chickens was quickly snatched from its coop and decapitated, so that the deficiency could be made up. One of the many neighbours spying upon these macabre doings from behind their window casements, says that at this point Perenze went to the door of the courtyard and vomited into the street.

*   *   *

At six o'clock the Minister of the Interior was awakened by a phone call from General D'Antoni, Chief of Police, who told him that Giuliano was dead. The morning was a busy one for the Minister, for soon after eight o'clock the Premier himself, De Gasperi, arrived with his congratulations. Shortly afterwards Scelba called a press conference, at which he made the following announcement: 'Last night Colonel Luca formed the opinion that the moment had come for the capture of the bandit Giuliano, and took measures accordingly. The bandit attempted to escape from a house in the centre of Castelvetrano where he had been in hiding, using firearms in an attempt to evade capture. After a long pursuit, he was finally killed in the gun battle which ensued.' The Minister could say nothing more than this, and he took the opportunity to exhort those present to do their best to play down the Giuliano episode from that time on. Italian newspapermen have never forgotten this emphatic recommendation, and ten years later they were still hammering away at him with the many questions arising out of that night's work at Castelvetrano which were never answered.

All day long the correspondents came pouring into Castelvetrano from every country in western Europe. The earliest of the cameramen to arrive were fortunate enough to capture the scene of dramatic anguish when Giuliano's mother and sister were conducted by the police to the mortuary for the routine identification of the body. Later the old mother asked to be taken to the courtyard of the De Maria house, and there, while the shutters of fifty cameras clicked, she went down on her hands and knees and kissed – some say licked – the dried blood on the flags. For latecomers of the Press, when the Giuliano family had been taken back to Montelepre, a black-shrouded crone was kept in readiness, who re-enacted the frantic scene for the payment of a few lire.

This trivial but ugly imposture set the mood for the day. The hundreds of excited but frustrated journalists who filled the streets of Castelvetrano, debarred from access to solid fact by a strange wall of official reticence, pieced together what rumours they could uncover and joined in an orgy of imaginative reconstruction of the events of the previous night. The evening editions of Italian papers carried detailed accounts, sometimes almost shot by shot, of street battles in which – according to the *Gazzetta del Popolo* – five hundred and thirty carabinieri were involved. The same newspaper described the remarkable weapon with which Giuliano defended himself in this fight to the death: a sub-machine-gun of his own invention carrying an extra magazine in its butt. The reports carried next day by such papers as *The Times* were more sober, but almost equally fantastic. A fog of lies had been released, like a genie from its bottle, and it was many months before the genie could be squeezed back again and the cork rammed home.

In Castelvetrano, sceptism was spreading like a contagious disease. Some of the old hands who had served a long stint as crime reporters and were familiar with all the commonplaces of violent death shook their heads over the *pièce de théâtre* in De Maria's courtyard. Somebody noticed that the blood from two wounds flowed upwards, and another reporter went round interviewing all the neighbours, who scornfully, and to a man, refuted the unofficial police story of a desperate gun battle.

The official story was given next day – by Captain Perenze in person. He explained to the representatives of the Press that it had come to Colonel Luca's knowledge that Giuliano had taken refuge in the Castelvetrano area, where he was awaiting an opportunity to get away to Tunis from the local airport. In an attempt to attract him into the town, and thus within reach of the police, the Colonel had hit on an ingenious idea. Knowing Giuliano's passion for publicity, and in particular for the publicity given by film appearances, he had rigged up a van complete with a cinema projector, a loudspeaker, and a number of advertising posters, and this was kept touring the streets of Castelvetrano at night. The crew of the van were supposed to be engaged in making a documentary film, but in fact they were Perenze himself and his carabinieri, and the belief was that this would be irresistible bait for Giuliano's vanity, and that sooner or later he would put in an appearance and allow himself to be interviewed.

And this, Captain Perenze told his listeners, was in fact how it went. 'After a long wait, at a quarter past three exactly, the carabiniere Renzi saw two men with sub-machine-guns on their backs passing along the Via Gaggini. Brigadiere Catalano held them up in front and Renzi cut off their retreat. The chase lasted fifty-four minutes. We recognised Giuliano because he was bareheaded. I and the carabiniere Giuffrida blocked the side turnings. For all this, one of the men succeeded in escaping, but it was not Giuliano. He in fact tried to hide in the courtyard of the De Maria house, where I was waiting for him. I opened fire and killed him.'

That Perenze was a man of feeling was made clear in a special interview granted to *Il Tempo* shortly afterwards:

> Giuliano died at ten minutes to four, after a death agony lasting ten minutes. I offered him water, but he was silent, mute in his agony, as if burdened by the presage of the hereafter. I can say that it is incorrect that only twenty shots were fired, as some people of the neighbourhood have stated. Giuliano alone fired fifty-two rounds, and then he took refuge in the courtyard, where he was brought down by a fusillade of seven shots, all of which struck vital parts.

For his part in this operation, which restored untroubled sleep to so many public persons, Perenze was promoted to major, while Luca became forthwith a general. But the climate of unbelief, far from being dissipated, seemed to grow murkier. At the end of the month, the Minister of the Interior was still sticking by his guns, and he dismissed a question in Parliament about the death of Giuliano with the reply: 'I fully confirm the version given by Colonel Luca.' Nearly a year later a sensational disclosure at the Viterbo trial of the bandits responsible for the massacre of Portella della Ginestra caused him to modify this view, but only slightly: 'I tell you quite frankly that I have no reason to doubt the version given me by the carabinieri. As a matter of native intuition and from what I have been able to ascertain, I can reconstruct the scene in this way: Pisciotta told Giuliano that the police were on his track and that he had better make his getaway. Giuliano got up, dressed in a hurry and went down into the courtyard. Then Pisciotta gave a whistle and the police hiding behind the wall opened fire. Pisciotta betrayed Giuliano. There's no doubt about it. But he didn't kill him. He wouldn't have had the courage.'

The true version of what took place on that stifling July night in Castelvetrano was supplied by De Maria, the mafioso lawyer. It took the form of a confession in writing handed to an examining magistrate, and coincidentally the confession was completed on the same day that Mario Scelba, aided by his intuition, was giving his latest account of Giuliano's end to the members of parliament in the House.

Like the shepherd Minasola, De Maria comes as a surprise as a man of respect. He was a youngish bachelor, living modestly in a shabby little house and looked after by a maid. As a mafioso, he would have got more than a fair share of Castelvetrano's legal business, but in such a poverty-stricken Mafia-run town this would hardly have amounted to much more than preparing a few legal documents such as leases and contracts. Disputes from which civil actions would normally arise would have been rapidly settled out of court in Castelvetrano, merely by submitting them to the arbitration of the town's capo-Mafia. De Maria was probably left to pick up the legal scraps, and there is a whiff of respectable near-poverty about him as he details in his confession the expenses involved in feeding Giuliano for the nine months, off and on, that this unwelcome guest stayed under his roof. Being a member of the 'Honoured Society' was not all beer and skittles, and De Maria lived to learn – as Dr Allegra had before him – that it could sometimes involve a man in some very tricky situations. De Maria's chief, Marotta, had simply brought Giuliano to the house one day and ordered De Maria to look after him. 'You're a bachelor,' Marotta said, when De Maria risked an objection. 'If you'd been a family man, I'd have taken him somewhere else.' 'It was a calvary,' De Maria writes – the confession has a faint scriptural flavour throughout – 'I felt myself slipping down into a bottomless pit. I searched my memory in an endeavour to discover some wrongdoing that might have justified the punishment of this cruel destiny, but could find nothing. My conscience cried my innocence aloud. I have lived for my Franciscan faith, for my books, and in the memory of the affection given me by my beloved mother . . . and yet I was forced to drain this bitter chalice to the dregs.'

Of his enforced association with Giuliano, De Maria says: 'He liked to be with me, because I spoke to him in an unknown language so far as he was concerned. Our conversations were of faith, good and evil, and redemption. He once told me that he was sure that if fate had brought our paths together earlier in his life, his destiny would have been a very different one.' De Maria added that Giuliano spent much of his time reading Shakespeare and Descartes. At that time De Maria was charged with complicity with banditry. Six months later another warrant was issued, this time for actual participation in an armed band. He was in due course acquitted for lack of proof.

13

GASPARE PISCIOTTA, second-in-command of the Giuliano band, Giuliano's cousin, his lifelong friend and his eventual assassin, remained at large for five months after Giuliano's death. He was eventually arrested in his own home in Montelepre by Questore Marzano, Chief of Police of Palermo – 'after months of tenacious investigation', Marzano said at his trial. Pisciotta himself said that he went to Marzano's office and asked to be arrested. By this time the mass trial of the Giuliano band for the massacre at Portella della Ginestra, held at the town of Viterbo, near Rome, had been dragging on for six months. Pisciotta was removed to the prison at Viterbo and kept there for three months virtually *incommunicado*. No attempt was made to interrogate him, and the long statement he had made to the examining magistrate at Palermo shortly after his arrest disappeared. Finally, Pisciotta was brought to court and placed in the cage with the twelve other regular members of the band. A second cage contained the *picciotti*, the 'boys' charged with sporadic association with the band, all of whom had been tortured into making some kind of damaging admission, and all of whom after spending four years in prison were found innocent.

From the moment of Pisciotta's first arrival in court, he dominated the proceedings. In place of the famous pullover patterned with rampant lions in which he had always been shown in his photographs, he now wore an elegant dark blue suit of imported English material. He was alert and watchful, his pale, handsome face stamped with an expression of mocking and occasionally ferocious good humour. His appearance had stirred up currents of nervous preoccupation. Pisciotta's presence was clearly a source of embarrassment. Captain Perenze's version of the killing of Giuliano was still officially valid, although rumours of the lurid truth of the matter were widespread, and had certainly reached the judge's ears. Day after day passed, and to the public's increasing amazement no attempt was made to interrogate Pisciotta, despite the assurance given to the Press by his counsel that the bandit was ready to make important revelations.

Matters came to a head when his defence counsel, Avvocato Crisafulli, asked the court's leave for Pisciotta to give evidence. The application was immediately opposed by the Attorney-General on the grounds that as Pisciotta had been the last member of the band to be arrested, his examination should be left to the last. The president of the court, D'Agostino, agreed – an extraordinary and almost unprecedented ruling under Italian judicial procedure, which assumes that an accused person volunteering to make a statement shows thereby his desire to collaborate with justice.

Avvocato Sotgiù, representing under the Italian system the interests of the persons who had suffered injury or loss in the massacre, then supported Crisafulli's application.

AVVOCATO SOTGIÙ: A campaign has been started in the Government Press to discredit in advance any evidence given by Pisciotta. Perhaps Giuliano signed his death warrant when he sent to you, Signor President, a declaration in which he denied the existence of instigators, but Pisciotta is here, and alive. Let us open our eyes to reality.

PRESIDENT D'AGOSTINO [showing signs of nervousness]: I have my own views, and shall do as I think fit. When the proper time comes, I will interrogate Pisciotta. First, I propose to interrogate the others.

AVVOCATO TINO [for the survivors]: I fully support the right of the accused to speak.

THE PRESIDENT: The accused can keep what he has to say in his stomach. His time will come.

ATTORNEY-GENERAL: Here we are trying those materially responsible for the crime of Portella della Ginestra. Anything irrelevant that may emerge does not concern us.

AVVOCATO CRISAFULLI: I ask the court's permission to read a statement by Gaspare Pisciotta. It is addressed to the Public Minister.

(The Public Minister has a species of watching brief for the State in Italian court procedure, and is supposed to hold the balance between prosecution and defence.)

THE PRESIDENT: Send it to him by post.

AVVOCATO CRISAFULLI: I will read it.

THE PRESIDENT: No you will not!

AVVOCATO CRISAFULLI: Article 444 of the Code of General Procedure –

THE PRESIDENT [interrupting]: Leave the Code of Penal Procedure out of this.

The Public Minister joined forces with the President at this point to insist that the declaration should not be read. Avvocato Crisafulli then went to the President and handed him the document, while a colleague gave a copy to the Public Minister. Finally, the statement went the rounds of the court. It said:

Dear Avvocato Crisafulli – Observing in you a man of conscience and of honesty, and reposing in you my most complete confidence, I feel that the moment has come to inform you of the following: by a personal agreement reached with the Minister of the Interior, Mario Scelba, Giuliano was killed by me. I reserve my explanation for this killing for the Court at Viterbo.

Gaspare Pisciotta

Now the veil had been torn away, and the ugly truths were to be displayed like the sores on a beggar's limbs. It was to be Pisciotta's tactic to waste no opportunity to demonstrate that the band had acted with the connivance, the complicity – and even the urging – of high authorities, and to show that the massacre was a political crime for which its instigators should be compelled to accept the responsibility. One after another the high officials of the Italian police came before the court to depose, and to run the gauntlet of Pisciotta's sardonic comments. They were old men with the grave burdened faces of the senators and bankers of Venice painted by Giovanni Bellini in the late *quattrocento*; the prisoners of a habit of subterfuge, the inheritors of minds assembled in the secret-agent factories of the petty Italian states. Shifty and hesitant in their evidence, nervously on their guard against the escape of some new disreputable fact, the police chiefs contradicted one another and often contradicted themselves, while that monumental liar Perenze was finally committed for perjury. By contrast, Pisciotta was a model of spontaneity in all his utterances. If Pisciotta told lies he made them sound like truth, but whatever truth lay buried in the policemen's account of these events seemed obscured by a general dingy patina of falsehood.

Inspector-General Ettore Messana was sixty-seven years of age when he appeared before the court, a man who spoke very slowly and in an absent, unconcerned manner of the recent tragedies, as if they had happened a long way back in history. In 1919 Messana had gained some notoriety and a good promotion for the bloody competence with which he had extinguished a small peasant revolt. After the Second World War he had commanded the first anti-bandit force formed in Sicily, and, working in collaboration with his old friend, Don Calò Vizzini, and the Mafia, it had taken him eighteen months to destroy some thirty bands, leaving only that of Giuliano intact. Now the Italian public was to know why. 'We were a single body,' Pisciotta said, 'bandits, police and Mafia, like the Father, the Son, and the Holy Ghost.' In this, perhaps the most celebrated of his utterances, he was supported by Frank Mannino, who said: 'Messana himself informed Giuliano when a police drive was in preparation. The same people who gave us our orders, gave the police theirs.'

Luca's rival Force for the Repression of Banditry got an equally rough handling. Pisciotta accused Luca's second-in-command of supplying the bandits with five machine-guns which were used at the massacre of Portella della Ginestra, and then of betraying Luca's operational plan to Giuliano.

THE PRESIDENT [sarcastically]: Perhaps you'd like to cross-examine the Colonel.
PISCIOTTA [with enthusiasm]: Yes, your lordship – if possible. Colonel Paolantonio calls himself a hero and says he's destroyed banditry. In

reality, banditry could have been wiped out in 1946. It was Colonel Paolantonio who handed over to Giuliano the CFRB's operational plan. It was Colonel Paolantonio who advised Giuliano to move to Castelvetrano outside General Luca's zone . . . Ask him what rake-off he got.

ATTORNEY-GENERAL: This is absurd.

PISCIOTTA: Gentlemen, it was they who created banditry in Sicily. They did everything they could to ensure that banditry should not be wiped out. From 1947 on I acted constantly as the link between the Inspectorate of Public Security and Giuliano.

It turned out not only that Giuliano, Pisciotta and Fra Diavolo had managed to establish a cosy *modus vivendi* with high police officials, but that most of the other leading lights of the band possessed their own protectors as well.

TERRANOVA [a leader of one of the bandit squads]: Signor President, Colonel Paolantonio once did me a service. He warned me at Monreale to go into hiding, otherwise I should have been arrested. I was at Monreale to kidnap somebody. Ask him how many times Provenzano was arrested, and released . . . I can tell you that when Colonel Paolantonio arrested Provenzano, a letter of extortion was found in his pocket and the Colonel himself tore it up.

PISCIOTTA gave his reason for killing Giuliano: As soon as he had written this statement accepting responsibility for the massacre and denying the existence of instigators, Inspector Verdiani promised to send his own son with the documents necessary for Giuliano to escape overseas. Giuliano told him that he would give the statement either to Scelba or Mattarella alone. I realised it was yet another betrayal, and I said to him, 'You're not only risking your own skin, but mine, and the others' too.' Then they got at him behind my back, and he handed over the document. That's why I made the approach to Luca. I realised that the Christian Democrats had fixed up everything for Giuliano to get away, and leave us to face the music. So I killed him.

This was the statement already referred to by Avvocato Sotgiù when he said that in sending it to the court, Giuliano had signed his death warrant. Up till then his immunity had been guaranteed by his famous memorial, a copy of which had been smuggled away to America by Giuliano's brother-in-law, Sciortino. It was described by Pisciotta: 'In that memorial was all Giuliano's life. It was written in pen and ink on twenty sheets of foolscap; the whole truth was there, even the names of the instigators.' Pisciotta said that he had had a copy himself. He asked Giuliano to give it to him 'because I knew what his end would be, and I wanted to have a document to defend myself and the others.' Sciortino had been arrested in the US and his copy was presumed to be in safe hands, but there was no way of deciding whether or not Pisciotta too had possessed a copy of the memorial, and, if so, whether it was still in existence. The court seemed obsessed with the fear that the highly incriminating document might still be produced. There was some suggestion that De Maria might have quietly abstracted it from Giuliano's papers in the hubbub that followed the killing. Evidence was given that he had promised to hand it over to the carabinieri for the payment of three million lire, but had taken the money and said that he had burned the memorial. There was nothing either conclusive or comforting in this.

*   *   *

Pisciotta was the most complex and the most interesting of the bandits – far more so than Giuliano himself. He boldly admitted to having killed by treachery the leader whom most of the bandits would have followed to their death, and yet he had been able, without the slightest difficulty, to replace Giuliano in their affections. More than that, he had established the legend of an untarnished personal honour. Those who dared to attack him in court, whatever their rank or position, inevitably came off worse, and as they beat a retreat the guilty secrets exploded like firecrackers round their ears. There were hard facts in writing, and the stamps, seals and signatures of men in high government office to prove most of Pisciotta's allegations. He produced in court permits and safe-conducts provided by every police authority in the country, plus a certificate of meritorious service issued by the Ministry of the Interior – a document that the most respectable citizen would have been proud to possess. Pisciotta had also come by a long and affectionate letter written by Inspector Verdiani to Giuliano, and this was exhibited in court. 'Dearest,' it began, and after some desultory intimacies, came to the point: 'As I wrote to our friend, in view of the loftiness of the ends we aim at, in the ultimate interests of Italy, I tell you that I can even settle the monetary questions on which your urgent decisions depend. In the national interest my word had been enough to procure adequate funds for you wherever you go. Just let me know what your requirements in cash are likely to be.' Speechless after the perusal of this, the judge passed on to shake his head sadly over a permit to 'carry firearms'. 'Were automatic weapons included?' he asked. 'Even a cannon,' Pisciotta replied, with his sardonic grin.

Meanwhile, the earlier antagonism of public opinion towards the bandit was calming, and eventually gave place to something like a bewildered respect. Pisciotta could even attempt with some success to represent himself as a devoted servant of the State – the instrument for the destruction of the banditry of which he had been a principal exponent. 'It is I, not Paolantonio, who put an end to banditry!' he cried from the cage, and the claim did not seem extraordinary. And again: 'I have done nothing but good in Sicily. The Giuliano band was the shame of the island, but it was not even the fault of Giuliano, but of the men of politics.'

Pisciotta was listened to in attentive silence, but when the police officers, those sad-eyed men of managed passions and the long years of distinguished service, gave their testimony, it was only too often greeted by ironic laughter from the body of the court. The public had been made the dupes of a foolish lie, and the lie had been abetted by a Minister of State. The police had lost face with Italians, and as a result the most improbable of Pisciotta's charges carried weight.

A DEFENCE COUNSEL FOR THE BANDITS' MINOR ASSOCIATES, THE *picciotti*: Did the accused men in the small cage form part of the Giuliano band?

PISCIOTTA [earnestly]: Some of them were only sixteen in those days. They were minors. The real culprits are already in the United States, or Venezuela, or the Argentine. All those boys are innocent. The men who fired at Portella left by plane from the airport of Palermo, supplied with regular passports issued by the Ministry of the Interior. At the airport the police saluted them with respect. Afterwards Giuliano received a letter from Inspector Verdiani, which said, 'Dear Salvatore, Two or three have already left. The others will go later.'

Pisciotta's testimony had frequently provoked excited comment and cries of indignation, but this new allegation, which was accepted at its face value by the public, caused a pandemonium. There were many attempts to silence him, but few succeeded.

AVVOCATO SOTGIÙ: Did Pisciotta go to Rome while he was a fugitive from justice?

THE PRESIDENT: The accused must not reply to the question.

PISCIOTTA [*shouting from the cage*]: I went to Rome, and I spoke to Minister Scelba.

AVVOCATO SOTGIÙ: Was it Inspector Verdiani who put Giuliano in contact with the various journalists who interviewed him?

[*The President signs to Pisciotta to be silent.*]

PISCIOTTA: Yes, he did it to damage the carabinieri. [*A few moments later Pisciotta said that he had warned General Luca of a plot by Inspector Verdiani to kill him. By this time the court seemed to have lost all power to be surprised at such allegations.*]

AVVOCATO CRISAFULLI: I call upon Pisciotta either to confirm or deny that he was charged with the responsibility of guarding the life of the Archbishop of Monreale.

THE PRESIDENT: It doesn't interest us.

PISCIOTTA [*from the cage*]: Certainly it interests us – and in connection with the massacre of Portella, as it happens. Padre Biondi, Padre

Giovanni and the Archbishop of Monreale owe their lives to me, and General Luca can confirm it.

THE PRESIDENT: Be quiet, Pisciotta, or I will send you back to prison.

PISCIOTTA: Do so by all means, but don't think I'll come back here again.

This exchange produced a happy bellow of laughter from Cucinella, one of the bandits in the main cage. (Cucinella was a handsome, pink-faced boy in his early twenties, who smiled continually and could not prevent himself from bursting out laughing at the slightest excuse. He was the most ferocious and the bravest of the bandits, and faced eighteen separate charges of homicide. He was the only member of the band who had been given the chance to put up a fight, and he had held off two hundred carabinieri, throwing hand-grenades, until one grenade had burst prematurely and mangled his leg.)

*   *   *

All the bandits obstinately denied taking part in the massacre. Most of them, schooled in the old Mafia tradition, simply denied everything, or invented some story by which they were miles from Portella at the time of the shooting, and then stuck to it through thick and thin, however infeasible it turned out to be. The technique was outstandingly demonstrated by Genovese, who answered almost every question put to him with the two words, 'Absolutely not.' Finally, the cross-examining counsel asked him ironically if he had ever seen Giuliano. Genovese's reply became famous. 'We passed in the street once or twice and greeted each other in the usual way, no more that that: "Good morning !" – "Good morning !" ' It was known that Giuliano had lived in Genovese's house for three years.

Pisciotta, on the other hand, produced a complex and ingenious alibi. He had been suffering off and on from a tubercular condition of one lung, and now eleven doctors, among them the four most celebrated chest specialists in Italy, foregathered to examine radiographs produced by the bandit and to argue learnedly – and to the court incomprehensibly

– over what they revealed. The date of the radiographs was stated by the medical evidence called for the defence to be May 1st, 1947 – precisely the fateful day of the massacre – and the two medical experts appointed by the court agreed that this might have been the case. The defence argued, too, that no one in the condition revealed by these radiographs could have expended the effort called for in a gruelling night march across the mountains to Portella. At this point the Sicilian peasants who had been injured or who had lost relations in the massacre applied for permission to employ their own experts. This being granted, two more distinguished doctors came on the scene, scrutinised the radiographs, examined Pisciotta, and declared themselves at variance on every point with the previous medical opinions.

The original radiographs had been made by a Dr Grado, a war-cripple and something of a hero, who was universally respected in Sicily. He entered the witness-box with difficulty, assisted by his nurse and leaning upon a stick, and immediately showed himself the possessor of a remarkable memory. Four years had gone by, and thousands of patients had passed through the doctor's consulting room, yet he remembered all the circumstances of Pisciotta's visit, although of course not having had the slightest suspicion of his patient's identity. Dr Grado's testimony seemed conclusive. Pisciotta could not have been at Portella on May 1st 1947 because that was the very day when the doctor had first seen him. Pisciotta had been brought in by his mother, coughing and very emaciated, and clinging to the woman for support. Dr Grado knew that it was May 1st because, being a public holiday, the electric current was unusually feeble – so much so, in fact, that he was unable to X-ray the patient and had to tell him to come back the next day. In so far as the doctor's testimony needed strengthening, this was taken care of by General Luca, who still seemed to regard Pisciotta as his protégé. The General said: 'I have been able to ascertain from my personal investigations that Pisciotta did not take part in the massacre at Portella because on that day he was extremely ill.'

CAPTAIN PERENZE: Colonel Angrisani also told me that he had

definite information to the effect that Pisciotta did not participate in the massacre.

COLONEL ANGRISANI [angrily]: I have never said anything of the kind to Captain Perenze.

But the memory of the highly respected Dr Grado turned out to be fallible after all, when the court decided to call the chief technician on duty at Monreale power station on the day of the massacre. To forestall any possibility of a slackening power output, the technician said, two extra transformers had been put into service on that day, and from his records, the electrical supply had been a little better than normal. There could have been nothing, therefore, to prevent a radiograph from being made on May 1st. The distinguished doctor might still have been acquitted of any suspicion of wishing to deflect the course of justice had a journalist, Jacopo Rizza, not entered the witness-box immediately afterwards. Rizza said that he had been telephoned by Pisciotta's counsel asking him to appear as a witness for the defence, and that he had refused, adding that if he appeared in court at all, it would be for the prosecution.

RIZZA: When Giuliano and I were together on the afternoon of December 11th, I asked him what he proposed to do for the bandits already under arrest, charged with participation in the massacre, and Giuliano said: 'I've told the boys to deny everything. I will accept the full responsibility.' I then asked Giuliano: 'How are you going to fix it so that your second-in-command, Pisciotta, is in the clear?' Giuliano replied: 'I've thought of everything. A doctor will produce an X-ray at the trial, say that he made it on May 1st, and confirm the identity of Pisciotta in court as the patient who visited him on that day.'

And yet how reliable was even this testimony? It seems extraordinary that Giuliano should have revealed his secret intentions so casually to a visiting journalist. Moreover, Rizza proved shortly after to be a not entirely satisfactory witness. That same day, the fashionable Romans who drove down to Viterbo for a picnic and a few hours of the excitements provided by the trial of the century were to see for the first time a real live mafioso in the flesh.

Domenico Albano, capo-Mafia of Borgetto, was a dumpy middle-aged man with a hooked nose and close-set eyes, who from his clothing and general appearance might have been a jobbing gardener. One newspaper even dared to describe him as having the face of an irritated rat, but his shadow fell across the court at Viterbo like that of a hawk over a brood of partridge chicks. Albano was said to have been the treasurer of the Giuliano band. It was also suggested that he had been the liaison between the Mafia and the Ministry of the Interior, and he admitted to having made several secret trips to Rome. It was Albano, too, who arranged for all the journalistic visits to Giuliano. But now, when brought face to face with Rizza in court, Rizza denied ever having seen him before. Even the President of the court seemed to be touched by the faint irradiations of menace from this man, and felt it necessary to say, as if to reassure himself, 'I can read what you are in your face, but do not think you can intimidate me.' Pisciotta's supreme self-confidence, too, failed for the first time when confronted with Albano, and turning pale and stammering, he denied all knowledge of him. By the following day he had recovered his nerve, and admitted to having been in close contact with the capo-Mafia for three years.

His alibi shaken, Pisciotta now fell back on blackmail as his next line of defence. He let it be known that he was holding in reserve far more damaging revelations than had so far been produced. In these frequent hints at the nature of the ammunition he had in store, Pisciotta clearly hoped to force his ex-collaborators in high places to find some way of extricating him from his predicament. It was a desperate manoeuvre indeed.

PISCIOTTA: Soon after my arrest Scelba transferred Marzano [the chief of police who had arrested him] not to Rome, but to Livorno, because he had been unsuccessful in obtaining what he had been ordered to obtain. [The veiled reference here is to Giuliano's memorial.] The Reds were at Livorno, and perhaps somebody thought that it was a good place where he could be quietly put out of the way. All these and other things I will reveal when the time comes for my trial at Palermo for the killing of Giuliano.

A LAWYER: They'll kill you first.

PISCIOTTA: I am now in the hands of public opinion. It's too late to think of killing me. Even if they killed me, the truth would come out just the same.

But Pisciotta had every reason to fear death. His capture alive by the Pubblica Sicurezza, in the first instance, seems only to have been in furtherance of their vendetta against the carabinieri, whose man Pisciotta had become. If the powerful enemies he had made had refrained from silencing him, it may well be that he had employed some manoeuvre like Giuliano's, encouraging them to believe that a memorial still existed in safe keeping somewhere beyond their reach. He began to be afraid that there would be attempts to poison him, and would not touch the prison food. At first his mother prepared all his meals and brought them to the prison, and when permission for her to do this was withdrawn, he tried everything that was given him on a tame sparrow before he would eat himself.

There were certainly many attempts to buy his silence. On almost the last occasion when he gave evidence, Pisciotta said: 'The first offer of fifty million to keep my mouth shut was made in my house by the Honourable Cusumano. I wrote to Prince Alliata after killing Giuliano, and Cusumano turned up straight away. He told me I could leave the country and that I would receive fifty million. Another offer was made in the prison of Palermo by a person whose name I don't wish to repeat. The third offer was made in the prison of Viterbo by the first counsel that defended me – the one I got rid of. Bucciante told me that the fifty million would be paid by the Minister Scelba.'

14

PISCIOTTA was found guilty of participation in the massacre at Portella della Ginestra and was sentenced to imprisonment for life, with hard labour. He received the sentence in silence, and with an ironic smile. The trial at Viterbo, he had made it quite clear, he considered as relatively unimportant. Almost all the things that Pisciotta had wanted to talk about had been excluded as irrelevant, but Pisciotta believed that this legal objection would no longer hold good when the motives for his killing of Giuliano had to be discussed. It was nearly ten years before the public was to learn of his stubborn rejection of a last chance given to him to withdraw his accusations of public men, and to accept his fate in silence. A clear cold light was directed for a moment on this murky corner of the postwar Italian scene, when the news-weekly *ABC* published a letter from an ex-partisan, Giovanni Polacco, who had been Pisciotta's neighbour for a short time in the prison at Viterbo. This letter, written from prison, may have cost Polacco his life, because as soon as he was released from gaol he disappeared and has never been seen again. The newspaper accepted full responsibility for the authenticity of the letter, and showed itself much impressed by the personality of the author in the respectful autobiographical note it published.

Giovanni Polacco was shown by his history to be another man of the stamp of the ill-starred Canepa, original leader of the Sicilian Separatists, and like him, he made many powerful enemies. Polacco had been victimised by the Fascists since the time in 1922 when he had gone to the rescue of an old man who was being beaten up by a gang of Blackshirts in the Piazza Colonna in Rome, spending thereafter most of the era of Fascism in gaol or in *confino*. Like Canepa, he became a partisan leader, and was addicted to extravagant exploits, such as arresting a whole hotelful of Fascist hierarchs in the centre of Rome on the day the

Armistice with Italy was declared. The citation accompanying his Italian Silver Medal for Military Valour gives some idea of his quality as a guerilla fighter. He took part in eighty-six actions against special SS units employed against the partisans, released one hundred and eighteen Allied prisoners, saved the lives of thirty-two Jews by hiding them in an apartment in Rome, was wounded five times, and taken prisoner. 'Miraculously he escaped,' the citation continues, 'and although suffering from his wounds, took over the command of his partisan band again. He continued to sabotage the enemy's war-potential until the arrival of the liberating forces... He set an admirable example of the highest patriotic virtue, of the disdain of personal danger, and of devotion to the national cause.'

Unhappily the time had arrived when it was not always possible to separate the sabotaging of the enemy's war-potential and the legitimate violences of war from actions which seemed to some onlookers to border upon criminality, and many things were being noted down for a day of reckoning. In 1944, during an operation for the capture of a war criminal, an Italian regular officer was killed, and Polacco was accused of his death. An Allied military court dismissed the case, but two years later, when the Italian civil authority had taken over, Polacco was arrested and sent for trial. He was sentenced to thirteen years.

Polacco had been languishing six years in prison at Soriano, near Viterbo, when he was approached with a singular proposition. He was visited by a counsel who had defended him at his trial, Ivo Coccia, who in the interim had become a Christian Democrat member of parliament. Coccia told Polacco that the infamous treatment he had received had been preying on his mind, and he had been to see 'the Minister' to argue his case once again. After a long discussion, the Minister had agreed to see to it that justice was done immediately, provided that Polacco, in return, would agree to carry out a confidential mission. Coccia then described to Polacco the increasing state of alarm and despondency in Christian Democrat inner circles caused by Pisciotta's revelations, 'which had damaged the Party's prestige and which, if allowed to continue, would jeopardise its future'. It had been decided in a discussion at Party headquarters that the only way to restore the public's confidence in their leaders would be to discover some way of inducing Pisciotta to make a public retraction of his charges. Coccia had then put forward Polacco's name as a 'serious-minded man, worthy of every confidence, and capable of fulfilling a task of this kind with the utmost discretion'. The job was consequently offered him, and it was implied that the reward for its successful completion would be his freedom. As his health was now seriously undermined, he agreed.

Next day he found himself transferred to the Viterbo prison – officially for a radiological examination. It seems that the prison authorities at Viterbo smelled a rat, were unhappy about the whole business, and did their best to get rid of him as soon as the examination was complete. In this, however, they were blocked by 'the Ministry', who gave orders that Polacco was to remain where he was 'until it was quite certain that no further radiographs were required'. But it turned out that the plan was still to be held up, because Polacco was kept in the sick bay while the bandits were held at the disposition of the Attorney-General in a separate wing of the prison. Coccia next went to work on the prison governor, who received him coldly. The Attorney-General's attitude was also 'negative'. However, pressure must have been brought to bear, for soon Polacco found himself in the cell next to Pisciotta's. There was a communicating passage between the two cells, and although the two men were kept apart by a steel-barred door across the passage, they could see and talk to each other as much as they liked.

For the first few days Polacco and Pisciotta eyed each other in silence through the door, Polacco cultivating an indifference to match what he called Pisciotta's natural Sicilian reserve. In the end, the ice was broken and Pisciotta unburdened himself. Polacco found him 'a person of slight culture', yet he says it was impossible not to be impressed by the coherence of his mind. He noticed that however often Pisciotta repeated a story, there was never the slightest variation in the details, and from this he judged that he was telling the truth. Polacco formed the opinion that Pisciotta was afraid of nobody and nothing on earth but the Mafia, 'whose tentacles could reach out and take a man in their grip wherever he hid himself'.

Pisciotta was in a state of constantly inflamed indignation about what he described as the trick played on him by Scelba, the Minister of the Interior. He had not been prepared to accept the assurances of the police or the carabinieri without receiving confirmation from the Minister himself. This condition had been accepted and he had been taken to Rome, where Scelba had received him and had given his word that the promises made to him would be kept. Pisciotta had then returned to Sicily and killed Giuliano. 'In killing him,' he said, 'I killed three birds with one stone. I obtained my free pardon, punished the man who had stained his hands with the blood of the innocent, and inherited all the explosive material that Giuliano had accumulated.' Pisciotta assured Polacco that he had retained possession of Giuliano's memorial – that hobgoblin of the Christian Democrats – and he would use it 'as the instrument of his vendetta against those who had cheated him'. 'Here I'm not on my home ground,' he explained, 'but back in Sicily, once my trial in Palermo starts, the earthquake will happen.'

And none of Polacco's blandishments nor any amount of playing on Pisciotta's fear of the vengeance of the Mafia could shake the bandit's resolution. It was weeks before the moment seemed propitious to sound Pisciotta on the possibility of his being prepared to eat his words. Pisciotta had been restless and depressed all day, pacing up and down in his cell, and in the evening he had dragged out a stool to sit by the gate with his head in his hands. Polacco thought that demoralisation might have set in. 'My dear fellow,' he said, 'I can't help feeling you've taken on something that is too big for you. It seems to me that what you've done is to get yourself mixed up in politics without having any idea of what politics are all about.'

'What would you have done in my place?' Pisciotta asked.

Polacco thought he was taking the bait. 'In your place,' he said, 'the first thing I'd do is to put myself right with all those people you've been attacking. Why not give it up, and say the Communists put you up to it? That way you'd avoid the certainty of reprisals, and you could count on a favourable verdict.'

But Polacco had mistaken his man. Pisciotta jumped to his feet, and shouted, 'You're mad. Nothing will ever make me take back a word of what I said because it's true!'

* * *

He had thrown away his last chance. What awaited him now was the prison of Ucciardone in Palermo, which must surely be one of the world's most remarkable penal institutions. When Pisciotta was sent there in 1951 it was controlled to the last detail of its organisation by the Mafia, and when in 1957 the prison was the subject of one of the many enquiries instituted during its history, it still was. The 1957 enquiry found that the prison guards were under the Mafia's orders, and even that the governor had been changed when he had not been to the Mafia's liking. The prison had been something of a rest-home for the Mafia potentates who had been incarcerated there. Some of them were past their prime, had made too many enemies, and knowing that a violent death was otherwise not to be avoided, had had themselves arrested, arranged for a longish sentence, and 'retired into private life' in the Ucciardone. They had been housed in comfortably furnished cells, had their meals sent in from the best restaurants in Palermo, and been visited as often as required by wives or prostitutes. As an illustration of the 'respect' accumulated by these men, it was noted that when one of them was once transferred to Brindisi to give evidence at a trial there, the witnesses lined up to kneel and kiss his ring. In collusion with the prison authorities, the mafiosi had run flourishing businesses from prison, for which the guards often acted as commission agents. Sometimes, while remaining on the register of inmates, they had succeeded in absenting themselves for long periods – as in the case of Salvatore Malta, who had organised an armed band for as long as two years while nominally a prisoner in the Ucciardone.

The prison of Palermo had in fact become almost a Mafia university, where apprentice members received refresher courses in the latest developments in crime, were rewarded for their zeal by promotion, and punished, when necessary, with ferocious beatings which often resulted in broken bones. These injuries were always entered in the hospital register as caused by a 'slip on the stairs', and over five hundred inmates had slipped on the stairs in twelve years. So complete, indeed, had Mafia control of the building become that it was possible to carry out the complex engineering project called for in tunnelling down to the petroleum pipeline that ran from the docks to the refinery, passing under the Ucciardone. This was skilfully tapped, and petrol pumped off for sale in the black market.

This was the wolves' den in which Pisciotta found himself, protected only by his own fearsome reputation and by the extreme precautions he took before eating or drinking anything that was brought to him. As part of these security measures, he was allowed to make his own coffee, and two days before he was to appear before the examining magistrate for preliminary questioning in preparation for the new trial, he did this, as usual, upon waking in the morning, but this time added a teaspoonful of vitamin concentrate prescribed for his chest trouble. Two minutes later he fell to the ground, but before the strychnine the medicine contained had had time to crush him in the constriction of his own muscles, he dragged himself to a jar of olive oil and drank it in the hope of vomiting the poison back. It was too late. Drooling blood from a chewed tongue, and screaming through the dreadful smirk of tetanus to every corner of the prison, he was rushed down to the infirmary – where the man into whose care he was committed was the very one who had poisoned his medicine. After half an hour of the most atrocious agony the human body is capable of knowing, Pisciotta died.

As an extra measure of precaution, the Mafia decided to suppress another key member of the Giuliano band imprisoned in the Ucciardone who was suspected of knowing too much. This was Angelo Russo, who was presented with a bottle of fine wine containing hemlock – chosen this time as being less noisy and spectacular in its physiological effects. After that the poisoner himself was removed from the scene, and with this discharge of buckshot and an extinguished cry in the night, the chapter of Giuliano, Pisciotta, and the massacre of Portella della Ginestra was almost concluded. The final page was turned when Inspector Verdiani, repository of so many perilous secrets, fell to the ground one day, clutching at his stomach, and was dead before he could be rushed to hospital. Suicide was the verdict, but not a Sicilian believed it.

Now all the voices were silenced, and the Mafia cloak of invisibility fell about the shoulders of the men who had sent the bandits to fire on the peasants.

15

THE MAFIA flourished exceedingly, but slowly it was changing its face. A great number of mafiosi American gangsters had been deprived of their citizenship and sent back to Sicily, where they immediately assumed leading positions in the Mafia hierarchy of the island. There was little about these spectacular and exuberant deportees that recalled the old-fashioned man of respect, but their influence over a new generation of Mafia novitiates was irresistible. The new island recruits to the Honoured Society were the product of war devastation, of hunger and the universal petty criminality of the black market, and of the grim anarchy of the postwar years, and they were devoid of illusion or sentiment. These young men in their bright shirts and loud ties who killed for a fixed rate of two hundred thousand lire (£130), totally lacked the capacity for self-deception so marked in men of the calibre of Don Calò Vizzini.

Traditionally the Mafia had lived off the scrawny monopolies based upon scarcity. It held back the land so as to create huge reservoirs of cheap labour. Rivers in their winter spate were allowed to empty into the sea – precious water that could have been dammed back and that would have transfigured a countryside, but would have damaged the interests of a few water monopolists. The mind of the old Mafia had been formed in a feudal past when there was not enough to go round, and it could never free itself from its philosophy of controlled dearth. Now it was opposed by an expansive and capitalistic young Mafia that had no patience with restrictive practices. The old Mafia vetoed dams because a hundred sleepy old villains made a fat living from water pumped up from artesian wells, but the new Mafia wanted them because of the huge profits to be made out of the contracts involved in their construction. For the same reason they wanted modern roads, bridges, transport systems, urban development and industrial expansion of any kind. Psychologically, Don

Calò Vizzini and his followers were still living in the eighteenth century – when not in the Bronze Age itself – whereas the cousins just back from Buffalo, New York or Kansas City were emphatically men of our times.

A clash was inevitable, and the deadly war that broke out between the exponents of the rival ideologies was epitomised by the happenings at Corleone. In this unhappy town where, as Dolci discovered, killing a man made no more impression than killing a goat, the sinister Dr Michele Navarra, head of the old Mafia, faced his young rival, Luciano Liggio, murderer of the trade union leader, Placido Rizzotto. With Dr Navarra in control in Corleone, nothing could change. A project had been under consideration for building a dam, but Navarra, the hidebound traditionalist, would not hear of it, and as he stood between Liggio and a huge fortune to be squeezed out of contractors, Liggio simply killed him. Unfortunately for that tormented population of Corleone, the numbers on both sides were about equal, so the struggle went on – and does to this day – with hardly a month going by without the news of some fresh massacre as the factions of conservatism and progress dismember each other.

In Palermo itself, the issue was less clean-cut between the several 'families' of the various districts of the market and of the port, but the results were the same. Violent death became a commonplace, and the city's homicide rate soon rose to be the highest in the world – exceeding that of the whole of Lombardy in the north, a province which contains all the great industrial towns of Italy. In the face of this bloody experience, the civil population maintained a stubborn reticence. On one occasion the police managed to cordon off the whole of a busy street after a killing, and every single person was questioned without even one admitting to having heard a shot. In another instance a passer-by took to his heels when the shooting started and had practically stumbled over a corpse when a policeman stopped him. Not only did he deny having noticed the body, lying practically between his feet, but while admitting to having heard alarming sounds, said he attributed them to thunder, and was running to avoid being caught in a storm.

These maladjustments and stresses within the Honoured Society's fabric were aggravated by the sudden death of that conciliatory genius, Don Calò, who had done so much in the cause of unity among the men of respect. Like so many mafiosi of the old school who were inclined to overeat and took little exercise, he had become increasingly sluggish and adipose in his declining years, and had suffered from a series of minor heart attacks. His end came one day while travelling home to Villalba by car. He asked to be carried out so that he could lie down in a more comfortable position on the road verge. A few minutes later he died peacefully, his last recorded words being, 'How beautiful life is!' When he lay in state, politicians, eminent clerics, and the heads of all the Mafia 'families' came to pay their respects, and there were ritual cries of wonderment at the delicacy of the fragrance the body was supposed to have exuded – 'even in death he's perfumed!' And just as in 1909 Don Calò had stood by the bier of Don Pietro of Camporeale and taken the cord of the black flag covering the coffin in his left hand so that the powerful influence of the dead capo-Mafia could flow into his body, now Don Calò's successor did the same. His memorial tablet in the church at Villalba says that he was chaste, temperate, forbearing, tireless in his defence of the weak, and that above all he was a gentleman. The nostalgic tributes of the hundreds of journalists who composed his obituaries went even further. One distinguished writer, speaking for them all, summed up: 'In any society a category of persons must exist capable of adjusting situations that become too complicated . . . Simply by picking up a telephone, he could reach the Cardinal, the Prefect, the General, the President of the Region, the Mayor, or any deputy. Don Calò himself remained aloof and inaccessible, like a samurai or a German field-marshal in the exercise of his functions.'

In the political field – even after the withdrawal of Don Calò's mesmeric influence from the Sicilian scene – things were going well for the Honoured Society. On April 10th, 1948, a conference of the heads of the Mafia of all Sicily had been held at a landowner's seaside villa just outside Palermo, and following this the order was given for all-out support for the Christian Democrats. After the meeting some fifty cars departed, heading for all parts of the island and carrying supplies of the

Party's emblem – a cross on a shield – for distribution among the Society's affiliates.

But comforting as it might have been to have the assurance that henceforward Sicilian voters would return to the disciplined frame of mind of old, when the time came to go the polls, it went against the grain of some Demochristian politicians to have to give what was expected of them in return. Among these was Alessi, President of the Regional Assembly. Although Alessi was a firm friend and admirer of Don Calò, and had once described the Mafia as Sicilian folklore – 'a matter of local colour' – the new arrangement was too much for his stomach, and he resigned. There followed seven years' rule by the Right Wing of the party, abetted by the Mafia with its authoritarian tactics. Not only was any prominent trade union leader slaughtered in this period, but even Demochristian politicians who stood for seats for which the Mafia wished to put forward its own candidate were resolutely eliminated by the double blast from the barrels of the *lupara*. All these numerous crimes went unpunished. The prize was control of the Regional Assembly and of the City Councils – as glittering an *el dorado* as the Spanish Conquistadors of the New World had ever dreamed of.

It was the men of the new Mafia who were to possess themselves of this treasure. The city of Palermo was entering a phase of huge postwar expansion, and all that was necessary to become a multimillionaire almost overnight was to know in advance – even better, to *decide* – just where the new suburbs were to be built, and then buy up the land. Instances have been quoted when land bought at sixty lire (9*d*.) per square yard became worth thirty thousand lire (£18) per square yard a few months later. Operating at this level, a capo-Mafia could make more in one single devastating coup than Don Calò had scraped together in five years of rigging the black market in olive oil, and more than the man who cornered the water supplies in a parched countryside could hope to extort in a lifetime. There were rich pickings, too, for the lower-grade mafioso in the city's modernisation. A man not yet big enough to pull strings at the City Hall might simply walk up to the proprietor of some half-finished block of apartments, or garage, or cinema, and say, 'I've decided to go into business with you. I'll pay for my shares out of salary – say half a million a week. I can save you money. You pay your contractors too much. They'll work for half the price for me.' Refusal, the man approached with this proposition knew, would almost certainly be punished by an explosion that might bring half the building down. The mafioso moved in.

*   *   *

Second only to the racket in land and building development as a source of spectacular profit was the traffic in drugs. Heroin, procured in the Middle East – principally the Lebanon – was shipped with reasonable security to Sicily, where the trickier business of arranging for its passage to the United States was organised. The rewards involved were so immense that a ten-pound parcel smuggled safely through to its final destination meant a small fortune for each man through whose hands it passed. The scale of these operations first became evident in 1958 through a pure accident. A league of Sicilian fishermen had been formed to put down fraudulent fishing by the use of dynamite, and by dragnets having an illegally fine mesh. The league bought its own fast motor-launch, and this, with its crew of sworn maritime police, patrolled likely waters on the lookout for offenders. One night, when just off Palermo, it detected the presence of a suspicious craft, but as soon as the patrol vessel approached with the intention of boarding, it was received with machine-gun fire. The stranger then made off at such a speed that it was quite clear from the power of its engines that it was no ordinary fishing-boat. The Mafia immediately moved in to suppress any possible repercussions of this encounter, and to rule out any possibility of a repetition of the incident. By order of the Customs authorities, the patrol boat was taken out of service, its captain was transferred to northern Italy, two NCOs of the Maritime Guard who made up the crew were also transferred, and a third found it necessary to resign.

Nowadays the traffic in drugs is accepted as commonplace. Everyone knows it goes on, and it is only new and ingenious methods, as they are occasionally brought to light, of concealing the heroin or cocaine on its way to the United States that excite any interest in the Press. Of these, the most celebrated involved the confection of false oranges out of wax. For some time whenever a shipment was made, every crate of selected oranges contained one of these counterfeits filled by syringe with a hundred grams of heroin. The device is supposed to have been the brainchild of Lucky Luciano – who died in 1962, with a dramatic suddenness that put many Sicilians in mind of the poisoned coffee of the Ucciardone.

For a short time after his homecoming Luciano went into partnership with Don Calò in an enterprise described as a confetti factory, but as this was protected by security measures adequate to an atomic project, it is supposed that the two men may have been engaged in processing locally the raw materials of narcotisation imported in the usual way. Luciano's other interest – prostitution – had had to be dropped because the white slave traffic was still *infamità* to the authentic Sicilian men of respect. Don Calò is supposed to have asked his partner once how ever he could have allowed himself to get mixed up in such an unpleasant business. Luciano excused himself on racial grounds. Foreign women, to him, were only half-human. He couldn't imagine them in the guise of Sicilian wives or mothers.

*   *   *

While in the towns the flashy young Americanised mafioso of the new school was making his fortune out of contraband and administrative corruption, the power was slowly slipping through the fingers of the old-fashioned man of respect of the feudal estates. The fact was that the peasant had become spiritually broken-winded through a decade of too-effective terror. A law had been passed which in theory demolished the estates, as no single proprietor was permitted to retain more than five hundred acres, but it was applied at a snail's pace, and with endless confusion. It was fifteen years, for example, after the law's passage – only in September 1963 – that the peasants of the Brontë estate, given to Nelson and his descendants by the contemptible King of Naples, were to receive their first allotment of land. By this time many Sicilian peasants

Bisaquino, almost a ghost town as a result of mass emigration

had lost the capacity for hope, and when emigration offered them a way of escape from what seemed a state of affairs that was never to be remedied, they took it.

Michele Pantaleone, in his book *Mafia e Politica*, describes the incident that perhaps finally broke the will to resist of the peasants in a huge area in central Sicily. A vast roundup of suspected criminals and mafiosi was carried out by a force of four hundred carabinieri and police, in the course of which 182 persons were arrested. Many stolen animals were recovered, and numerous firearms were seized, among them three sawn-off shotguns and a number of cartridges loaded with the special shot traditionally employed in Mafia killings. The peasants showed their eagerness to co-operate with the police and gave so much useful information that peace returned at last to an area where murders had been an almost daily occurrence. 'In that zone,' Pantaleone says, 'the presence of the State had destroyed the myth of the Mafia's indestructibility – a myth which unfortunately was re-established when all the persons arrested were released for "lack of sufficient proof". This produced a wave of emigrations to the north, and abroad.'

The first batches of emigrants to leave Sicily for northern Italy or Western Germany are said to have gone reluctantly, and saw themselves as the victims of an enforced expulsion; but once the movement was under way its character changed. What followed has been called by Italian sociologists a psychological collapse. There was an almost neurotic abandonment of the land. Where land from the estates was in the end made available, in many cases it was not taken up. Between 1951 and 1961, four hundred thousand Sicilians – more than ten per cent of the population – decided to emigrate. The majority of these were males who could expect to find work, and in large areas only old people, women and children were left behind. In the province of Messina women and children now make up eighty-five per cent of the population. For the first time since their creation a thousand years ago, some of the feudal estates – which still comprise twenty per cent of the cultivable surface of Sicily – are without labour; a situation which has compelled one land-owner at Catolica Eraclea to hand the whole of his land over to the Forestry Commission. Parallel to this flight from the land is a growing process of 'dis-industrialisation'. Potential investors from the mainland have come to sniff the Sicilian atmosphere and quickly departed. Northern capitalists do not take kindly to the notion of having to pay for 'protection' for their enterprises. Thus the so-called miracle of Italy's economic expansion passed Sicily by. In 1962 the *per capita* income remained by far the lowest of any region – only £130 per annum, as compared with £250 in northern Italy, and £350 for the town of Milan. This figure, of course, included the incomes of relatively affluent city dwellers. A peasant's income would be very much lower.

The climate for many of those Sicilians that remain is one in which the familiar *omertà* has slowly deepened into a real and paralysing fear, which has finally penetrated the Sicilian subconscious. From this has developed an almost pathological aptitude for suffering in silence, incredibly illustrated in the recent case of a whole community bowing its neck in resignation under the depredations of a handful of mafiosi monks.

It was 1958 before the activities of the Franciscan fathers of

Poster condemning release of Mafia killers

Mazzarino received any publicity, although they had by that time been terrorising the neighbourhood for some years. Bandit monks and mafiosi monks were nothing new to the long-suffering inhabitants of rural Sicily. Time and again one reads of sinister Friar Tucks riding with outlaw bands to waylay travellers or attack farms. At the beginning of the century there had been a pitched battle between the peasants of Santo Stefano and robber monks from the local monastery, and in 1923 a mafioso Benedictine father who was a member of the same monastery beheaded the Abbot on the refectory table. The Abbot was capo-Mafia of the whole valley. Yet again in 1945 at Santo Stefano the Bishop of Agrigento was shot and nearly killed by a mafioso brother, while the Franciscan convent of Mazzarino had in the past sheltered a band of robbers and the monks had shared in the proceeds of their crimes.

What seems so extraordinary to the outsider is that only one man ever stood up to the monks, and even he never seems to have considered going to the authorities. This was Mazzarino's richest citizen, Angelo Cannada, one of the many – including affluent monks in neighbouring monasteries – who received letters of extortion, but the only victim who refused to pay up. For this obduracy he paid with his life.

The principal villain in the case was Padre Carmelo, the prior of the convent, who was a personal friend of Cannada's and had often said mass in the private chapel in the Cannada house. At this time the Prior was approaching his eightieth year, a man of exceedingly fragile appearance but possessed of a sort of macabre, skipping vitality. Padre Carmelo was considered the best preacher in the province, a great quoter in his sermons of the *Divina Commedia*, but off-duty habitually expressing himself in the thieves'-slang of the Mafia. Cannada had received a succession of letters demanding ten million lire and ordering him to get in touch with the Franciscans, who would tell him how the money was to be paid. In the end he rang up Padre Carmelo, who came over in a taxi to discuss the matter with him. The old Prior's story was that the monks had been forced by some mysterious organisation to act as agents for the collection of the money. He advised Cannada to pay up, did his best to make his friend's flesh creep with an account of the ferocity of the extortioner's character, and offended Cannada by a blasphemous outburst when Cannada said that he put his trust in God. All the old Prior's arguments were without avail. Cannada said that nothing would make him pay a single lira. In the end Padre Carmelo went off in a fury. Some days later four masked men called at Cannada's house, dragged him out and shot him in his own vineyard. Padre Carmelo officiated at the funeral service and preached movingly on the theme of the transience of human satisfactions, including wealth.

Now it was the turn of Cannada's widow to receive the usual threatening letters, and the inevitable visit from Padre Carmelo. The widow's brother was present at this meeting when ten million lire was again demanded, and he made a counter-offer of a hundred thousand lire. This produced the sarcastic suggestion from Padre Carmelo that he should keep it to buy cigarettes. However, on behalf of the extortioners he agreed to drop the asking price to three million. As a friend of the family, Padre Carmelo knew something of the Cannadas' financial background, and he suggested to the widow that she should sell a piece of her property which he valued at seven million. If the demand were not met, he warned her that some tragic fate was likely to overtake her only son. At this point the terrified woman agreed to hand over a million lire, and Padre Carmelo, who appears to have entered with relish into the mechanics of extortion, warned her to see to it that she kept no record of the numbers of the banknotes.

Thereafter the monks continued to terrorise the cowed citizenry of Mazzarino for two full years. A witness at the preliminary hearing of their trial described the fear, almost amounting to panic, provoked by the mere appearance of Franciscans in the streets of the town. A new police chief, Maresciallo Di Stefano, called in to investigate the killing of Cannada, ran up immediately against the usual barrier of silence. Isolated as he was from the population, an occasional rumour reached him of the goings-on at the convent, and finally induced him to investigate the monks' financial background. The result of this enquiry produced some surprises. The Franciscans of Mazzarino depended for their revenue on public charity, on the produce of a small orchard, and, he discovered, on regular but smallish subscriptions they received from political sources for persuading the citizens of Mazzarino to vote Christian Democrat – which they did, almost to a man. Despite what was in theory a somewhat meagre income, all the monks he was investigating turned out to be lira millionaires, having large sums of money held in their original lay names in banking accounts dispersed about the country.

Anonymous letters began to reach the Maresciallo, and some of these contained fascinating accounts of the nature of monastic life at Mazzarino. Some of the monks carried guns. One in particular, Padre Guglielmo, delighted in blazing away at night with a heavy automatic from the window of his cell 'at the stars'. One anonymous letter was probably from a domestic employed in the monastery, because it mentioned a monk who had been expelled after a row with Padre Carmelo, the old Prior, and who was seen to pack a sub-machine-gun away in his luggage before departing. The fathers were keen business-men, and bought and sold property, loaned money at high interest, and in one case dealt in pigs. Vows of chastity received scant attention at

Mazzarino. For years, Di Stefano discovered, women had been visiting the monastery at night, disguised in Franciscan habits. The monks were interested in pornography, too, and had established a network of correspondents with whom they exchanged obscene letters. A girl working as a servant at a school in Gela was arrested, according to Di Stefano's testimony, with enough such material in her possession furnished by the monks to constitute an anthology of pornographic literature. These revelations of life in a religious establishment, ventilated at the preliminary hearing, were debarred by a pact established between prosecution and defence when the case came up before the assize court.

It was two years before Di Stefano could be quite certain that the monks were carrying on an extortion racket, but even then the certainty that no witnesses could be induced to come forward prevented him from taking action. Di Stefano knew that it would have been fatal to move without overwhelming proof. The situation almost resolved itself when a member of the urban police force, who may well have been acting as a spy for the carabinieri, was ambushed and shot while prowling in the vicinity of the monastery. The three attackers took to their heels, and one of them in his panic dropped his gun. The gun was recognised, and the three men arrested. They confessed not only to the attack on the policeman, but also to the murder of Cannada, but said that they had acted under the domination of the monks' gardener, Carmine Lo Bartolo. The news of his accomplices' arrest reached Lo Bartolo before the police arrived. He disappeared, and it has since been proved that the monks managed to conceal him for several weeks, moving him from monastery to monastery, until he was smuggled away to Genoa, where the police finally picked him up.

Lo Bartolo's arrest caused great excitement back in Mazzarino, where his criminal association with the monks had been a matter of common knowledge for years, and sensational revelations were expected. Nothing of this came to pass, for Lo Bartolo's mouth was quickly sealed by death. Within hours of his arrival in Sicily, he was found hanged in his cell of the Caltanissetta gaol. Few Sicilians were surprised when an autopsy was refused and Lo Bartolo's brother was denied permission to see the body.

Di Stefano, however, now took the bit in his teeth. He searched the monastery and found the typewriter with which he was able to prove the letters of extortion had been written. Padre Carmelo and three other fathers were arrested and brought to trial.

At the preliminary hearing the issue was quite simple. The Franciscans blandly admitted to all charges except complicity in the murder of Cannada, but claimed, like the three men already under arrest, to have been the helpless tools of their gardener, Lo Bartolo. A witness cast some doubt on this picture of the monastery's enslavement to an illiterate labourer by recalling a conversation he had had with Padre Carmelo. He had asked the Prior how he got on with Lo Bartolo, who seems to have been a Caliban-like creature. Replying in Mafia jargon of quite untranslatable vulgarity, the formidable old man had said something like: 'He responds well to a good kick up the backside.' Among the monks' victims had been the Father Superior of the Capucines of Syracusa, who was despoiled to the tune of 600,000 lire – a sum which he was later accused of abstracting from the monastery's funds. Apart from the typed letters of extortion, the Franciscans of Mazzarino had habitually employed the confessional box to transmit their threats, and Padre Carmelo usually suggested that it would be convenient for payment to be made in church.

In March 1962 the monks were brought to trial, and for several weeks the Assizes at Messina offered a spectacle of entrancement and domination. What staggered the Press correspondents who attended from the Italian mainland was not so much that it was soon clear that the monks would slip through the fingers of justice – they had been warned that this was to be expected in such trials held in Sicily – but the servility and obsequiousness of the public's attitude towards them. The atmosphere in court was fevered and ecstatic, and old Padre Carmelo acknowledged the applause that greeted his appearance by tracing the sign of the cross with a diaphanous hand. The carabinieri who escorted the fathers into the dock were cordiality and respect itself. Benefit of Clergy had seen to it that the monks were relieved of the ignominy of appearing in chains, although this privilege was not extended to the three members of the laity who were on trial at the same time. It had not been considered necessary to suspend Padre Carmelo and his fellow defendants from the exercise of their sacerdotal functions, and while awaiting trial at the Assizes, they had continued to say mass and hear confessions. The corridors and antechambers of the courthouse at Messina were full of prominent ecclesiastics who seemed on good terms with the fathers, and whose presence was therefore taken to mean that the Church was expressing its solidarity with the accused men. Maestro Francesco Carnelutti, one of Italy's most famous counsels, had announced that he would conduct Padre Carmelo's defence without charge. His every sally in court was greeted with a rumble of *sotto voce* approbation which the judges were unable to suppress, and outside the courtroom members of the public struggled for the privilege of pressing the famous advocate's hand and thanking him for the generosity of his action.

Later, an unnamed witness for the prosecution gave a newspaper some idea of what it felt like to stand up and give evidence against the monks in this atmosphere. He was unnerved by the concentrated hostility of which he was the target, and made almost to feel that he was a perjurer. He found that he could not stop trembling while giving evidence, and in the end, was hardly able to produce his words. When he left the court, all backs were turned as he passed. Disapproval was expressed in other ways, too. Another prosecution witness was found half-dead with a hand cut off. When the prosecution suggested that this had been an act of vengeance, counsel for the defence waved the allegation aside and supposed that the man had cut his hand off himself. The court did not seem to find this theory especially surprising.

At an early stage in the trial the prosecution suffered a body-blow through the refusal of the murdered Cannada's widow and her brother to give evidence – which necessitated their treatment as hostile witnesses. In conformity with the laws of *omertà*, the three men charged directly with Cannada's murder blamed it all on the unfortunate Lo Bartolo, and refused to admit that the monks, of whom they spoke with the greatest respect, were in any way involved. A year's respite had transformed the

Padre Carmelo and the monks of Mazzarino

monks of Mazzarino from criminals into victims. There was not a whisper of the orgies at the monastery, or of the extorted money spent on debauchery. The secret banking accounts were forgotten. The monks were found not guilty of complicity in the murder of Cannada, and were acquitted on all charges of extortion as having acted under duress. The three lay criminals got thirty years apiece, and when the sentence was read out there were screams from them of 'assassins' – directed at whom, nobody could be sure. They clearly had been led to expect milder treatment. Of the trial's outcome, the Honourable Leone, President of the Sicilian House of Deputies, wrote: 'This verdict almost upsets the glorious legend of the Little Flowers of St Francis.'

The verdict was, of course, grotesque. A state of duress, as defined under Italian law, is ruled out by the circumstances of the crimes committed by the monks of Mazzarino. Duress, as pointed out by the Public Prosecutor in presenting the arguments for a retrial, involves a physical impossibility of escape. If a man in the middle of a desert covers another with a gun and orders him to commit a crime, there is duress. In this instance, even supposing that an illiterate gardener could have imposed his will on the sophisticated men who employed him, nothing would have been easier than to escape from his clutches by asking to be transferred to some convent in another part of Italy, or even abroad.

What this verdict reflected, in fact, was the condition of the Sicilian mind – the state of mass hypnosis under which it lay. Sicilians accepted these men – even if not as mafiosi themselves – as protected by the Mafia. But there was one other factor in the composition of their invulnerability – and this was their appeal to an atavistic layer in the Sicilian subconscious. To this, the fact that the monks were immoral would be unimportant. What was important was that they were the human vehicles of magic power. The supernatural offices they per-formed were in no way lessened in their efficacy by the monks' own extreme human fallibility. The Medicine Man or the African Head of Bush Society is not expected to be virtuous, but to be a successful practitioner in the art of compelling rainfall or driving away devils. This is the survival of the primeval mentality which carved the ferocious lions on the front of the Cathedral of Cefalù, created in mosaic the severe Norman-faced Christ that stares down on the worshippers in the same cathedral, and covered the pillars of the Palatine Chapel of Palermo with its mouthing gargoyles. It was, and still is, the power of exorcism that counts. The monks were not good men, but they were powerful men, and it was their power to which the Sicilian subconscious automatically responded.

16

THE FACT THAT an appeal by the prosecution was allowed, and that when a year later the monks of Mazzarino appeared once again in court at Messina they were hastily found guilty and sentenced to thirteen years apiece, is to be ascribed to an extraordinary new circumstance. Suddenly an urgent adjustment of the local scene was called for. After years of obstruction by Right-wing politicians, a Parliamentary Commission had been formed to investigate the Mafia, and this was about to arrive in Sicily to begin its work.

The line consistently taken by the Commission's opponents, and by the thirty Demochristian members who had voted against it in the Sicilian Regional Assembly, had been that the Mafia was a myth – a defamatory legend invented by the Italians of the north in their contempt for the ancient, mellow, but little understood civilisation of the country's deep south. It was considered advisable, therefore, that such family scandals as that of the monks should be cleaned up as quickly and quietly as possible. No doubt it was hoped, too, that the members of the Anti-Mafia, as it was called, would be given the chance to conclude that the lurid side of the island life had been much exaggerated. Consequently, with the Commission's imminent appearance, an extraordinary peace fell upon Sicily. For weeks and months on end, almost every case of a life being suddenly cut short by the brusque double blast from the *lupara* proved, on investigation, to have respectable motivation in some story of love betrayed. In Palermo, a winter of tranquil nights came and went. An embarrassing discovery was made of a whole collection of skeletons in a disused well near Marsala, but the local doctors who examined them soon agreed that they belonged to the victims of a hardly remembered typhus epidemic. The fact that there were holes in every skull was passed over as the result of accidental *post-mortem* damage.

Then, suddenly, the almost wistful serenity of the city of Palermo was disrupted by an assassination so elaborately and expensively prepared as to be quite evidently an act of war between men or factions of exceptional power. The dead man, Cesare Manzella, was a capo-Mafia of a rather special kind – a mafioso of the stamp of Don Antonio Cottone, shot to death in 1949, whose eccentric generosity had won for him the affectionate nickname *U Patre Nostru* (Our Heavenly Father). Manzella's prickly conscience and his desire to perform good works had survived thirty years spent as an organiser of gambling houses in Chicago. His weakness was children. He found it difficult to pass one in the street without stopping to pop a sweet into its mouth, and he had devoted a high proportion of the wealth gained in recent years from the traffic in narcotics to the building of an orphanage. It was in acknowledgment of his many benefactions that he had been almost unanimously elected President of the Catholic Action of Cinesi – the suburb of Palermo where he had established himself. In his activities in the Honoured Society, however, Manzella had shown himself a disciplinarian.

In January 1962, Lucky Lucanio, then living in princely style in Naples and allegedly supreme organiser of the world traffic in narcotics, died at the Naples Airport restaurant. It was the time and place chosen by the narcotics bureau of Interpol to swoop on their most slippery adversary, but by the time they reached him, he was dead. Officially death was due to heart-failure, but rumour had it that his associates, fearful of the revelations that might follow their chief's arrest, had quickly poisoned his coffee. Manzella stepped into the breach left by Luciano's disappearance from the scene. In the office he now held he was served by a spirited following that could only be kept in control by a man with a flair for dictatorial methods.

One evening in April 1963, Manzella returned home with a hench-man, but found it impossible to drive his car into the courtyard of his villa as another car – a brand-new Alfa-Romeo – had been parked there, inside his ornamental wrought-iron gates. Manzella and his man went to investigate, opened the door of the Alfa-Romeo, and there was an explosion of the kind produced by a one-hundred-pound bomb in the

An Alfa-Romeo Giulietta. Below the same car after a Mafia-planted bomb has exploded.

last war. Of Manzella, all that was discovered was his wide-brimmed, American-style hat and a single shoe, and these in due course were placed in the sumptuous coffin subscribed for by his friends and enemies, together with a dummy dressed in one of his suits. Nothing at all of significance was found of his companion. The details of the interlocking histories that led to Manzella's death were unravelled by the police after they had found a satchel containing his papers in the branches of a tree some twenty yards from the explosion.

From these documents, and from the further investigations they inspired, the police learned that with the threat of the Anti-Mafia looming ahead, the Honoured Society had taken its dispositions in an intelligent manner. A General Council had been called which had immediately ordered a truce covering all dissensions between the various Mafia families. A standing committee was created to which disputes were to be submitted for arbitration, and crimes of violence were forbidden. The Mafia now stood back and took a look at its recent history, and examined certain *causes célèbres* that might conceivably be of interest to the Commission in the light of the possibility of strengthening defences by newly confected evidence and alibis. Political ties were to be strengthened by all possible means, and prominent persons who might come under attack as accomplices of the Honoured Society were to receive all possible assistance. For the organisation of its resistance the Mafia wanted, above all, a long interim of peace, and no publicity. But this, to its wrath, had been denied by an unhappy incident, also alluded to in the dead Manzella's papers.

The chain-reaction of preposterous violence that in the end was to nullify all the forethought and planning of the Mafia Grand Council was provoked by a misunderstanding arising from the purchase and resale of a valuable parcel of heroin. This had been acquired by the Manzella organisation from its normal suppliers in the Middle East, but a difficulty had arisen over its delivery. Previously the heroin had been shipped across to Sicily by a well-known and highly-thought-of specialist, Joseph Molinelli, known as 'Richard', who was quite prepared to bring his yacht in to within a mile or two of the port of Palermo for the transfer of the heroin to one of the Mafia's fishing-boats. This time Richard had an objection. It seemed that somebody in authority had baulked at the blatancy of these deliveries of contraband being made within sight of the lights of the capital, and in future arrangements would have to be made to take over the heroin at some point at sea on the south side of the island.

A suitable person had to be found to carry out this operation, and Manzella put forward the name of Calcedonio Di Pisa to the syndicate who had purchased the heroin. Di Pisa was a garish young freebooter, habitually be-gloved, shirted in puce silk, and with a coat of the palest of camel hair – a kind of latter-day George Raft. He drove a butter-coloured, gadget-festooned Alfa-Romeo, and in his dandified presence he was anathema to the mafiosi of the old school, whose minds had not been broadened by travel. Di Pisa was a contrabandist by profession but had recently moved into the even more flourishing real estate racket, thereby making a number of enemies. He was given the job, went down to Agrigento, hired a boat, met the scrupulous Richard at sea, and a few hours later reported back to his employers at Palermo with the heroin. This was in due course handed over to a member of the crew of a transatlantic vessel, who smuggled it safely into the United States through the port of New York. Shortly afterwards the Mafia syndicate in Palermo received their payment, but the sum remitted was far below the agreed amount. Manzella promptly put through a transatlantic call to his friends and was told that a short-weight package had been delivered. Both parties agreed there and then to investigate at their own ends. In New York the member of the ship's crew was kidnapped, and, succeeding in convincing his interrogators of his innocence, was released. Manzella and company believed Richard to be above suspicion, so Di Pisa, as the only other man who had handled the parcel since it left the Middle East, was picked up and tried before a Mafia court.

In finding Di Pisa not guilty, this tribunal may have been influenced by the recent decision of the Grand Council, realising too well that a death sentence imposed at this delicate moment might jeopardise the general truce. The verdict exculpating Di Pisa was bitterly contested by two members of the court – the brothers La Barbera, leaders of an immensely powerful minority faction of the New Mafia. Their reluctance, and as it subsequently turned out, their refusal to accept the ruling of the majority, epitomised the struggle between the divergent Mafias: a struggle which was on the verge of becoming – truce or no truce – a war to the knife.

Angelo and Salvatore La Barbera were the chief and vice-chief respectively of the Mafia of 'Palermo-Central', the richest of all the Mafia 'families' through its control of most of the city's building expansion. They were business operators of genius; ex-slum-urchins who had made huge fortunes in fifteen years, and – as the picturesque Sicilian expression goes – they had put the city through their winepress. At the same time they were craftsmen of death, killing with the forethought and intellectual concentration of chess players, in observance of the Machiavellian principle of never allowing an enemy to live – to which they added a corollary of their own, which called for the extermination even of friends of enemies. They lived in the select suburb known as Rose Garden City, populated by the cream of Palerman bourgeois society, and were highly respected by the High Court judges, the medical consultants, and the titled landowners who were their neighbours. The opinion of one of these – who had never dreamed that Angelo La Barbera was anything other than a successful building contractor – suggests that 'the man in the flat above' had a chameleon-like personality. 'Capo-Mafia? Killer? . . . Personally I couldn't even imagine him lifting his hand to anyone. I always regarded him first and foremost as a *considerate* man. In fact, he carried his kindness to others almost to the point of exaggeration. Not only with the big people he used to go round with, either. He was the same with everybody, it didn't matter how unimportant they happened to be. As for money, he quite obviously didn't care about it. He simply threw it away. La Barbera was a soft touch if ever there was one. Never heard of any poor devil going to him and being sent away empty-handed.'

Di Pisa was shot down by La Barbera's killers. It is unlikely that the missing heroin was his undoing, although it provided the excuse. By La Barbera's severe standards Di Pisa was a brash and noisy fellow, lacking in proper respect. He had tried to force his way into the building expansion racket, the preserve of the highest level of the Mafia hierarchy, '*prima di aversi fatte le ossa* – before making his bones'. (La Barbera had made his bones at the age of twenty-five, in a bloody episode straight out of the Pentateuch, by killing the famous capo-Mafia who had been his protector.) Getting out of his car in a main square of Palermo and making for a tobacco kiosk, Di Pisa found himself suddenly in the company of two silent strangers. He made no attempt to escape. Among the many people questioned by the police was a garage-hand who had been filling up a car's tank on the other side of the road when Di Pisa had met his end. The pressmen were fascinated to discover that this was none other than the bandit Giuliano's brother. He had not heard the shots.

In this assassination the verdict of the Mafia Court had been ignored, and the truce broken. This was the moment, if ever, in the Mafia's history when the cool counsels and the statesmanship of Don Calò Vizzini were called for to avert the threat of anarchy and civil war. But Don Calò was no longer there, and his successors could no more dominate the dynamic and explosive young Mafia of Palermo than an ageing bomber pilot of the last war could be expected to take over the controls of a modern jet airliner.

The old Mafia had had all they could take of high-handedness of this kind. Compared to the newcomers who had appropriated the city of Palermo, they were an unimaginative and poverty-stricken collection, but they could still fight their own battles in their own way. Salvatore La Barbera simply vanished and only the charred remains of his car were found. His brother Angelo left Sicily and got as far as Milan, and was there ambushed – ineffectively – as, although severely wounded, he survived. It was the benevolent Manzella who was held responsible by the La Barbera faction for ordering the elimination of the two irksome brothers. It was for this that he was called to account in so macabre a fashion when, returning on that April evening from a visit to the nuns of the Convent of the Sacred Heart, he discovered the unfamiliar car in his courtyard.

Now the war was on in earnest, and it was fought on two levels: the ideological conflict of the ancient blood-feud, and the battle for the material rewards offered by the succession to the chieftainship of Palermo-Central. The struggle for the seizure to high office of any kind where no official successor has been appointed is likely to be ruthless, but in more polite spheres of society blow and counterblow are delivered behind a screen of outward sanctity. In Palermo at war, the passions engaged are identical, but the contestants are a law unto themselves – therefore they simply kill each other in the confident belief that they can do so with impunity.

The manner of Manzella's death had set a new fashion in assassination, and within a few weeks several more Alfa-Romeo cars exploded with murderous results in various parts of the city of Palermo and its suburbs. This particular *marque*, sleek, speedy and outstandingly manageable in a getaway dash through traffic, has always been the favourite of the mafioso owner-driver, and it possessed an additional advantage where death by a dynamited car was planned. This lay in the placing of the car's battery in the boot, which much facilitated the wiring called for in rigging up any engine of destruction. When the men of the New Mafia packed a hundredweight of dynamite into the boot of a Giulietta and arranged for it to be blown to smithereens, the attack was not only on life, but on property, and it was not long before the mere leaving of a car of this type unattended for a suspiciously long time was enough to panic the police into cordoning off the street and evacuating nearby buildings. The old Mafia could not afford this expensive modern version of the assassin's dagger, but retaliated in the traditional manner, and with considerable success. Quietly and economically, the friends and relations of the brothers La Barbera, as well as the pressing candidates for their office, began to disappear. Among them was the supposedly invulnerable Don Mommo Grasso, capo-Mafia of Miselmeri. For many years in the past Don Mommo had played the part of Our Lord in the annual Good Friday mystery-play performed in his town, but even the great prestige based on this additional count was insufficient to outweigh a fatal relationship with the La Barberas, and he and his son vanished, to be seen no more.

It began to seem now to some observers that the Honoured Society was fast sliding into a phase of self-destruction, and the impression was strengthened by the wild savageries perpetrated at the end of June 1963. On the morning of the 29th two bakers on their way to work in the small town of Villabate, near Palermo, noticed smoke coming from an Alfa-Romeo car parked outside a garage. Incredibly enough, they did not run for their lives, as they probably would had they known that the garage was the property of the Di Peri family – a notorious dynasty of mafiosi. While one of the bakers sauntered on a few paces, the other went to find the watchman in charge of the garage, and was just returning with him when the car exploded, blowing them both to pieces. The second baker was crippled for life.

Next day, with the police department in a state of rising hysteria, a telephone call was taken at headquarters from Ciaculli – also a few miles from Palermo – to say that another dubious-looking Alfa-Romeo had been found abandoned in a lane. A few minutes later a second call was received. 'Don't touch the Alfa-Romeo,' the caller said, and then rang off. No one would have dreamed of touching the Alfa-Romeo in the ordinary way, but when the squad of policemen and army engineers reached Ciaculli, they were relieved to find that this was not an occasion when they would be expected to risk their lives exploring the intricacies of the wiring of an explosive charge. For once, the bomb – a primitive affair with a fuse – had been left on the car's back seat, and the fuse had been lighted and had gone out. One of the rear tyres was flat, and that, quite clearly, was why the car had been abandoned. Having removed the bomb from the back seat, somebody then opened the boot, and the real charge exploded. The bomb on the seat had been only a decoy. All seven soldiers and policemen were killed.

Thus had the Mafia played into the hands of the investigatory Commission. Or so it seemed. A wave of arrests began, only equalled before in the days of Mussolini's Prefect Mori and his celebrated 'Plan Attila', and within a few days some three hundred new prisoners had been crammed into the lugubrious cells of Ucciardone. The newspapers published row after row of photographs of the arrested persons, but studying these glowering and unshaven faces, the public began to wonder just what was happening. Nobody seemed to have heard of most of these men, and people studied these almost daily rogues' galleries in vain for any appearance of a politician-manipulating, cocktail-sipping capo-Mafia of the La Barbera type. These faces were those of the foredoomed, half-demented, gallows-fodder of François Villon – 'rags', as the Sicilians call them. A confident rumour spread abroad that all the mafiosi who mattered were 'on holiday in Switzerland, and that a four-star hotel in Lugano was full of them'.

And then suddenly the public mood veered round towards hope, for once again peace returned to Palermo – and now, too, to the confounding of the cynics, the big names began to appear in the headlines: Di Peri, Passalacqua, Nicoletti. 'Zu Tanu' Filippone was arrested – an octogenarian man of respect of the highest rank. When Zu Tanu was approached by a subordinate the man bent to kiss his ring, and if he only had a foot on one of the lower rungs in the organisation, he actually knelt. Zu Tanu was a chronic asthmatic, and it was said of him that the sound of his laborious breathing was as comforting to his followers as that of the gentle pounding of the surf to a fisherman. Hearing that a warrant had been issued for his arrest, Zu Tanu disappeared. He was found hiding in a lavatory, and all the newspapers published pictures of him, a mountainous patriarch with a slightly oriental cast of features, like one of the old Chinese gods of good fortune caught in an unguarded moment of ill-humour. It was generally agreed that at last the police were doing their job.

*　　*　　*

The trial of the thirty mafiosi of Tommaso Natale was to be the proving-ground of the bright new millennium to be ushered in by the Parliamentary Commission of Inquiry into the Activities of the Mafia, which in September 1963 presented its first proposals for anti-Mafia laws for the approbation of the Senate in Rome. By this time this case – one of the most publicised and closely followed of the century – had for several months been passing through its preliminary stages. Much of its fame, which had spread beyond the confines of Sicily, was due to the circumstance that a woman, Rosa Messina, who had lost her husband and two sons in Mafia killings, had dared to break with the tradition of *omertà* and had told the magistrates all she knew. Her courage had been acclaimed in the Press of five continents, and she had been photographed over and over again in her widow's weeds, her face ravaged by grief, as she called down vengeance on those who had bereaved her of her family. And what was more to the purpose, thirty mafiosi, charged with a total of nine murders, were to appear in dock as the result of her denunciations. Here, then, the moment had clearly come for the trial of strength between a renascent and invigorated justice and a seemingly enfeebled Mafia.

Tommaso Natale is a mountain village only fifteen minutes by bus from Palermo, and its inhabitants are the inheritors of a parsimonious land supporting a few olive trees and a scraggy miscellany of animals. In these primitive places where water and pasture and fertile earth are precious, strong families arise, and in the end establish some sort of squatters' rights to the use of a well, or to the pasturing of sheep on a mountainside. Where the central authority is able to impose little restraint, they frequently punish infringement of their privileges with death, so that the blood feud winds intricately, like a scarlet thread, through the brief moment of their history. There are a hundred places on the edges of the deserts of Africa and Asia where a comparable situation exists. The mafiosi of Tommaso Natale are Bedouins in double-breasted suits and gaudy pullovers, with nomad faces and eyes still screwed up from searching the depths of hallucinatory landscapes for their straying beasts. Without realising it, they have killed each other as far back as anybody can remember, and still kill each other, not so much out of bloodthirsty sentiment, but from economic necessity. There has never been enough to go round, so the vendetta becomes a device for keeping down the population.

By the time the new sequence of murders began, a few droplets of the industrial prosperity of Palermo had spilled over into these outlying regions. Now, with an impudent travesty of affluence, the men of the strong families drove about in worn-out Fiat cars instead of riding their mules, but nothing in their minds had changed. Scorn, previously demonstrated by stealing a man's cow and then depositing its horns and hooves outside his door, was now translated into the slashing of tyres, or setting light to a car. The lesser families, the plebeians of wrath who were excluded from participation in the Mafia's vengeance, still set about an enemy's ruin by getting possession of his photograph and placing on it a lamb's heart stuck through with skewers.

Francesco Riccobono was the head of one of the strong families, and he used his official position as forest guard to keep his neighbours' sheep off the best grazing sites in the mountains. He was a village Esau, a huge, hairy fellow with a knack of improvising boisterous and bawdy verse with which he lampooned his enemies. One day he was found with half his head blown away. His wife, Rosa Messina, went to the police, and they listened and did nothing, so his son, Natale, decided to take the law into his own hands, shouldered his *lupara*, and departed to hunt down the men responsible for his father's death. Several members of the rival Cracolici family were slaughtered by Natale before the police captured him, and locked him safely away. Now it was the turn of the surviving Cracolicis to counter-attack; Natale's younger brother disappeared and his decomposed body was found in a crevice a month later.

But in the bookkeeping of the vendetta, accounts still failed to balance, and in their determination to see to it that they did, the Cracolici faction ran up against a minor difficulty. Four of the Cracolici clan and their allies had been killed, and there was a shortage of male Riccobonos within reach of the *lupara* or the sub-machine-gun. Francesco Riccobono and one of his sons were dead, two more sons were in prison, and another was a fugitive from justice, hiding out in the mountains somewhere nearby. A further adjustment in the score was made by the murder of Pietro Messina, a close relation of Rosa Messina's, but this still left a debit balance on the Cracolici side of one life. It was therefore decided that in the absence of any accessible adult male, the thirteen-year-old Paolino, youngest of the Riccobono family, should be dispatched to even the accounts.

Pitilessness apart, only patience was required to accomplish this. Local intelligence sources were well aware that young Paolino paid occasional visits in secret to his fugitive brother, so a watch was kept on

Paolino Riccobono, aged fourteen – a Mafia victim

the house, and the next time Paolino slipped away along the path to the mountains he was followed and riddled with bullets, just out of sight of the village. Three men took part in this assassination, one of them bearing the baptismal name Crocefisso (Crucifix), commonly given to the child of an exceptionally devout family. On their way home the execution squad caught sight of a youth whom they feared might have heard the shooting, and who had seen and recognised them. He was chased with wild bursts of machine-gun fire, staggering and bleeding from his wounds, all the way back to the final haven of his home.

It was the death of her boy that drove Rosa Messina to do what she did. She went to the police, and to them – and thereafter to the examining magistrate – she gave the voluminous, detailed, and largely verifiable evidence that led to the arrest of the mafiosi. She was supported by Anna Galletti, the widow of Pietro Messina, whose evidence was even more damaging to the Mafia's cause. Anna Galletti was a native of the northern Italian town of Perugia, and therefore less susceptible to the intimidating climate of a Sicilian village. Both women spoke as freely to the news papermen as they did to the police, and it seemed to those who saw them that they wore their immense sorrow like an armour that not even the deadly hostility of the Mafia could penetrate.

On September 19th at the Assize Court of Palermo, Rosa Messina was called to give evidence against the men she accused of the murder of her husband and her two sons. It was a moment of supreme dramatic suspense, as this was expected to be one of the few cases in the history of Mafia trials when a witness did not retract the evidence given in hot blood, before the Mafia had had time to undermine their will to resist. The usher called Rosa Messina's name again, but there was silence, followed by a babble of excitement. The accuser did not appear. A reporter tracked her down in Tommaso Natale a few hours later, where, through a door opened only a few inches, she told him that even if the carabinieri came for her she would refuse to testify in court. Anna Galletti, the woman of Perugia, however, did appear. Entering the witness-box, she said in a loud clear voice, which rose almost to a shriek: 'I live alone at Tommaso Natale. I have four children. Therefore I know

The man who talked: Simone Mansueto

nothing about anything.' The next week was spent in hearing the fifty witnesses for the defence, who were unanimous in describing the thirty mafiosi, chained together in the dock, but now relaxed and smiling, as 'decent working men who never gave anybody any trouble'.

But justice, put on its mettle, had not yet admitted defeat, and when all appeared to be lost, it produced an even greater surprise than Rosa Messina had been before her collapse. An inhabitant of Tommaso Natale had been found in a remote gaol who was prepared to confirm all Rosa Messina had said, and to add to it even more conclusive evidence of his own. This man, Simone Mansueto, announced that he had been on the mountainside on the evening of the killing of the Riccobono boy, had heard the gunfire, and had seen the three murderers returning from their bloody errand.

The new champion of the law had written to the President from prison, an ill-spelled and unpunctuated letter which was read out in court: '. . . and therefore I beg Your Excellency to allow me to come and declare all I know this being of the greatest importance and I shall be proud to be able to serve the cause of justice if Your Excellency will allow me to appear before the court . . . '

The reading of the letter was interrupted by a scream from the man's wife, present in the public gallery. 'He's mad! Anybody who listens to him will go to hell!'

'There is God in these people,' Danilo Dolci once said, 'like the fire beneath the ashes.' At this moment it looked as though yet another generation might be used up before the flame could break through.

*   *   *

At the time when the Riccobonos and Cracolicis of Tommaso Natale were engaged in the last rabid phase of mutual extermination, a commission of experts appointed by the European Parliament in Luxembourg arrived in Sicily. The Commission had come to investigate the island's economic predicament with a view to reporting on the feasibility of aid by the European Bank. All the members of the Commission were northerners, and the spectacle to these men from France, Belgium and the German Federal Republic of a member nation where the Middle Ages still kept a foothold was novel and disconcerting. The visitors were briefly entertained among the baroque splendours of Palermo, taken on a round of the Greek temples of Agrigento, and then without further ado plunged into the island's austere hinterland. The harshness of the contrast evoked a heartfelt comment in the Commission's report: 'Sicily reminds one of a gloomy picture in a gilded frame.'

This penetration of the Sicilian interior – seeming as it did to the visiting specialists something akin to an exploration back into social history – produced a succession of surprises. The report noted the nonexistence of European- style villages. People lived as they had done a thousand years before in small townships, perched for the most part on laboriously accessible hilltops, and to these they returned at nightfall, leaving the countryside deserted. The peasants cultivated tiny holdings, often widely separated, the farthest of them located at huge distances from the town. Thus much of their working lives was taken up in sterile journeyings from one patch to another, and back to their homes. A governmental programme of land reform had set out to rectify this absurdity by building small colonies of houses for agricultural workers in

Agrigento, with ruins of the Greek temple perched upon its bare, eroded hills

between the widely spaced towns, and the Commission was invited to inspect several of these. It found that not a single house was inhabited. Observing this phenomenon through northern eyes, the experts drew what was almost certainly a mistaken conclusion. The peasants, they supposed, had rejected the houses because they lacked electricity and water and, as the report put it, were 'too small to live in, and too large to be buried in'. No one thought fit to explain to them the grim legend of the bandit on every mountain-top who had been there throughout the centuries and might at any moment return.

The much publicised land-reform had been going now for fifteen years, but the foreign experts took a hard, professional look at its paper achievements and kept their scepticism intact. Some of the best legal brains in Italy had been employed to discover and enlarge the many loopholes in the law. Statistically the feudal *latifundia* had been abolished, but in reality it was in business almost as before. The great bulk of fertile acres had been put beyond the reach of expropriation by such simple devices as disposing of the land on long leases. 'It was left to the great proprietors to decide which land they should hand over for distribution under the provisions of the land-reform law, and they did not always part with the best.' In nine cases out of ten the Commission found that the maximum grant of fifteen acres to which a peasant was entitled consisted of land that was too arid to support a family.

It appeared to the representatives of the European Parliament that the benefits ascribed to the land reform were largely fictitious. Despite the huge and continuing wave of emigration, Sicilians who remained could be divided into the unemployed and the partially employed. Sharecropping, described by the investigators as without social or economic justification, was as widespread as ever. The report recommended the establishment of co-operatives based upon properly mechanised farming as the only remedy for the country's economic near-prostration. They were told by their hosts that the excessive individualism of the Sicilian character made the solution difficult, but they heard nothing of these individualists' bitter experiences of co-operatives in the past – the co-operatives organised by Don Calò and his Mafia imitators. The Mafia, indeed, is nowhere mentioned in this otherwise penetrating analysis, although – whether the members of the Commission realised it or not – they were confronted with monumental evidence of its presence. 'We were given the opportunity of visiting two dams in construction. For the members of the delegation they offered a singular spectacle, as the dams were being constructed in zones of almost total drought, and it was logical to ask oneself if these basins would ever fill with water.' It was evident that the dams' builders, too, hardly expected them to fulfil their presumed function, as no plans had been made to distribute any water they collected.

The European Parliamentary Commission's report concludes with a not unexpected verdict. 'The unhealthy economic situation of the country must be blamed on the persistence of feudalism. Even if this is to be explained by historical causation, the delegation feels that it must not be allowed to evade censure.' It was as much as a body of economists could say, but in reality how much the charge might have been expanded, and how many more of the sorrows of Sicily could have been laid at the door of the feudal system – that mangy but imperishable tiger.

For centuries, and as a matter of coolly considered policy, the feudalists had kept back huge areas of Sicily from cultivation. They had developed a neatly effective system for suffocating the periodic outbursts of despair this policy engendered: the desperate spirit turned bandit was enlisted in emergency in the feudalists' private armies, employed like a prison camp trusty to quell the mutinies of his fellow sufferers, and then, the crisis past, coldly destroyed. The men who manipulated the levers of this ancient engine of oppression had stood between the King of Spain's Viceroy and justice, had deluded the foolish Bourbons, tamed the socialism of Garibaldi, made a laughing-stock of parliamentary democracy, and done a profitable deal with Fascism. Slowly they had fused with the Mafia – detached from the peasants it once protected – as the richest men of honour became landowners and the most astute of the feudalists joined the Honoured Society. The Mafia-feudalist combination had pulled the wool over the Allies' eyes in 1943, and the Allies had been tricked into assisting in the Mafia's reanimation. Giuliano had been the puppet of the Mafia-feudalists, and *their* finger had been on the trigger of his machine-gun when he set out at Portella della Ginestra to teach the peasants what they must expect whenever they dared to vote as free men. The supporters of the feudal system had littered the streets and the waste places of Sicily with the corpses of their opponents, but the damage done by outright violence was nothing by comparison to the crushing of the Sicilian spirit and the anaesthetising of the Sicilian conscience in an artificially prolonged climate of illiteracy, ignorance and fear.

And now the final irony emerges. Sicily, dominated for all time by landlord, Church and Mafia, was to provide a reservoir of docile right-wing voters. But the reservoir had cracked open under intolerable pressures, and was fast emptying; thus the conspiracy so carefully prepared was bound to fail. Moreover, the Sicilians who escaped their island prison carried with them an ineradicable resentment, and in the north they were to become ardent recruits to the world's numerically largest Communist Party outside the Eastern bloc – voting Communist almost to a man. Thus, by their stubborn mistakes, the backward-looking men who believed they could rule Sicily for ever prepared their nemesis.

The assertion on page 149 concerning the actions of Prince Alliata and his colleagues in the Christian Democratic Party are based and based only upon the testimony of Pisciotta at his trial at Viterbo. No history of the matters discussed in this book would be complete without a full account of the trial and, in particular, of Pisciotta's evidence. However, Pisciotta's evidence on a great many matters is almost certainly unreliable and must be treated with the greatest reserve. Prince Alliata has categorically denied the allegations made against him.

Epilogue

by Marcello Cimino

Marcello Cimino has spent the last twenty-five years on the staff of L'Ora, Palermo's afternoon daily, known for its stand against the Mafia. He was acquainted with several of the honest men who have been eliminated by the Mafia in recent years. He was particularly close to Mauro De Mauro and Giuseppe Fava, both journalists, Cesare Terranova, judge, and Pio La Torre, member of parliament. This epilogue is dedicated to their memory.

TWENTY YEARS have passed since the appearance of the penetrating and accurate report by Norman Lewis on the Sicilian Mafia, ironically entitled *The Honoured Society*. To read it again today one finds little there to alter or correct; the question that remains to be answered is what happened to the personalities who featured in Norman Lewis's story and what has happened to the Honoured Society itself?

As was to be foreseen, many mafiosi active in 1963 are dead, and not all of them peacefully in their beds. The Mafia, on the other hand, survives, and, not only that, but has grown and changed its form. It is no longer a feudal, but a capitalist organisation, based not only in Sicily but in Italy as a whole, from which it has extended the range of its operations to neighbouring countries, as well as retaining its strong links in the United States.

It has strengthened its defences because the antagonistic forces it faced have strengthened theirs. Its enemies now include not only the Left, but significant sectors of the Catholic and liberal world, as well as the judiciary and the forces of law and order.

The present phase of the struggle between the Mafia and the Italian state began in 1963 with the beginning of the operation of the Parliamentary Commission of Enquiry into the Mafia, mentioned by Norman

Lewis in the last chapter of this book. The work of the Commission went ahead until 1976 – thirteen years of difficult navigation – encountering innumerable obstacles and thwarted by secret protection from within the governing parties, above all of the Christian Democrats, who in the past have been charged with favouring the Mafia in return for electoral support. In the end, the Commission may be said to have failed, largely through having been unable to expose the suspected collusion between the Mafia and politicians.

Today, it is possible to say that the mere fact that such a commission could operate at all has at least acted as a curb on the most brazen manifestations of criminality. It has also encouraged the servants of the state in Sicily, and in particular the police, the Carabinieri, and the judiciary in the execution of their duty.

During these years mafiosi were from time to time at least arrested and put on trial, although few were found guilty and sentenced. The few who were sentenced were often banished to other regions of Italy. The intention was to sever their connections with the criminal elements in their original surroundings. It was a wholly unsuccessful device: those who were banished not only maintained their old connections, but created new links locally, with the result that today the Mafia operates just as effectively in any part of Italy as in Sicily itself.

In the course of its thirteen-year investigations the Commission accumulated an enormous quantity of documents, only a part of which have been published. Senator Donato Pafundi, Social Democrat, who for some time was president of the body, said the archives contained material that would cause a national catastrophe if they ever came to light. This is unlikely to happen as the major parts of the material remain categorised as state secrets. Those documents published up till now fill thirty large volumes. They confirm and supplement the account given us by Norman Lewis.

In favour of the Commission it can at least be said that it has jettisoned the famous, but long outmoded, definition of the Mafia as 'a secret society of persons sharing a pronounced sense of honour' and all such descriptions which tend to elevate and remove it from organised criminality. Gone, too, are the romantic fallacies of those who wish to find the origin of the Mafia in the resistance of the poor against the oppression of the rich. Amazingly the Commission is unable to give us a new definition of the Mafia, and on this point it remains vague and imprecise, as if faced with a threshold across which it has feared to tread.

The decision presented by the left-wing minority in the Commission makes some attempt to arrive at a conclusion, when it describes the Mafia as 'a great financial power', 'a system of power', 'a widespread plot, of which the roots, the terrain of financial accumulation, and the recruiting ground of its leadership, remains in Sicily.' This is the nucleus of a definition adequate to fit the daily reality of the Mafia, the characteristics of which Norman Lewis had understood more than twenty years before the Parliamentary Commission, when he spoke of 'an expansive and capitalistic young Mafia which had no patience with restrictive practices.'

Nobody twenty years ago could have associated the image of the Mafia with that of capitalism. Latterly, however, it has become the object of scientific investigation, not only by sociologists but by historians, jurists, and economists. They speak nowadays of a mafia economy and of mafioso enterprises. The Mafia, in fact, can be studied as a true form of bourgeois capitalism in formation.

From halfway through the Seventies an immense and rapid accumulation of capital has been achieved by the Sicilian Mafia through the international traffic in drugs. It is one that offers staggering profits, due to the disproportion between the cost of raw material, opium, and the price of the final product, the white powder that the addicts call 'La roba' (the stuff).

The last report worked out by an Italian expert (basing his figures on the year 1982) contains the following data: for a kilo of morphine-base the Turkish price is $3,500, the Greek $8,000, and the Milan price $12,000. The transformation of morphine into heroin is extremely simple and costs little; but this transformation is all that is necessary to produce a leap in value from $12,000 to over $120,000 on the European market, and $250,000 (at wholesale prices) on the United States market.

During the Seventies the Mafia was able to establish in Sicily a large, but unknown, number of morphine refineries, only three of which were discovered by the police. The productive capacity of Sicilian refineries has been calculated at five tons of pure heroin per annum, a quantity corresponding to about thirty per cent of American consumption.

A part of the enormous profits made in this way are being reinvested in the same trade, but another more significant part filters through into the general Sicilian economy. It is through these investments that the mafiosi traffickers in drugs are transforming themselves into capitalists.

There is nothing new under the sun. Profits on this scale were made in the sixteenth and seventeenth centuries, the formative phase of English bourgeois capitalism, by the ship owners who dedicated themselves to the slave trade between Africa and America, and who, having thus enriched themselves, became paragons of social respectability.

Once in a while a newspaper story provides one with hints of what happen to the huge profits generated by heroin. There was the story of the international banker Michele Sindona, so closely involved with Roberto Calvi, who on June 17, 1982 was found hanging under Blackfriars Bridge. Or the story of a well known capo-Mafia who disappeared from Sicily in 1981, and turned up in 1984 in Madrid, where he had passed as a rich Brazilian, owner of a construction complex in the Costa del Sol. Frequently police investigations have led them to the discovery of Mafia capital invested in the names of private individuals, the owners of chains of hotels, businesses and famous casinos.

Violence is the method through which the Mafia promotes its business interests and settles internal disputes. After the warfare, described in the last pages of Norman Lewis's book, there was a temporary lull in the violence. This was in part through the activities of the Parliamentary Commission, but also through a temporary stability following the drastic elimination of the young mafiosi rebels under the leadership of the La Barbera brothers.

At that time, the drug traffic had not yet become the colossal affair it is now, and the Mafia continued to extract its major profits from the construction industry and tobacco contraband. A few mafiosi who moved to North Italy involved themselves in kidnapping and extortion. A shoot-out between rival Mafia factions in the Viale Lazio, Palermo, produced five corpses. Some time in 1975 Angelo La Barbera, who in the meanwhile had been arrested, was stabbed to death in the prison of Perugia. There was, in fact, not a great deal to report.

Then a year after the killings at Viale Lazio an incident took place in Palermo that produced a sensation throughout Italy. Mauro De Mauro, an extremely brave reporter for the daily *L'Ora di Palermo*, was kidnapped outside his house, and of him nothing more has been heard. Two explanations for his disappearance were current: one that he had been kidnapped and killed because he was about to disclose a Mafia arrangement with high finance or politics; the other that he had stumbled across some dangerous secret in connection with the drug trade.

Hardly a year had gone since the disappearance of De Mauro when, on May 6 1971, Judge Pietro Scaglione of the Palermo court was killed. In this case, too, the investigations have produced no result, nor has there ever been any plausible explanation as to the motives of his killing. Certain strange circumstances came to light in the course of the enquiries. It is known, for example, that Mauro De Mauro had a secret meeting with Judge Scaglione shortly before being kidnapped. There are reports, too, of involvements by the Judge in episodes connecting the Mafia with banditry. He was placed in charge of investigating the death of the bandit Giuliano, and helped foster the erroneous rumour, according to which the bandit was killed in a battle with the Carabinieri. Later it was known that he was murdered in cold blood in his sleep, probably by his lieutenant Gaspare Pisciotta. Pisciotta was interrogated in prison by the same Scaglione, the very day before being poisoned with the famous coffee laced with strychnine.

Scaglione was promoted to another post, but murdered before he left Palermo. One of the last people to see him was the journalist Mario Francese of the *Giornale di Sicilia*, an able reporter who specialised in legal affairs. Scaglione told him: "before going I propose to show you some letters from which you'll have an idea how difficult a judge's job is in this city". It has never been known what these letters were about.

What is known is that eight years later Mario Francese, too, was killed by the Mafia.

After the disappearance of De Mauro and the murder of Scaglione there followed several years of relative truce, during which Mafia action seemed to go underground. It is known that these were the years in which the Mafia bosses were establishing new international connections – above all with the heroin traffickers in Marseilles.

This new activity enormously increased the stakes involved and, automatically, the violence of internal conflict. A new war between mafiosi broke out in Palermo at the end of 1980. The first hostile act was singular indeed. A monk, known as Fra' Giacinto, was stabbed to death in his cell in the convent of Santa Maria di Gesù, on the outskirts of Palermo, and the policeman called to the scene at the time made some surprising discoveries. The monk, despite his vows of poverty and Franciscan humility, occupied not one but seven cells in the convent. In these were found a colour television, perfumes, expensive liquor, whips, an automatic pistol, and 4 million lire. His brother monks refused to aid the police in any way, but it was not difficult to learn that Fra' Giacinto had been an intimate of the famous capo-Mafia Don Paolino Bontà, whose family controlled the area round the convent, besides being a close collaborator with Bontà's son, Stefano, a trafficker on his own account in heroin.

This recalls Norman Lewis's story of the monks of Mazzarino who belonged to the same conventual order as Fra' Giacinto, and of other old stories of mafioso monks, like those of the convent of Tagliavia, near Corleone, where the police believe that the Giuliano band hid its weapons, and where the bandits were frequently given hospitality. There is the case, too, of Padre Agostino Coppola, the priest of Cinisi, arrested and sentenced in 1970 for complicity in a number of mafia-associated kidnappings. He was in the habit of paying the ransoms into his bank account.

The killing of Fra' Giacinto in the convent of Santa Maria di Gesù was only a first warning. In the space of a few months his elimination was followed by that of Stefano Bontà himself and of dozens of his friends and followers. Whole families were eliminated in these vendettas. The war was carried to Milan and other Northern cities and produced a chain of murders in prisons, even in the United States where certain high-ranking mafiosi had taken refuge.

Although it was of unprecedented violence there was nothing new about this conflict. The whole story of the Mafia in Sicily, as in the United States, is a succession of wars and pacifications. War is the means by which the Mafia carries out internal changes, finds new blood and enlists promising recruits. One might well decide that such fratricidal struggles are a sign of vitality rather than of weakness. As soon as internal differences are settled, the Mafia is free, as in this case, to resume its attacks on society.

Here is a list of those who have fallen at the hands of the Mafia in these last years.

1977 GIUSEPPE RUSSO, Colonel of the Carabinieri, sent to Sicily from the North, 'to clear up'. He had a profound insight into the world of the Mafia and had led the investigations into the kidnapping of the journalist De Mauro and the murder of Judge Scaglione.

1978 GIUSEPPE IMPASTATO, young militant of the Left. He ran a private radio station, through which he attacked the mafiosi of his home town, Cinisi, dominated by the capo-Mafia Don Tanu Badalamenti (recently arrested in Madrid).

1979 MARIO FRANCESE, a journalist specialising in legal and criminal matters. BORIS GIULIANO, head of the PUBBLICA SICUREZZA, specialising in Mafia connections between Sicily and the United States. FILADELFIO APARO, Sergeant of Police. MICHELE REINA, Provincial Secretary of the Christian Democrats. CESARE TERRANOVA, judge. He had been prosecutor in many trials of mafiosi. Elected to parliament as an independent deputy, in the Communist party's list. He had taken part in the Parliamentary Commission.

1980 PIERSANTI MATTARELLA, Christian Democrat, President of the Sicilian Region in parliament. With the aid of the parliamentary party of the Left, he initiated government action with the intention of reforming public building enterprises and fighting corruption. EMANUELE BASILE, Carabinieri Captain. He was investigating the relationship between the Mafia and banking personalities. GAETANO COSTA, Attorney General of Palermo. He had signed a number of orders for the arrest of leading mafiosi.

1981   PAOLO GIACCONE, forensic specialist attached to the court. SEBASTIANO BOSIO, surgeon, director of a university clinic. PIERRE MICHEL (killed in Marseilles), a French judge who collaborated with his counterparts in Palermo to investigate the heroin laboratories in Sicily. VITO JEVOLELLA, Carabinieri Sergeant Major.

At the end of 1981 the Mafia threat reached an extreme phase, more than one hundred persons having been assassinated in Palermo alone in that year. The Rome Government's counter attack began with the decision to name General Carlo Alberto Dalla Chiesa as Prefect of Palermo, with the task of carrying the war into Mafia territory. Dalla Chiesa had had some previous experience of the Mafia, having served as a captain of Carabinieri in Sicily in the days of banditry, and returned there with the rank of Colonel in the year 1970. He was then transferred to the North and placed in charge of the struggle against the *Brigate Rosse* and the other terrorists, a task which he brought to its conclusion so successfully as to warrant his promotion to the rank of General.

In 1982, before the General's arrival in Palermo, the year opened with a sensational crime, the killing of Pio La Torre, a Communist deputy, who had recently been sent to Sicily to direct the regional organisation of his party. La Torre had been one of the most active members of the Parliamentary Anti-Mafia Commission and had proposed the passing of a special law permitting magistrates to investigate the bank accounts of persons suspected of laundering Mafia funds. This law was approved and applied only several months after his assassination.

There persists in the heart of the Italian world of politics an obscure area of resistance to the fight against the Mafia, for even the granting of the necessary special powers to General Dalla Chiesa met with opposition in Rome. As soon as La Torre arrived in Palermo he began his attack on the Mafia, as well as a campaign against the NATO installation of atomic missiles in Sicily. He had been a strong supporter of General Dalla Chiesa, welcoming his appointment, and promising his party's support. However, before Dalla Chiesa could arrive in Palermo, La Torre had already been assassinated and the General arrived barely in time to be present at his funeral. Precisely one hundred days later he and his wife were ambushed and killed while driving their little car on the way home.

After the killing of the Communist Deputy and of the new Prefect, the Mafia challenge continued in 1983 with the murders of Judge Giacomo Ciaccio Montalto, Mario D'Aleo (Captain of the Carabinieri), and of Judge Rocco Chinnici. The latter was well-known for his encouragement of civilian resistance to the Mafia. He took part in public meetings, spoke in schools, wrote to the Press to denounce the immorality of the Mafia traffickers, and to urge Sicilians not to give in to threats and intimidation. Realising that he was in constant danger he went everywhere protected by a strong police escort. Being unable to kill him in ambush, the killer used remote control to explode a car parked outside his house, just as he was passing through the door. Two policemen died with him and also an innocent passer-by.

1984 opened with a disturbing portent: the killing of a journalist, not in Palermo but in Catania, where it had been believed that the Mafia had little following, but where they were now firmly entrenched. The dead man, Giuseppe Fava, was an author and journalist, who, for some years, had directed his own paper, in which he carried an open campaign against the Mafia, particularly against Catania's drug traffickers.

It cannot be claimed that in the years following the publication of Norman Lewis's book the Mafia has been defeated, or even held in check. Indeed some economists forecast that in Sicily the Mafia economy will, in the end, expel the normal one, as it extends its empire even further into business, banking, and drugs. The implications of the relative silence which followed the thirteen years investigation of the Parliamentary Anti-Mafia Commission are that it has retained protective links in the political parties. Disquieting questions arise from the strong US presence in Sicilian bases, when from recent history we know that collaboration between the United States military and the Mafia can exist. In Palermo, too, it should be remembered that, according to police estimates, about 30,000 citizens derive benefits, either directly or indirectly, from the narcotics trade, and that many young people working at present for Mafia undertakings, would otherwise be on the streets.

On the other hand the Mafia has ceased to be useful to the right-wing parties as an instrument of political power, employed to capture votes in exchange for a certain tolerance on the part of the police. Moreover, for the Italian state it is intolerable that a savage, uncontrollable and aggressive neo-capitalism should be allowed to develop in the South. Hence the likelihood of more and more drastic repressive action by the government, and more and more ferocious counter-attacks by the forces of the Mafia. This is an impasse from which there is no end in sight. We shall be obliged to await a further epilogue to *The Honoured Society*.

The Death of Boris Giuliano

A postscript by Norman Lewis

SCANNING THROUGH Marcello Cimino's epilogue to this book and its most recent extensions to the interminable catalogue of Sicilian death by violence, my eye was suddenly caught by a familiar name. The first instant reaction was of refusal to accept an intolerable fact. Strangers who had no real flesh and blood existence for me might be cut off in the huge abruptness of a Mafia ambush. This could never happen to a friend, upon whom our friendship itself ought to have conferred a kind of invulnerability. But here was the name, fourth on the fatal list. There could be no mistake here, no confusion. There were Giulianos in abundance in Sicily, but certainly only one Sicilian mother of the numerous Giuliano clan could have ever taken it into her head to name her son Boris.

I first met Boris Giuliano on an extraordinary day in June 1968, the morning of which I had spent in the Assize Court of Palermo, where a trial that was supposed to have made history had just faltered to an end. It had been advertised as unique on two counts. The first was the awesome reputation of the prisoners in the dock, supposed until this moment to be wholly beyond the reach of the law. They were described in the newspapers as 'princes of the underworld'. Joe Bananas (Giuseppe Bonnano), in close association with them, the Al Capone of his day, had been tried *in absentia* in the same court, but John Bonventre, his lieutenant, trapped while on a visit from the States, was here in the flesh, shackled in Italian style to the nine other men in the dock, a confident half-smile barely absent from his face.

The presence here of three men holding dual American and Italian nationality provided the second reason for widespread excitement. These, including Bonventre, were reputed to be heads of Cosa Nostra 'families' in the United States, and the trial was to provide the opportunity for uncovering the tenuous association between the formidable Sicilian parent and its evil American offspring, described in President Johnson's *Task Force Report on Organised Crime* as the most powerful and successful criminal organisation the world has ever known.

Hopes of astounding revelations to be followed by drastic action were dissipated as the trial degenerated into farce. It turned out that to have legally established the suspected relationship between Sicilian and American gangsterdom would have necessitated the translation from English into Italian of seven volumes of evidence (comprising 1,497 pages) gathered in the United States, and that this would take a year. Furthermore the multifarious and often horrific crimes of which these men were accused became as insubstantial as legends of the Nibelungs when the defence counsels went to work. Witnesses had second thoughts as to what they had claimed to have seen or heard, urgently retracting all or part of their previous evidence. Police files had gone missing, and alibis winged like doves through the stagnant spaces of the seedy courtroom. Many of the accused were presented as men of exemplary conduct, intensely engaged in religious and charitable work. Several were known for their long association with the heads of the Church in Sicily. Two had sons training for the priesthood, and one had founded an orphanage.

On July 25th, in an atmosphere of boredom and derision, the charade came to an end. For the last time impudent press photographers, who had no right to be there, poked their camera lenses into the face of the somnolent judge. For the last time, deferential as ever, the guards unshackled the prisoners – so relaxed, so debonair, and, after so many months spent in prison on remand, so amazingly suntanned – to allow them to embrace their wives and press sweets upon their children.

The long foreseen verdict had to be Not Guilty, through lack of proof, and once more justice bowed its head in defeat.

Later that day I called on Colonel Giuseppe Russo of the Carabinieri who was understandably outraged that his efforts should have come to naught. Although he had been sent down from the North and given all the powers he asked, the ten men that he and Boris Giuliano, of the

Squadra Mobile, had between them sent on remand to the Ucciardone Prison had been freed with nothing to show but spectacular suntans from the months of their captivity. Russo was a handsome man, very much of a soldier, who used handcuffs of his own design as paper-weights, and surrounded himself with underlings and spit-and-polish. For the local Pubblica Sicurezza, including Boris Giuliano, its chief, he showed unconcealed contempt. In handling the Mafia he favoured a no-nonsense approach and described with relish the way he had dealt with the powerful Frank Copolla, one of the men released that day. 'I took a couple of carabinieri and went to his house, chained him up, and had them drag him away,' he said. 'I made sure that as many people as possible were there to see it. Respect – as they call it – is what they live for, and that's just what I make it my business to see that they lose.'

Leaving Russo, I called on Boris Giuliano. He was a young man, full of potentially mischievous humour, a Sicilian by birth who had once worked – illegally, as he was delighted to assure me – as a waiter in a Soho restaurant, speaking excellent English, as a result with something of a Cockney accent.

He admitted to being no more impressed by Colonel Russo of the rival police force than Russo had been with him, and was deeply shocked at he way Russo had boasted about the circumstances of Frank Coppola's arrest. 'He's signed his own death warrant,' he said. 'He'll end up on a slab. Apart from that, it does no good.'

'Let me explain the way I play it,' Boris said. 'First of all I take a plain car to the house. If there's a woman there I bow to her and excuse myself. "*Mi dispiace assai*, Signora," I say, and should there be a kid in sight, I give it a pat on the head. The man is given time to get his things together, and then we go off. That way the thing is kept on an impersonal level, and I don't make an enemy. Why should I die before my time? A man like Frank Coppola is too heavy to drag around on a chain.'

We were sitting in the bar of the best hotel in Palermo, which was not only good but extremely reasonable in its prices, and we both knew only too well who owned it. A few minutes before I had asked the barman if he had ever met Lucky Luciano, once a frequenter of the place, to which his reply was, 'Many times, and if you ask me my opinion of him it is this. He was on all counts the most exquisite man I have ever met.'

Boris was determined to bore me with all the stale old arguments for the historical reason for the Mafia's existence. 'You English have only been invaded once. In Sicily we've gone through the mill six times. Every time a new lot of foreigners took over they changed the laws, naturally in their favour. Supposing a Spaniard took your orchard away and then told you all the old title deeds had been cancelled, what would *you* do? The Mafia had to exist.'

'I've heard it so often, before,' I told him. 'Surely you don't really believe that stuff.'

'Put it this way, the big money these days is in development and construction. The Mafia controls the City planning department, so no one outside the mob gets planning permission. This way they make thousands of millions. But does it really matter all that much? If they didn't cash in, the Roman bankers and investment companies would. We'd be no better off. They kill each other, but what of it? The main thing is to see to it they don't kill us.'

'Sometimes you sound just like a mafiosi,' I said.

'In my trade you have to be a realist. No one will stop this thing. The most you can ever hope to do is to keep it within bounds. This is a game. It's like chess. I give a piece here and I take a piece there, but I know it's a game I'm never going to be able to win. I have to do business with them, and they can be helpful in small ways. Among other things they hate to have small-time villains spoil the atmosphere of the place. You can leave your car unlocked in the parking space outside this hotel. Can you think of any hotel on the mainland where you could do that?'

'They still kill judges. And chiefs of police.'

'Outsiders who don't bother to learn the rules of the game. We try to explain to them, but they refuse to listen. It's a great help to have been born here.'

Boris and I got on tremendously well. He wanted to talk about Soho, and I about the Mafia, and we had a half dozen such meetings at that time. We exchanged letters and a few years later I spent an hour with him when he stopped off in London on his way to Washington for a conference with the FBI. An earlier visit to the United States had had to do with the assassination of President Kennedy. His opinion as to the possibility of a Sicilian connection in this case suggested the plot of a book based on the assassination I subsequently wrote.

In the early part of 1979 Boris's letters stopped. I assumed that he was too busy a man to continue a desultory correspondence, but the reason proved later to be different. Ten years earlier the wealth of the Mafia came from the expansion and the rebuilding of cities like Palermo. Since then it had been discovered that no business had ever been known to compare with the trade in narcotics, and the secret laboratories of Sicily stepped up production to meet a quarter of the world demand in heroin. It was no longer possible for a policeman to stand on the sidelines and exercise any measure of control over this explosion of criminality. In July Boris visited Marseilles and Milan, engaged in a crucial investigation into a reallocation between the Italian and American Mafia families of spheres of influence in the narcotics trade.

A few days after his return he went as usual at exactly eight o'clock for his morning cup of coffee in the Bar Lux, a few yards from his home. He was alone as ever. Boris never bothered with bodyguards, as confident as always in his knowledge of the ways of the enemy who opposed him. He shook hands with one or two of the regulars, finished his coffee and turned to go. Only one of the twenty odd men in the bar at the time would admit to having seen what happened next. 'I noticed a man who was trembling,' the witness said. 'He was white in the face. He must be ill, I thought. My first impulse was to offer to help. When the *commissario* went towards the door the man followed him. He drew a pistol and shot him three times in the neck. Signor Giuliano fell face downwards, and the man then shot him four more times in the back.'

Colonel Giuseppe Russo, the man from Milan who did all the wrong things and could therefore expect to take the consequences, died with his bodyguard in an ambush in July 1977. The assassination in the Bar Lux, of the man who had mastered all the intricate moves in the eternal chess game with the Mafia, took place only two years later, almost to the day.

Publisher's Note 2003

Since these two epilogues, the law of attrition by the Mafia has continued.

Among many other atrocities, the most famous was committed in May 1992, when Judge Giovanni Falcone, his wife and three bodyguards were all killed by a two-thousand-pound car-bomb. In the judge's biggest case, the maxi-trial of 1986–7 involving four hundred and seventy-six suspected mafiosi, all of the seven officials involved in investigations were murdered. Two months later Judge Paolo Borsellino, Chief Public Prosecutor of Palermo, was also killed by a car-bomb.

Index

About the Author

Norman Lewis's early childhood, as recalled in *Jackdaw Cake* (1985), was spent partly with his Welsh spiritualist parents in Enfield, North London, and partly with his eccentric aunts in Wales. Forgoing a place at university for lack of funds, he used the income from wedding photography and various petty trading to finance travels to Spain, Italy and the Balkans, before being approached by the Colonial Office to spy for them with his camera in Yemen.

He moved to Cuba in 1939, but was recalled for duty in the Intelligence Corps during the Second World War. It was from this that Norman Lewis's masterpiece, *Naples '44*, emerged, a resurrection of his wartime diary only finally published in 1978.

Before that came a number of novels and travel books, notably *A Dragon Apparent* (1951) and *Golden Earth* (1952), both of which were best sellers in their day. His novel *The Volcanoes Above Us*, based on personal experiences in Central America, sold six million copies in paperback in Russia and *The Honoured Society* (1964), a non-fiction study of the Sicilian Mafia, was serialised in six instalments by the *New Yorker*.

Norman Lewis wrote thirteen novels and thirteen works of non-fiction, mostly travel books, but he regarded his life's major achievement to be the reaction to an article written by him entitled *Genocide in Brazil*, published in the *Sunday Times* in 1968. This led to a change in the Brazilian law relating to the treatment of Indians, and to the formation of Survival International, the influential international organisation which campaigns for the rights of tribal peoples. He later published a very successful book called *The Missionaries* (1988) which is set amongst the Indians of Central and Latin America.

More recent books included *Voices of the Old Sea* (1984), *Goddess in the Stones: Travels in India* (1991), *An Empire of the East: Travels in Indonesia* (1993) and *The World the World* (1996), which concluded his autobiography, as well as collections of pieces in *The Happy Ant Heap* (1998) and *Voyage by Dhow* (2001). With *In Sicily* (2002) he returned to his much-loved Italy, and in 2003 his last book, *A Tomb in Seville*, was published.

Lewis travelled to off-beat parts of the world well into his nineties, returning to the calm of rural Essex where he lived with his second wife. He died in July 2003 at the age of ninety-five.

ELAND

61 Exmouth Market, London EC1R 4QL
Email: info@travelbooks.co.uk

Eland was started in 1982 to revive great travel books that
had fallen out of print. Although the list has diversified into
biography and fiction, it is united by a quest to define the spirit of place.
These are books for travellers, and for readers who aspire to explore the
world but who are also content to travel in their own minds.

Eland books open out our understanding of other
cultures, interpret the unknown and reveal different environments
as well as celebrating the humour and occasional horrors of travel. We
take immense trouble to select only the most readable
books and therefore many readers collect the entire series.

All our books are printed on fine, pliable, cream-coloured paper.
Most are still gathered in sections by our printer and sewn as well
as glued, almost unheard of for a paperback book these days.
This gives larger margins in the gutter, as well as
making the books stronger.

You will find a very brief description of all our books on the
following pages. Extracts from each and every one of them can be
read on our website, at www.travelbooks.co.uk. If you would
like a free copy of our catalogue, email us
or send a postcard.

ELAND

'One of the very best travel lists' WILLIAM DALRYMPLE

Memoirs of a Bengal Civilian
JOHN BEAMES
Sketches of nineteenth-century India
painted with the richness of Dickens

Jigsaw
SYBILLE BEDFORD
An intensely remembered autobiographical
novel about an inter-war childhood

A Visit to Don Otavio
SYBILLE BEDFORD
The hell of travel and the Eden of arrival
in post-war Mexico

Journey into the Mind's Eye
LESLEY BLANCH
An obsessive love affair with Russia and
one particular Russian

Japanese Chronicles
NICOLAS BOUVIER
Three decades of intimate experiences
throughout Japan

The Way of the World
NICOLAS BOUVIER
Two men in a car from Serbia to Afghanistan

Persia: through writers' eyes
ED. DAVID BLOW
Guidebooks for the mind: a selection
of the best travel writing on Iran

The Devil Drives
FAWN BRODIE
Biography of Sir Richard Burton,
explorer, linguist and pornographer

Turkish Letters
OGIER DE BUSBECQ
Eyewitness history at its best:
Istanbul during the reign of Suleyman
the Magnificent

My Early Life
WINSTON CHURCHILL
From North-West Frontier to Boer War
by the age of twenty-five

Sicily: through writers' eyes
ED. HORATIO CLARE
Guidebooks for the mind: a selection
of the best travel writing on Sicily

A Square of Sky
JANINA DAVID
A Jewish childhood in the Warsaw
ghetto and hiding from the Nazis

Chantemesle
ROBIN FEDDEN
A lyrical evocation of childhood
in Normandy

Croatia: through writers' eyes
ED. FRANKOPAN, GOODING & LAVINGTON
Guidebooks for the mind: a selection
of the best travel writing on Croatia

Viva Mexico!
CHARLES FLANDRAU
A traveller's account of life in Mexico

Travels with Myself and Another
MARTHA GELLHORN
Five journeys from hell by a great
war correspondent

The Weather in Africa
MARTHA GELLHORN
Three novellas set amongst the
white settlers of East Africa

The Last Leopard
DAVID GILMOUR
The biography of Giuseppe di Lampedusa,
author of The Leopard

Walled Gardens
ANNABEL GOFF
An Anglo-Irish childhood

Africa Dances
GEOFFREY GORER
The magic of indigenous culture
and the banality of colonisation

Ask Sir James
MICHAELA REID
The life of Sir James Reid,
personal physician to Queen Victoria

A Funny Old Quist
EVAN ROGERS
A gamekeeper's passionate evocation
of a now-vanished English rural lifestyle

Meetings with Remarkable Muslims
ED. ROGERSON & BARING
A collection of contemporary travel
writing that celebrates cultural difference
and the Islamic world

Marrakesh: through writers' eyes
ED. ROGERSON & LAVINGTON
Guidebooks for the mind: a selection
of the best travel writing on Marrakesh

Turkish Aegean: through writers' eyes
ED. RUPERT SCOTT
Guidebooks for the mind: a selection
of the best travel writing on Turkey

Valse des Fleurs
SACHEVERELL SITWELL
A day in St Petersburg in 1868

Living Poor
MORITZ THOMSEN
An American's encounter with
poverty in Ecuador

Hermit of Peking
HUGH TREVOR-ROPER
The hidden life of the scholar
Sir Edmund Backhouse

The Law
ROGER VAILLAND
The harsh game of life played in
the taverns of southern Italy

Bangkok
ALEC WAUGH
The story of a city

The Road to Nab End
WILLIAM WOODRUFF
The best selling story of poverty and
survival in a Lancashire mill town

The Village in the Jungle
LEONARD WOOLF
A dark novel of native villagers struggling
to survive in colonial Ceylon

Death's Other Kingdom
GAMEL WOOLSEY
The tragic arrival of civil war in an
Andalucian village in 1936

The Ginger Tree
OSWALD WYND
A Scotswoman's love and survival
in early twentieth-century Japan

Poetry of Place series

London: Poetry of Place
ED. BARING & ROGERSON
A poetry collection like the city itself, full of
grief, irony and delight

Andalus: Poetry of Place
ED. TED GORTON
Moorish songs of love and wine

Venice: Poetry of Place
ED. HETTY MEYRIC HUGHES
Eavesdrop on the first remembered glimpses
of the city, and meditations on her history

Desert Air: Poetry of Place
ED. MUNRO & ROGERSON
On Arabia, deserts and the Orient of
the imagination

Istanbul: Poetry of Place
ED. ATES ORGA
Poetry from her long history, from paupers to
sultans, natives and visitors alike

The Ruins of Time
ED. ANTHONY THWAITE
Sized to fit any purse or pocket, this is just the
book to complement a picnic amongst the
ruins of time